Transform Your Destiny

Advance Praise for Dale Halaway

"This amazing book is loaded with many lessons and much wisdom! Let the wisdom found within these pages change your life for the better."
—Brian Tracy, *New York Times* Bestselling Author of
Eat That Frog

"This is a game changer for me! Dale has an incredible way of articulating truths in a way that breaks down the complexity of our human experience, like no other. He helps it make sense. He provides a safe environment for people to look at themselves in a productive way to make real and lasting changes in their lives. It is valuable beyond measure!"
—Janell Simonson

"If you know that something needs to change in your life but don't know what it is and/or how to change it, let Dale help you. He has a natural gift that will assist you in finding the answers you are looking for. I guarantee that your life will change for the better if you are willing to be open and honest with yourself."
—Tina Piazza

"These are amazing teachings where I have found true support for my life! Not just my ordinary life, but the deepest yearning I have to know myself and grow!"
—Dorbe Holden

"Dale's teachings on karma have had THE most positive impact on my life!"
—Nancy O'Connell

"I'm taking so much value away from this! I learned so much about myself and my unconscious resistance and how it has simply been keeping me from making the steps forward that I need to in my business. It was life changing for me! Thank you so much, Dale!"
—Misty Olsen

"Dales classes and teachings are designed to help you move the needle forward in a practical, hands-on, simple way. They will change your life!"
—David Forestieri

"From seeing Dale teach in just one seminar, I could sense the authenticity. His teachings are pure gold! This is the best thing I've done in years!"
—Anthony Kasner

"I have never been able to get THIS deep into my limiting beliefs and I felt more energetically prepared to actually accomplish and manifest the goals that I've been sitting on and self-sabotaging for so long. I really cannot recommend this highly applicable training more. Life-changing information and learning!"
—Cynthia Mirabelli

"I'm so grateful for you, Dale! These teachings have really spoken to my heart and soul. With the practical exercises you give, I've been able to clearly see why I've lagged in certain places in my life and how I can get back on track with full and deep love from myself. Thank you, Dale!!"
—Rachel Petkus

"This has given me a renewal in the sense of who I am, what I am, and where I'm going in life! It's given me a deeper understanding of myself as a human being here on Earth as well as the strength to move forward in my life's journey with newfound knowledge. Thank you, Dale!"
—Chris Montigny

"Dale Halaway has amazing ways of articulating high-level teachings just about anyone can comprehend and practically apply in their life. And yet, his teachings are so powerful and life altering. I am beyond grateful and already feel so empowered!"
—Aurelio De Robles

"Inspiring, profound higher teachings with amazingly practical action steps!"
—Heidi Goodwin

"The time is now, the teacher is Dale, and the place is within your body, mind, and soul. Everything else is a distraction from uncovering your true self. It's the only way of breaking out of the sleepy matrix."
—Genevieve Burciaga

"These seminars have definitely impacted my life with money, relationships, and my own transformation. Dale is a true master teacher and his teachings will change your life for the better."
—Jaime De Robles

"Be prepared for an impactful and empowering experience in bettering your life—which includes your personal and business life. If you're asking questions, and are ready for the answers, you'll get it here."
—Candice Park

TRANSFORM

your

DESTINY

Embrace the Life You Are Meant to Live in Partnership with The Divine

BOOK 2 IN THE TRANSFORMATION TRILOGY

DALE HALAWAY

ISBN: 978-19-5-315348-7

Published by

LIFESTYLE
ENTREPRENEURS
P R E S S

If you are interested in publishing through Lifestyle Entrepreneurs Press, write to: *Publishing@LifestyleEntrepreneursPress.com*

Publications or foreign rights acquisition of our catalog books.
Learn More: *www.LifestyleEntrepreneursPress.com*

Printed in the USA

DESTINY

"I would not interfere with any creed of yours
or want to appear that I have all the cures.
There is so much to know...
So many things are true...
The way my feet must go may not be best for you.
And so, I give this spark of what is light to me,
to guide you through the dark,
but not tell you what to see."

—Author Unknown

Contents

CONTENTS

FOREWORD

By Ronald L. Greenawalt D.C., F.A.C.O.

D ale Halaway is the type of person you would really like to know, master teacher, transformational teacher, teacher of life's journeys, teacher of authenticity, teacher of realization, teacher of life's potential, and to have as a dear friend. Anyone can benefit from his words, written or spoken. This book, *Transform Your Destiny*, is no different when it comes to the type of impact it will have on many.

I have known Dale for over twenty years now, and it is refreshing to interact with someone who doesn't operate from a place of ego. He was a patient of mine for seven years before I even knew about his work or the seminars he conducted. I will never forget that Monday morning when I found out. A patient of mine was beaming as she described a seminar she had attended over the weekend. When I asked her what seminar she attended, she stated it was a Dale Halaway seminar. I was taken aback—he'd never spoken to me about his success in his career. She had such a great experience there. After my bringing this up to him and seeing how he simply had no ego involved in his work, another level of friendship began to emerge. We have even done seminars together to share our experiences with others.

His ability to communicate self-transformational information to the common man or the most sophisticated philosopher is such a gift. Anyone can gain insights in finding their personal destiny from his messages by looking into their inner being, their soul. Just that little nudge from Dale can allow our true authenticity to emerge, and by tearing away the masks that we all hide behind consciously and unconsciously, who we really are and the person we were born to be is exposed.

Over the years, I have witnessed Dale's personal journeys that he has so expertly been able to communicate to others; the lessons he has learned now can become your lessons, and we can all grow from this transformation. Destiny is something we cannot avoid but can try and optimize through the special teachings that resonate with us to become the best functioning us: physically, biochemically, emotionally, and spiritually. Through all of the conflicts in life there are always lessons to learn to progress in our own enlightenment. Dale draws from his own experience, from other mentors, from having turned his life personally and professionally into his own laboratory where he has learned as much from other people's experiences as he has his own. His way of presenting self-transformational ideas is very clear and easy to apply in one's life, as real transformation all starts inside of us. Blaming the environment we live in is not the way forward. The goal is to embrace the environment; to learn and adapt to it, not blame it for our issues. We are not to avoid the challenges in life but to embrace them and learn from them to propel us through our self-transformations. All adaptation mechanisms in working through life begin within us physically, biochemically, emotionally, and spiritually.

This second book in Dale's trilogy follows his first book, *Being Called to Change*, which set the pace for this type of education. In this book, Dale evaluates several aspects of the self and creates a pathway for self-transformation to occur with knowledge and understanding. Being able to tap into your innate intelligence and allowing yourself to express who you truly are with authenticity is the gift Dale offers in his teachings and written words. I can only hope you will enjoy your own personal journey to expose the true inner power that we all have as much as I, along with countless others, have.

In *Transform Your Destiny*, Dale answers the most important question: What is destiny? He follows this up with a deep dive into the other pertinent questions: Can we affect our destiny? Where does choice or free will come into play? Does karma have anything to do with our destiny?

Scientific research has shown that destiny is pretty much determined, with some wiggle room for change. Dale's teachings can assist in some of those changes. This book will allow you to explore aspects of your own destiny; something that Dale has been exploring in his own life for decades. In this book, he has put together what he has found out about himself as well as his findings from studying others to share with you. Let the journey begin and continue!

Ronald L. Greenawalt D.C., F.A.C.O.
Chiropractic Kinesiologist
Diplomat of the American Board of Chiropractic Orthopedists

INTRODUCTION

A lot of people think they know their Greater Destiny, but what I've noticed with a number of the people I've supported along the way is that many don't really know what it is yet. It's there. They just don't know what it is. They might start off thinking they know what their Greater Destiny is, but after they've had a couple of hard knocks, all of a sudden, they're no longer sure what it is, or if they even have one. Once stuff starts to hit the fan in their world, then they begin to question things. They find themselves feeling confused and bewildered, and often they set off on a path that detours them from their mission entirely—sometimes for years, or sometimes for their entire lifetime.

Destiny is a greatly misunderstood topic. Contrary to what you may (or may not) believe, it is the way you use your free will, or freedom of choice, not chance, that can alter it. Some people assume that their destiny is dictated by a higher power. But that is only an assumption. If that were the case, then we'd pretty much have everybody on the planet in alignment with a Greater Destiny, having a great time or having a more powerful life. But no one has to look all that far to realize that yeah, most people might think they have a Greater Destiny, but they obviously haven't tapped into it yet. So, then what does that imply? It implies that free will is only part of the equation.

You see, there are two points of destiny. For the purpose of this teaching, I call them Lower Destiny and Higher Destiny or Lower Destiny and Greater Destiny. Where most people get caught up is that they think there's only the Greater Destiny. But that is not the case since this Greater Destiny seems to elude them throughout most of their life.

This could be because they don't understand the other point of destiny—Lower Destiny. This other point of destiny is where your free will comes into play.

Destiny is
a greatly
misunderstood
topic.

When we don't understand all the parts of our destiny, we can find ourselves getting really jammed up—and then we start making choices from this place. We start wondering why we feel so stuck in our lives, or why we can't achieve the goals that we keep setting for ourselves. When we have a greater understanding of what destiny is, we are better able to understand the bigger picture of our lives. This saves us a lot of pain and confusion.

When our bodies go through growing pains, a lot of times they hurt and they're uncomfortable—but, over time, we can see that our bodies have matured and are now more capable. Well, the experiences that we have in this lifetime are there to help us learn our lessons. We chose these lessons for ourselves at soul level so they could help us mature, expand, and evolve. They might hurt or be a little uncomfortable, but they were written into our destiny for our expansion, our growth and our evolution.

This book is devoted to exploring all the facets of our destiny in our current lifetime. As you will soon come to see, these facets overwhelmingly center on the quality of our choices. This is why it is so important for us to be able to stop from time to time and reflect upon whether our choices are leading us to the life we truly desire.

WHY I WROTE THIS BOOK

I wanted to write this book, in large part, because I've lost a lot of people who were very dear to me. A handful of times, those deaths took the form of suicide. Because I knew these people quite well, I had a front row seat, so to speak, when it came to watching them make choices in their lives. I watched as they eventually got to that choice to give up—to take their own life.

Even though that was painful for me, the pain that I experienced through the loss of someone dear to me would always take me deeper—not just into wanting to uncover more of what had happened to them but to find some way to make a significant difference in the lives of other people who get stuck. I wanted to find a way to help people before they began to make those lower, weaker choices that often lead to some form of destruction within their world. Eventually, I came to a place where I could.

I can now name a number of people who often say that I've literally helped save their life. I helped them by teaching them and guiding them to illuminate their pathway forward. As their understanding of destiny became deeper, it started to genuinely empower them, and then, over time, they started to get their lives back. They started learning again and started doing what they were meant to be doing all along, and that boiled down to improving their decision making.

As the quality of our decision making improves, our quality of our life improves. This is because every time our choices improve, we become closer and closer to that Greater Destiny that is within the DNA of our souls.

As you get a better understanding of what's really going on in your own personal universe, it will help you to become unstuck and enable you to get back on the path that's in alignment with your destiny. There will always be challenges along the way, but they will be challenges that you can now stand up to because the quality of your choices has been increased.

MY PERSONAL JOURNEY WITH DESTINY

Since I was young, I knew that I wanted to help people and that I needed to help them in a very specific way: through teaching. That showed up very early for me in this life. Heck, I taught my first five-day class just as I was coming into my twentieth year. Can you imagine that? There I was, giving a nearly week-long class on sales and personal development to a group of forty or fifty people when I was just twenty years of age—and they just loved it. It was so well-received. But the more important thing was that it helped them.

Even before that, I was always helping people to understand things that were going on in their worlds. I would always support my friends and the people around me, and from a young age, I've also supported my employees in the various businesses I've had over the years.

My first really clear memory of helping people was when I was about 13 years of age. It was at that time that I started helping some of my mother's friends to better understand some of the things that were going on in their lives. They thought I was someone really special. They were in their mid to late thirties at the time and just didn't know how it was possible for a thirteen year old to help them the way that I did.

I remember it as if it as if it happened just yesterday.

My mother's dearest soul sister and girlfriend was also her first cousin. She had a troubling dream—it really scared her. They were sitting in the kitchen, having a normal conversation, and I was in the other room. My mother, at some point, asked me if I had any thoughts on what they were talking about because she had no idea how to help her friend with this troubling dream.

I asked her about it, and once she told me, I began responding to her dream and helped her to understand the content of the dream. More specifically, I helped her understand how the content in the dream was related to what was going on in her life.

When that happened that day, it really helped her understand a problem that she was experiencing in her day-to-day life, and it became a nostalgic moment for me because it was my very first experience in translating somebody's dream in this life. From that point on, I did this on an ongoing basis.

Not long after I helped her, my mom's friend had another dream. She asked if I would spend some time with her on it once again. Next thing you know, another one of my mother's friends was asking me about her own dream. Obviously, they all talked, as people do when they find something that's working for them.

They thought I was special. I didn't think so at the time, but they seemed to think so—whether I did or not. The best thing to come out of those experiences is that to this very day, I'm still helping all kinds of people in interpreting their dreams.

From a young age, I knew that part of my Greater Destiny was to help people to better understand themselves, what they were challenged with, and what they were struggling through so that they could better navigate through life's big challenges successfully.

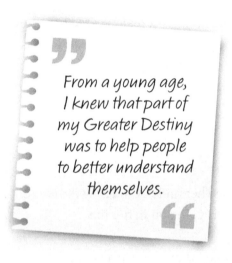

From a young age, I knew that part of my Greater Destiny was to help people to better understand themselves.

In addition to becoming a person who could help people in their personal lives, I also became known rather quickly in the earlier part of this life as a highly effective problem solver. All kinds of people wanted me to come into their companies and help them solve issues they were facing. But whether it was on a personal level or a professional level, it all came down to helping people to understand their problems so they could better work with them and through them to improve their lives and/or businesses.

Remember that very first class on sales and personal development that I mentioned? That evolved into doing seminars for my own sales organization. And next thing you know, some of our salespeople asked if they could bring their husbands or wives to my trainings—these spouses included a sales manager of an insurance company, a sales manager of a car dealership, a business owner who managed his own string of dry-cleaning shops, etc. And, of course, I said yes.

Next thing you know, I'm being asked to come into their companies to help them solve their problems and increase their levels of productivity. At some point, I started to say yes, and that's what I moved into doing on a more regular basis. I would go into other people's organizations helping them clearly identify what problems they were experiencing and then how to help solve them, which always resulted in a notable leveling up of their overall productivity and success.

So if you look at the evolution, there I was, a young adolescent, thirteen years of age, literally translating somebody's dream in an era when there weren't yet professional dream interpreters (or at least there weren't many of them). Then, in my early twenties, a few years later, suddenly, I'm being invited into other people's companies to help those business owners solve some of their problems. You can see that my Greater Destiny was showing itself very early in this lifetime.

Back then, I never did any marketing. I never knocked on anybody's door. I didn't ask anybody if I could interpret their dream. I didn't even know I could interpret somebody's dream, no more than I knew if I could help somebody solve a problem in their life or in their business. But it came to me effortlessly. And that's the whole point here; that your Greater Destiny will come to you. In other words, we don't have to go looking for our Greater Destiny, as it will find us, in a way that is unique and in divine time for us.

At that time, of course, I didn't see it as a Greater Destiny. But clearly now, after more than a half a century has passed, it's really obvious that my Greater Destiny was already revealing itself when I was a child. The things I was doing were in complete alignment with my Greater Destiny in terms of helping people.

Maybe now you, the reader, are starting to make your own connections as well to those types of experiences in your own life that reveal alignments to your Greater Destiny?

Those things evolved almost effortlessly in the earlier part of my life as part of my Greater Destiny. And from there it just continued to morph and expand and evolve to the place I am now, where I can help a lot more people than ever before through my online courses, my coaching programs, my seminars—and my books, like this one!

Sometimes people will ask me if there was ever a time along my path when I began to question my destiny—if my destiny was always clear to me, or if there were points when things got rocky and I wasn't so sure what my Greater Destiny was. And I always tell them, "Of course! I was challenged by those questions the same as anybody else."

When I was younger, it was like I was on fire. I was just unstoppable. People who knew me really well back then would refer to me as the man with the Midas touch; everything I touched seemed to turn to gold. I was helping to lead people and businesses to a brighter place, and everything was going great.

But as I moved towards the latter part of my twenties, I started to experience blocks, or challenges, that I didn't really understand yet— and boy, were they intense. By the time I reached my late twenties, I couldn't even begin to count how many times I'd been hospitalized. I had many physical health issues. In my early thirties, it developed into something life-threatening.

And that's just what was happening on a physical level. I had a couple of businesses, and outwardly, it looked like no matter what I did, I would succeed. But behind that appearance of success, I was setting myself up for ruin. Deep down, I was afraid and sabotaging myself on some level.

I was terrified because I could not put my finger on why I was succeeding. With the level of success I'd experienced since my late twenties, I'd have people want to interview me. One of the most common questions was: "You're so young. What's your formula? What's your secret?" Back then, my number one answer was you work hard. And I was working hard, but I knew inside that was not the only answer. I just didn't know what the other answer was. People constantly told me I was special, from a young age, but I didn't feel special. Because of that, I became very afraid that I was going to lose all of this in the blink of an eye.

And so, I was one of those people who was climbing the ladder of success, and then something shifted, and it started to go downhill.

The other issue to note was that I also had a speech impediment back then. Imagine standing up in front of six hundred people and all of a sudden, you start stuttering. Even though people seemed to benefit a lot from what I was teaching back in those days, what many did not know is that inside I was terrified that this was all going to come crashing down.

So my big thing was fear. I was afraid of losing everything and that people would find out that I wasn't who they thought I was. And back in those days, I didn't even know who I was yet. I just couldn't answer those deeper questions at that time.

As those blocks started to come, I never really questioned whether I was meant to continue teaching people and continue helping them to understand what was going on in their own lives. My bigger challenge was not understanding what was going on with my own life.

I learned later that these darker, denser feelings, challenging events, and my own self-sabotaging patterns were a part of Lower Destiny, which most people have very little understanding of. In fact, it would take me a good ten years to start to even understand it myself. It was, if you will, the underbelly of my consciousness that I had to deal with. That underbelly had been buried for a long time, but it was in my mid to late twenties that it started to surface. And there was a lot of stuff in there that needed to be resolved—old dynamics, lower energy patterns, limiting, restricting beliefs, and unresolved past negative karma that I didn't even know I had, let alone chose at soul level, to resolve, release, and ultimately heal in this life.

As I look back on that time in my life, I know that I never would have made it if I hadn't learned to recognize—and then resolve—that under-belly. Like a lot of people, I could have easily gotten lost in it. If I hadn't deepened my understanding of what was going on in terms of that part of my destiny, it would have swallowed me up—and then I would have lived the rest of my life on autopilot. It would have been like that movie *Groundhog Day*, just repeating the same thing over and over again for the rest of my time on this planet.

As all that started to surface into the experience of my day-to-day life, it definitely challenged me. It brought me down to my knees more than once. A few times, I wasn't even sure if I'd come out on the other side. I had bouts with long-term depression, which led to thoughts of suicide. I was experiencing a period of rejection in sales, but I was determined to break through it. Little did I know that the amount of rejection I was experiencing was more than most people could handle. It was almost more than I could handle.

I would find myself getting really down and depressed and wondering, "Why is this happening? This doesn't happen to anyone else." It didn't make any sense at the time.

I dropped into a deeper, darker depression, and it reached a peak where my mother literally did save my life because I came really close to suicide on one particular day.

> This book is for anyone and everyone who has the desire to reconnect to their greater truth as a soul.

Due to this series of events and lack of self-worth at that time, things got really dark for me—all because I didn't understand what was going on. I didn't have anybody around who could help me because back when I was young, nobody taught what I teach today.

So I was left on my own to figure things out. After a number of years, I started to break through—and as I did, that's when my understanding of all this grew to a deeper level.

Once I began to understand what I had been dealing with was what I eventually came to know as my Lower Destiny, it helped me to better navigate it. This process continued for some time because as it turned out, I had a lot of stuff I needed to clear out from inside myself; I had a lot of that underbelly that needed to get resolved.

But even though it took me a while, it still played into my Greater Destiny as a leader and as a teacher. The deeper I went into that understanding of my own Lower Destiny, the more I was able to help others navigate through theirs.

Now, this shift didn't just happen overnight; this was definitely a process that needed to take place over time. But I suppose that was another piece of the puzzle—the fact that, at least on my path, none of this came easy to me. And yet, that's also what has allowed me to be as effective as I am today in helping to serve people along the course of their journeys.

For a large part of this process, it felt like I was trying to plow through molasses. But at a certain point, I learned how to transform that uglier part of my destiny—and that's what caused the light inside of me to become brighter. Once I could start to feel myself transforming that part of my destiny on a cellular level, it was like I had struck gold. And ever since then, it has served me wonderfully well.

That's where the title of this book comes from—it comes from that experience in my twenties when I was first beginning the process to transform my own destiny. And when you learn how to do this, that is going to alter everything for you in the biggest, the best, and the brightest of ways.

WHO SHOULD READ THIS BOOK

This book is for anyone and everyone who has the desire to reconnect to their greater truth as a soul. To transform your destiny is to ultimately meet this deeper part of yourself that you are perhaps not as connected to as you could be. Once we have established this reconnection, we're going to figure out how we can strengthen and enrich it. This book is for those who want to become unstuck and find their happiness again. It's for those who have become stagnant in their lives and want to start growing again.

This book is also for those people who want to level up their lives. It's for anybody who wants to have a more meaningful life, or who finds themselves thinking that maybe there's a better way. It's for anybody who wants to better understand why their life is how it is right now and how to transform it.

After learning about some of my struggles, I do hope that you see that if I can do this, anyone can do this. By opening myself up to going into the stuff in my life that wasn't working and being willing to face my fears and be vulnerable, I was able to transform my destiny.

During this transformation, I hit several milestones that upleveled my journey and brought some of my abilities back online that were dormant and waiting to be released and expressed.

Every one of us has these abilities within us, and they are different for each of us. It's just a matter of doing the work to get to them. Later in this book, I share one of these transformational moments in which my mystical abilities came online. I use these abilities in my work and throughout this book to reach a deeper place and realm than most people know is possible. You have the same potential inside of you; it's just a matter of choosing to consciously move towards your Greater Destiny.

My belief is that on a soul level you have already done so, just by finding this book...

CHAPTER 1

WHAT IS DESTINY?

So, you think you know about destiny?

Let's take a look at the general consensus about destiny and some dictionary definitions.

From *The American Heritage® Dictionary of the English Language, 5ᵗʰ Edition*:

des·ti·ny   dĕs´tə-nē

- *n.* The inevitable or necessary fate to which a particular person or thing is destined; one's lot.

- *n.* A predetermined course of events considered as something beyond human power or control.

- *n.* The power or agency thought to predetermine events.

From the MerriamWebster.com dictionary:

destiny
des·ti·ny | \ˈde-stə-nē\

1. something to which a person or thing is destined
2. a predetermined course of events often held to be an irresistible power or agency

Now, if your concept of destiny is limited to one of the dictionary definitions listed above, I encourage you to be open to expanding it. Throughout this book, I am going to take you on a much deeper dive into the true nature of destiny and impart some deep wisdom that you can carry forward with you.

How am I going to do this? By breaking destiny down into all of its parts and pieces so that you will not only understand it but use it in a lasting way that will create deep and permanent change.

But, of course, that kind of change won't just come from me—you'll have a significant role of your own to play in it as well! I strongly recommend that you take the exercises that are in this book to heart and complete them all. Don't let your ego trick you. It might say, "Oh, you should just concentrate on reading it on the first go-around. We'll do the exercises later." You may never return to do them again later—and even if you do, you won't feel the same way on your second read as you do on this one.

Your best results will come by creating a snapshot of where you are now and immersing yourself into the present. So, before you go any further, make sure to get a notebook that you can dedicate to working on the exercises. You will be more deeply committed to the work, and completing the exercise portion of the book will help impart and solidify this knowledge neurologically, transforming it into the wisdom that you seek.

Take this work seriously and treat it as if your life depends upon it—because, in reality, it does! If we don't learn to understand destiny, then not only can life become boring by repeating itself over and over again, but it can become one big crapshoot.

TWO LEVELS OF DESTINY

As I mentioned in the Introduction, destiny is such a misunderstood topic on our planet. People who believe in destiny think that there is only one path—God's destiny—when, in fact, there are two different levels of destiny: our Lower Destiny and our Greater Destiny.

LEVEL 1: YOUR GREATER DESTINY

When you are in complete alignment and/or resonance with your Greater Destiny, you will have morphed into a divine human. In other words, when you are truly at one with your Greater Destiny, there will no longer be a separation between you and the Divine ever again. The Divine has a much bigger plan for all of us, and the only way you can start to access that plan is in the sacred act of becoming one with the Divine.

What your soul wants most is growth for the purpose of evolving and expanding itself. Your ego, or your personality, also wants to be in charge, however, which means the soul takes a back seat when the ego starts steering your ship. Now, the cool thing is, just so you don't get too hung up on this, if that's how this life plays out for you, then you'll get another chance—and the soul knows that.

Eventually, in this lifetime or another after it, the soul is going to get its way. The soul is going to evolve. Why? Because it's destined to evolve. It might very well be in your destiny to become a divine human in this lifetime. Only you can know that by going inside, checking in with yourself, and examining your life.

What are the results in your life telling you? Is there a possibility that you are going to move into complete alignment with the Divine? What that means is you've got to bring your humanness into alignment with your divinity—you've got to unify these two.

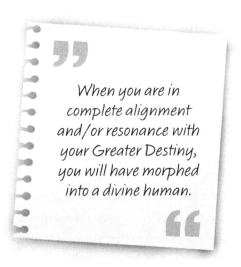

> When you are in complete alignment and/or resonance with your Greater Destiny, you will have morphed into a divine human.

What it also means is that you're going to have to let go of your self-centered ways, whatever that takes and however long it takes. You're going to have to get better at moving into the centered self, the realm of the soul, and then stay there for as long as you can. You might lose it again for possibly an hour or two, a day or two, or a period of time. Then you'll shift back into the centered self again—and eventually, it becomes a lifestyle. Others have gone before us and actually accomplished this, which means that we can all do it as well.

THE DIVINE AGENDA

When we look at our Greater Destiny, we operate under a Divine Agenda. Now, this Divine Agenda is a key element because what it ultimately represents is things like higher desires. A higher desire could be the desire to become really healthy or to become really conscious. A higher desire could be to have truly loving relationships or to be of greater service to your family, your community, or your company. A higher desire could be to be wealthy or to be a philanthropist. A higher desire could be to do the right things even when they feel most uncomfortable. These are the things that truly move us towards the positive.

Another aspect of the Divine Agenda is the genuine needs of the soul. Pretty much everyone's soul has a genuine need to grow, but beyond that, there are other needs that your soul came into this life with. You might have a genuine need as a soul to master love—both the giving of love and the receiving of love. Maybe you're not very good at receiving love. Or perhaps you're not very good at giving love.

Maybe your love is conditional, and you don't even know it—and before you took your first breath, your soul said, "You know what? We're going to develop a genuine need to experience love, and we're going to master it this time. We're going to master what love really is—and in doing that, we're really going to explore what it's like to give love from a conditional point of view versus an unconditional point of view. And we're going to explore what it's like to receive love—to really open ourselves up and let ourselves be loved by someone else."

The Divine Agenda is such where we're really dialing into a higher desire and choosing to align our life with it. We are dialing into a genuine need of our soul-self. That need might be the need to evolve, which means the need to grow, which really means the need to heal and resolve. Evolution is a stairstep process.

23

Another part of the Divine Agenda has to do with your higher energy patterns. When you are in alignment with your Greater Destiny, you can access higher energy patterns. For example, one of the higher energy patterns is the pattern of perfection, which basically says with anything that happens, there's perfection in it all—and when you're operating from this level, you'll rather quickly see the perfection even in the most chaotic of situations. Sometimes you'll see it before it even plays out. But that's because you're now the embodiment of that higher energy pattern. Most people on the planet are trapped in the lower energy world. They don't even know what a higher energy pattern is. They don't even know it exists. They've temporarily lost the awareness that this is all available because to access a higher energy pattern, you've got to start tapping into your Greater Destiny.

MULTI-DIMENSIONAL ASPECTS OF YOUR SOUL

Your soul is multidimensional, not only in the sense that there are many facets that make up your unique soul, but you as a soul also exist in different dimensions simultaneously. How cool is that?

Have you ever heard the expression that someone is an "old soul"? The age of your soul will determine how many aspects of your soul are alive and well somewhere, waiting for you to call them in. These aspects could be parts of your soul that exist in other times, living out their expressions in other dimensions. This is a mind-bending concept for some and a comforting one for others. How one perceives this concept often has to do with the age of their soul. An example of this might be someone rejecting this idea, which could be an indicator that they are a very young soul and this information is just completely foreign to them.

As you morph into your divine humanness—as you morph into your Higher Self—you're going to have an experience with those other parts

24

of you. What might this look like? You might experience a knowing of another lifetime where you are a specific person—a person of great prominence. Or perhaps you were a dynamic healer in another lifetime. In this case, there's going to be another natural higher ability that this part of you has already developed. But, up until now, you've had no access to it at all. Upon discovering this, you might be able to tap into this ability in this lifetime. It all comes back to the age of you as a soul.

The Divine Agenda is such where we're really dialing into a higher desire and choosing to align our life with it.

At some point, as you're embodying your Higher Self and becoming more divine in your human form, other facets of you are going to make themselves known, and you're going to have an experience with them. If this has never happened to you before, I can almost assure you that your first experience is going to leave you feeling somewhat disoriented— partly because it's been foreign and an unfamiliar concept thus far.

Once one of these facets opens and starts to make itself known to you, you can't stop the process. It can be a little shocking, unsettling, and potentially disorienting. Though you may not feel like you're ready for this to happen, the only way it will happen is if you're truly ready for it. It must be deemed by your Higher Self—which is very much like a guardian angel that's with you all the time and knows whether you're ready for it or not.

LEVEL 2: LOWER DESTINY

The second level of destiny is your Lower Destiny. This is the destiny of your Lower Self. Energetically, your Lower Self exists in the same column as your Higher Self; as **you** move up in vibrational frequency, you find your Higher Self, and as you go down in frequency, you find your Lower Self.

If we haven't opened ourselves up yet, or perhaps we're not yet willing to open ourselves up yet to a greater possibility, then at Lower-Destiny level, we remain basic humans instead of moving into becoming divine humans.

The basic human is just playing it safe. That's all they're doing because they have a deep-seated need for safety that they haven't fully recognized yet or ultimately worked through, released, or resolved.

If we're at basic-human status, we're not going to ascend to divine-human status overnight. But what we can do—what any of us can do once we become aware of this—is start working through whatever we need to work through.

What I've noticed over four decades of working with thousands of people from all walks of life is that if a person simply starts the process of transforming some part of their life that they have acknowledged they want to change, and then they identify the very next thing that's required of them, they are able to move the needle forward and change that particular part of their life.

Let's say that someone is in an unfulfilling career. They're in a career that's no longer working for them, and they've now identified that it's time to change this. Should they choose to stay in this career that's no longer working, this will have its own negative affect on them and their life. However, should they choose to declare that it's now time to change this, the very next thing would be identifying the next step they're going to need to engage in to begin to move that needle forward in changing their career.

So if they recognize that this is what they now want to change in their life, then what is that very next thing that they're going to need to do? Maybe the next thing could be that they hand in their resignation. Making a move like that is probably going to require them to have a significant amount of trust in themselves, their Higher Self, or a higher power. Or if that's not the best move for them at this juncture, maybe they decide to start looking for a new career. Or maybe they go to a career counselor.

Whatever it is, they've now identified that this is something that's up for them to change. And now they're beginning to move forward in doing something proactive about it.

This reminds me of how some people were when they attended their first seminar with me. Looking back, so many of them were just unfulfilled. Some were in a lot of pain because they were in a job or a career that they did not like. They would blatantly state: "I don't like it" or "It's not for me." It was clearly up for them to change.

Remember that one of the ways to rise into your Greater Destiny is to choose to get out of those Lower Destiny patterns and areas where you are not fulfilled. Those are basic human characteristics. Ideally, we want to shift our thinking towards making divine human choices.

When it comes to this second level of destiny, or Lower Destiny, we don't have a Divine Agenda—we have a personal agenda. When someone is operating purely on human agenda, they are driven exclusively by their own self-centered desires.

Lower Destiny is also where we have those lower energy patterns and karmic patterns. The karmic patterns are the heavier ones. Now be aware that someone who's operating completely at the level of Lower Destiny might actually believe it's their Greater Destiny. They might think this is what God wants. They might think: "If it happened, it was meant to be." God wanted them to break their leg or God wanted them to have an abusive, toxic relationship. No—God did not want that. The Divine did not want that.

When it comes to Lower Destiny, we don't have a Divine Agenda—we have a personal agenda.

This is an example of a 100 percent personal self-centered agenda at the level of Lower Destiny. They were going to do it their way. They weren't going to listen to anybody or even to listen to their Higher Self. They weren't going to listen to their own intuition. They were going to do this no matter what. They were convinced this was the right thing to do because they had already justified it in their mind, not their heart, that they were right—that they deserve this—still not picking up the clues that they were operating from their own personal agenda. They were going down that track like a train at 85 miles an hour. Nobody could stop them.

RISING UP FROM YOUR LOWER DESTINY INTO YOUR GREATER DESTINY

As you are rising from your Lower Destiny into your Greater Destiny, you will likely discover aspects of your soul that you were unaware of or that were dormant. As you're rising up, at some point, you're going to make a connection with another aspect of your soul. That aspect of your soul is a part of your Higher Self—just like an aspect of your ego is a part of your Lower Self.

You'll be discovering more of yourself as you start to access other soul aspects during this rise. Whatever you see as you stand in front of the mirror is not even a tenth of who you truly are, but you've got to rise into this higher frequency to access all of you. This is all part of the rising-up process from your Lower Destiny into your Greater Destiny.

If there's more than one soul aspect, then the next aspect comes in—then another aspect comes in, and so on. For each soul, it's going to be different. Where your soul is at and where my soul is at could be two completely different places; not that one is better than the other or less than the other—they are just at different places along that of our respective journeys. Now as an aspect of our soul integrates, we may realize: "Wow, I'm different—I've changed in the best of ways."

One of my soul aspects is problem solving. What that means is when I was born into this life, I already had it. Another soul aspect would be my ability to interpret dreams. There's been no training whatsoever in my life for these aspects; they just came naturally to me. Another example of this would be that I'm an entrepreneur. Entrepreneurialism is a soul aspect.

So, as a soul aspect is being realized, there's not a lot of work involved to actually manifest it. Rather this becomes a discovery process, just like it was with me when it came to interpreting dreams, problem solving, and starting businesses.

Other soul aspects could be a creative cook or creative chef. We've all come across somebody like that who, when they cook a meal, it is phenomenal. Or the parent of all parents could be a soul aspect. They just parent like no one's business. And yet they've had no training in their lifetime for parenting. There are countless other soul aspects. The point is that as a soul aspect fully integrates, these are the things that come with great ease to us, as in the chef of all chefs or the parent of all parents.

All of us get to rise up from our Lower Destiny regardless of who we are or our soul's age. When we were born into this life, we signed on to go through this. The question becomes, how long will it take us to understand what's really going on—and then to fully embrace our Lower Destiny as a way to rise up into our Greater Destiny? Will it take ten years? Will it take fifty years? Will it take a whole lifetime? Might it take five lifetimes? What will it take? Again, everybody is going to experience this differently and in a way that is unique to their soul.

As you start to rise into your Greater Destiny, once again, you might feel disoriented because it could shock your system a bit. Then there's going to be an integration. You're going to start to feel more of the magnitude of who you are because your Higher Self encompasses all of this. But nobody can go from zero to one hundred overnight.

The Higher Self is very powerful, and that power is electric. When it starts entering your physical vessel, you will feel larger and more formidable. You will feel stronger in your body. It will actually start working at a higher level and functioning in a way that it has never functioned before.

The process of becoming your Higher Self, little by little, slowly but surely, starts to take over the physical vessel over time. Your Higher Self takes over your brain. Your Higher Self takes over your personality. At some point, there is no more personal agenda. You begin operating 100 percent from Divine Agenda. Everything is cleared in your partnership with the Divine before anything's acted upon.

There are a set of talents, abilities, and gifts that we have that are a part of our Greater Destiny.

It's not because you're trying to force it anymore, rather this has become a natural expression of your soul as your Higher Self.

One final point here is that there are a set of talents, abilities, and gifts that we have that are a part of our Greater Destiny. That said, it's important to develop an awareness around the fact that those talents, abilities, and gifts could also be used against us if we are in our Lower Destiny thinking it's our Greater Destiny.

For example, some of the celebrities who have committed suicide due to overdose were using one of their abilities to make people laugh. They were the best of the best, right? This was a higher ability—no doubt about it. It was a super ability, and yet that ability ended up being used against them and that became their own demise. You can have a famous movie star who's a superb actor, and yet that can be used against them in the end.

So, whatever your abilities are—and you have at least a couple of abilities and talents that you were born into this life to utilize for a higher and greater good—however, if they are being used solely for personal agenda, they can ultimately be detrimental. Another example could be someone making a lot of money from an innate gift, talent, or ability they have, then they go and buy a lot of drugs, have a lot of sex, or believe they can have anybody they want. They'll make some big mistake along the way. They'll possibly hurt somebody and in the process, destroy themselves. Why? Because their ability, their gift, was being misused under the influence of their personal agenda. It was never being used under the influence of their Divine Agenda.

When you become a divine human, you have the same abilities that you had when you were in your Lower Destiny. When you're a basic human and you rise in your Greater Destiny, every talent, ability, and gift that you have is utilized for one reason, and that's to accomplish a higher and greater good. There's nothing self-centered about it anymore. It all comes out of a centered self. Now it's all being utilized in the best of ways—in the highest of ways—where it's going to make a difference in the life of another individual outside yourself or in another aspect of life.

Whatever they are, the abilities that you are born in this life with will be utilized at that highest level. But you've got to rise into your Greater Destiny, which means you've got to do the work. You've got to get a better handle on your Lower Self. You've got to get a better handle on your basic human tendencies and on your own personal agenda. If you're not aware that you're under the influence of your personal agenda, then your abilities, your talents, and your gifts are likely being used for self-centered reasons. That's what keeps you at the level of a basic human.

You might happen to make a couple of poor choices along the way. These can get you stuck at the level of destiny where you'll stay at the status of basic human. You might stay at this level for the rest of your life—until next time, when you get another chance to show up differently. But since you're reading this book, you will have a newfound awareness around these concepts so that this doesn't have to happen to you.

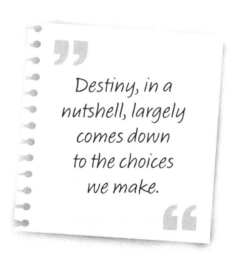

Destiny, in a nutshell, largely comes down to the choices we make.

The unhealed parts of us that have not yet been fully integrated can keep us trapped in our Lower Destiny for years—maybe even decades. If we don't get to it, it doesn't just naturally come to us. For example, our ego is not going to come to us and say, "Hey! I'm your ego. Please heal me." The ego's going to be very secretive with us. It's going to pretend like it's not even there so that we keep on doing what we've been doing. That's how it gets more of our power, so it can get its way with us more often under that personal agenda. We will learn more about how this happens with the ego later in the book.

At this stage there can't be a partnership with the Divine yet because the ego is not interested in being in a partnership with anyone. A negative aspect of the ego is being self-centered. The ego is not about anything outside of itself. It's only when we're in that place of the centered self that in those moments, we can connect with the Divine. In those moments, if we listen, we can hear and feel the Divine—we can maybe even feel the nudging of the Divine to do something towards becoming it. That's really the greater goal here. The ultimate destiny, should we choose it in this lifetime, is to become that divine human—to bring our life into alignment with the Divine. It's like the phoenix rising out of the ashes.

Once you step in, you'll start to feel the early experiences of becoming a little sliver of your Higher Self/Divine Self. And when that happens, you cannot mistake it because the feeling is so profound in every one of your seventy trillion cells that make up your physical form—again, you cannot deny it. Even just a little piece of it will expand you immediately. It's an amazing experience.

At that point, your inner life becomes so incredibly rich that you wouldn't dream of avoiding your inner life ever again. You'll want more, and now you'll know what it takes to have more, so you'll become even more devoted.

Then, at some future point, it will happen again, and you'll feel another aspect of your Higher Self/Divine Self that has made entry into your body temple. And again, you'll know it because it just naturally expands you. You're going to feel the largeness of it.

As wonderful as this all sounds, the question remains: How much can you handle of your Higher Self at any given point along your life's journey? There's a reason why the masters who have gone before us often took multiple lifetimes of dedication in order to master all parts of self and their overall field of consciousness. When they finally did become masters, everything became so simple, easier, and more powerful. Their life was harmonious and in complete resonance with the Divine.

FREE WILL, KARMA & WISDOM

There are some major events that are pre-written into our lives, such as the majority of our significant relationships. However, destiny, in a nutshell largely comes down to the choices we make. If, for example, something unexpected happens to me in my life, I have the choice to show up one way or another. I could act crazy, become very reactive, and literally get swallowed up in this unexpected event, or I could choose to stay in my center, behave responsibly, and show up maturely. Those are two different responses to the same event that will impact what will happen next in my life. One thing we're going to do in this book is take a deep dive into free will, how you exercise it, and how it influences and plays into your destiny.

There are also lessons that we've come here to this planet to learn—and this is where karma comes into play. Nearly everyone has heard of karma, but few understand what it really means. So, one of our goals for this book is to help you deepen your understanding of karma and how it, too, relates to destiny.

Another area that we're going to be exploring is wisdom. Someone who is truly becoming wiser makes healthier choices, and these choices align better with their Greater Destiny. And if they do start to veer off of their path, their newly earned and embodied wisdom will help them to sense this; they'll be able to make a quick U-turn and choose again.

COURSE CORRECTING YOUR PATH OF DESTINY

Whenever you find yourself veering off your path, it's important for you to recognize this so you can begin to course correct and come back to a place of centeredness, joy, and happiness again. For so many people, once they go off their path, the joys in their world—the meaning, the happiness, the fulfillment—go away. This is where they can lose hope. I've spent years working to serve people in the best and brightest of ways to try to minimize the number of people that find themselves in these places—especially in the darkest of places, where they're thinking about taking their life because they've lost all hope.

In my view, someone who has strayed off the path that was written by their soul has lost that ray of hope. They don't have that happiness; and at this juncture there's very little light in their life. And the longer they stay off their path, the darker and heavier and denser their life becomes. Sometimes they reach a place where the only way they can get happy is to go out and have five or six drinks. They have to stimulate their system one way or another; to some degree, choices like these become a survival mechanism for them.

A significant part of my mission is to minimize that as much as possible. Too many times we find people getting stuck in their own lives. They can get stuck in that heavier, darker place and then even stay there for some time. This is where things can become very risky, as they could give up on themselves entirely. I believe it would make a huge, lasting difference on this planet to help change this.

So if you really are up to this mission of transforming your destiny, then you've got to get both feet in—and more importantly, you've got to keep them in. You can read this book with casual interest, or you can take the words in these pages to heart on a much deeper level and make this quest a part of your daily life.

If you choose to put both feet in and keep them in, then you're going to stay there. When you get both feet in and planted into your healing and transformation, you cut off all the escape routes. You cut them off on purpose because if you don't, you will be tempted to go back.

So take a moment right now to examine where you are at. This is a crucial point in your journey. Do you have both feet in the game, or are you still operating with one foot in and one foot out? Because if you aren't all in, you'll never get there.

> If you really are up to transforming your destiny, then you've got to get both feet in—and keep them in.

Regardless of what you decide right now, throughout the coming pages you will discover where you are really at with your commitment level and if that needs to be deepened. The results don't lie! So keep documenting your progress, do the exercises, and continue journaling what comes up along the way. Then, your self-centered, negative ego can't trick you. This documentation will minimize the possibility of defaulting to one of your lower energy patterns that can distract you from your higher path.

You're going to be prompted by your soul to choose how vulnerable you are willing to be or if you'd rather let those lower energy patterns continue to run you and your life. Whatever your truth is in current time, that's exactly what's going to reveal itself to you. Don't let that scare you—this is exciting! This journey that you have chosen at soul level, some time ago, is ultimately about moving towards the greater version of you that is simply waiting to reveal itself, as in your most authentic self.

EXERCISES

1. So, before you go any further, make sure to get a notebook that you can dedicate to using for these exercises. By doing this you will be more engaged and committed to the work. Completing the exercise portion at the end of each chapter of this book will help to impart and solidify this knowledge on a neurological level, transforming it into the wisdom that I know you seek.

2. How well do you know yourself? Write a description of how you see yourself in current time: your temperament, your level of joy, your productivity, your follow through, your choices, etc. This will serve you well as you progress on your journey to your Greater Destiny. Be sure to date it for later reference!

3. What are the results in your life currently telling you? The results never lie—so it's time to be honest and start getting real with yourself.

4. Think of a time that you had your mind made up and no one was going to tell you otherwise, but, upon later reflection, it turned out poorly and you can see in retrospect that it was a Lower-Destiny path choice. Describe what happened.

5. Now think of a time that you chose something that truly turned out wonderful and self-nurturing. As you reflect on this, you can

see that it was a Greater Destiny path choice. Describe what happened.

6. What is one your soul aspects that you have already discovered (something that is effortless or comes naturally for you)? Write out how this soul aspect has shown up in your life.

7. What is one of your abilities or talents? Do you use it in a Greater Destiny or Lower Destiny way? (Be honest.)

8. Continue documenting and journaling what comes up for you as you work through this book. Every time you get activated, that is a little gem trying to reveal something to you—treat it as such!

CHAPTER 2

WHAT DOES IT MEAN TO TRANSFORM YOUR DESTINY?

S o, when we say that we want to transform our destiny, what does that really entail? When most people hear the words "transform your destiny," they want to jump right into that more pleasant part. They want to get right to the part of their destiny where they're having the time of their lives because they finally get to be their most authentic self and do whatever it is that only they know how to do so well. That is definitely part of it, but we've got to be ready to do some work to get to that wonderful place. You know that saying that the best things in life are worth fighting for? Well, just remember that and keep that reminder in the forefront as you embark on the path of transforming your destiny.

For a lot of people, their destiny transformation means working in a career that makes them happy because that's a big part of what destiny is. That's the higher part, or that more joyous part of your destiny, where you really get to utilize your unique talents and abilities—and you get to do so in a way where you're in service to people, whether it's your customers or the other people in your company. It's where you get to be a part of a group, or a family, and where you get to be acknowledged and honored and celebrated. That's going to feel just absolutely amazing to anybody on this planet. It's something that everybody ought to experience—and boy, just imagine what a beautiful society we'd have if everybody on the planet *was* experiencing that!

We must be
willing to see
it in order
to clear it.

But there's a whole other piece to destiny, and it has to do with what goes on underneath that higher, more joyous part. This is where I'll make further distinction between Higher Destiny and Lower Destiny. It is essential to raise the vibrational frequency of the lower part of our destiny, as in working through the underbelly of our consciousness. I refer to this process as our inner work. This part of our journey is often challenging and hard work, but also is the most rewarding. Unfortunately, a lot of people aren't willing to do that for whatever reason—but there are a lot of people that won't work hard in any area of their lives. Others are stuck, some feel like it will be way too much work, some are afraid, and some just don't understand it. But we're all meant to be working to transform that lower part of our destiny so that we can move towards obtaining the higher path of our Greater Destiny.

So claim it! Proclaim, "I want this. I can do this. I am doing this." By declaring this out loud and putting it out into the Universe, it comes back to you. This is supported by the Universal Law that says what I send out comes back to me. So keep sending it out!

We all have blind spots, and these arise from the temptations that are part of our Lower Destiny. If we can be tempted, be assured it will happen, and these temptations, if acted upon, are what can then hold up our progress in transforming our destiny. It's important to remember that we must be willing to see it in order to clear it.

Some people have a lot of blind spots, which means they really can't see what's going on in relation to themselves or their own life. It's usually easier to see what's going on in relation to somebody else than it is when we put the focus on ourselves. And when we are putting the focus on others, it generally is a distraction we are creating under the influence of our own ego to postpone looking at ourselves. It's also good to note that what we notice most in others is usually a reflection of something that is within us. Now that might be tough to hear, but it's true! So keep that in mind when you get hung up on something about someone else. Simply ask yourself, "What is this trying to tell me about myself?" The answer might be very revealing should you be willing to go there. Remember, it's not as easy to bring the focus onto us—to really put ourselves in the hot seat. This in itself is a scary thing for some, as this could amplify that fear inside of us if we have not transformed or healed yet. But the rewards are waiting for us within our Greater Destiny once we do.

CONFRONTING ONE OF MY DARKEST FEARS – PART 1

Speaking of fear, I had confronted many of my fears, which eventually led me to going face to face with my own fear of death.

Now I have had a few personal experiences with death in this lifetime; not only near-death experiences, but I have actually died as well. Each experience was profound and revealing in different ways. Some of my greatest discoveries and deepest insights came from these experiences.

One of them was the time I did a long-standing liver cleanse. I was about halfway through what ended up being a year-long cleanse; little did I know that this cleanse would lead me to my most impactful and insightful of all my brushes with death.

I had rented a hotel suite and created a cave-like setting that I could have this experience in. I knew this was coming, I knew what I needed to do, and I created an environment that I could do it in.

My doctor, Dr. Ron Greenawalt, who was to become one of my dearest friends, was the only person who knew what I was up to. I wanted at least one person to know because I was confronting some deep and dark stuff at the time. I knew I was going through some things that most people never go through in the course of their life. I knew I was not so much in foreign territory, but I was in the type of territory that the majority of people would never understand. Neither did Dr. Greenawalt. When I shared some of the deeper experiences with him throughout that year, he would respond, "All I know is that you're speaking truth." Some of the things I was sharing with him he didn't fully understand because he had no reference point for them at the time. But he would do applied kinesiology tests every time I shared anything with him, and they confirmed that, as he put it, "What you are sharing with me is rare, remarkable, and authentic."

I was about maybe a third or almost halfway through this cleanse, when one night I went to bed, having just done one of my evening rituals. This was the first time in which I became aware of a mystical ability, that I've now fully embraced. But I didn't make the connection to what it was at that moment. It was around 10:30 that night when I was lying in bed, and the room was pitch black on purpose. I had it all set up so it would be literally like a cave in dirt—similar to my experience when I was in the pit that is 750 feet into the earth, below the base of the great pyramid in Egypt.

I was sitting up at a 40-degree angle because I had just completed my ritual, and my body was doing some amazing things at that point. I was experiencing a lot of high-level sensations, such as my inner eye was opening, and I was seeing things beyond the room that were not of this world.

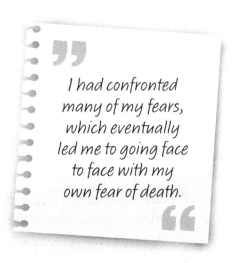

> *I had confronted many of my fears, which eventually led me to going face to face with my own fear of death.*

Next thing, you know, I could see my liver—and I could see my liver exactly as it was. (Someone who is a medical intuitive has a similar ability.) Then my liver started to speak to me. It began telling me about the memory it was holding from this life. I started getting flashbacks, and suddenly, I knew I was literally dying. My liver was releasing memories from different periods of my life that were flashing right before me in full living color.

When someone dies, sometimes it takes a few months for that person to actually transition. Sometimes it takes longer, sometimes it's shorter, and sometimes it's immediate. But, once the transition occurs, we go through a number of different steps—and one of them is that we get a review of our life as we've lived it.

What happens is things are being set up for us to go into something like a reevaluation chamber where we're going to evaluate how well we did or what we did in the course of our life. It's the time where we're remembering what we at soul level put into motion prior to taking our first breath for that life. Then, we're comparing it to how well we did. This process of seeing our life happens in a manner of a couple of minutes. All of the significant periods and significant people flash by us at the speed of light. Like we're in a movie theater watching something incredibly fascinating, engaging, and totally captivating. In this process, time as we know it here in the physical world collapses; therefore the experiencing of our own transition becomes far more accelerated and can pass quickly.

In my case, I discovered this some time ago. As I previously mentioned, I have had a few experiences with death. And so, right away I knew I was dying, and I started thinking of some of my kids and students and thought, "Whoa—am I really ready to go?" I knew then that I wasn't ready to go, but I had all the sensations, all the experiences, that one would have when they're literally physically dying. I was fully aware of it. My liver came on, and just like a highly skilled medical intuitive, I was reading my liver at the speed of light.

I was just fascinated with this whole thing. This went on for a while. Next thing you know, I went off into an altered state, and then sometime early in the morning, I felt a set of hands on my chest like I was being revived. I had died in the middle of the night...

This story continues and is completed later in the book.

PARTNERSHIP WITH THE DIVINE

If you're going to live the life you were meant to live—if you're going to become the person you were meant to be from the very beginning of this life—then you're going to need the Divine. More specifically, you're going to need to be in a partnership with the Divine, and you're going to need to be conscious of that partnership. You'll need to know how to work that partnership in the best of ways. In other words, you're not going to do this all by yourself. No one does it all by themselves, including me or anyone who's gone before us.

When you're part of something that's bigger than yourself, you can be assured the Divine has a part to play in that. When you're a part of something that's self-centered, it's not that it's bad, but the Divine did not play a part in that. The Divine is interested in helping you heal, transform, and grow. The Divine is interested in the difference it can make through you whether it's with your children, your grandchildren, your employees, your partner, your friends, your clients, or even a stranger. That's where the partnership aspect comes in.

When you see that someone you love is calling you, what do you do? You pick up the phone. Why do you pick up the phone? Because it's important to you—very simple. This partnership I've been speaking of begins when you can see the Divine in the same way. The Divine becomes important to you, and when the Divine calls, you pick up. And the Divine will call. Did you pick up the phone the last time the Divine called you? Did you listen and follow through on what it said to you? The message may have been, "Get out of this relationship," and you actually followed through on it—or maybe you chose not to listen, and that produced a different result and possibly some unnecessary pain.

When you've got the Divine on your side, you can pretty much accomplish anything because the Divine can influence anything whenever it genuinely needs to—where you can maybe only influence a couple of people or a couple of things. Now, think for a moment about what your partnership with the Divine is like. If it suddenly hit you that you haven't been listening very well to the messages you get from the Divine, then maybe this is a wakeup call to begin doing so. Listening and following through on a message that the Divine gives you can propel the trajectory of your destiny into higher and higher levels, but you have to be willing and ready to do it.

The Divine wants us to have a heavenly experience.

The Divine wants us to have a heavenly experience. All of us are all destined for this. And yet some of us will fight this tooth and nail because that hardness takes over, and hardness and heaven don't seem to go together.

So, we've got to let go of our hard, fixated, or obsessive ways because those things make life difficult when it doesn't really have to be. Can heaven be a place on earth for you?

Take a look at your relationship with the Divine. Do you have one? If so, could it be improved? What do you want this relationship to look like? And what are you willing to do differently to up-level, deepen, strengthen, and expand your relationship with the Divine—with the ultimate goal being to become a divine human?

WHAT IT TAKES TO TRANSFORM YOUR DESTINY

First of all, you are the captain of your own ship. Whether you like this position or not, you are it—there is nobody else! So, for those who are waiting for somebody to come in and save them, it would really be in your best interest to let that go because no one's going to save you but you. Now this doesn't mean that you can't get help. Rather what it means is that once you decide to save yourself, the right kind of help can come in to assist you.

An example of this might be someone coming in to rescue us if we are about to take our life. Or someone could come in and save us if we are about to destroy ourselves or destroy some part of our lives that we really value. But let's be clear—they can't do the work for us. As we've often heard, the Universe, Spirit, or God can only help those who are willing to help themselves.

In order to truly transform our destiny, there are three things that would be beneficial for us to commit to doing for ourselves.

1. GIVE YOURSELF PERMISSION TO WAKE UP

I'm inviting you to give yourself permission to wake up so you can begin to see how your life has been set up and why it's been set up in such a way where your default state is to be asleep. Waking up is incremental; it doesn't happen overnight. No one wakes up one morning and suddenly gets an incredible flash of light that causes them to remember all that they are and all that they've ever been.

You see, there's a process of awakening that we all get to go through, when we're ready or when we choose to, and that process can go on for months or years—and with some of us, even decades before we come to that last initiation where we know all of who we are.

2. TURN TRANSFORMATION INTO A LIFESTYLE

So, what does it mean to turn transformation into a lifestyle? Well, what do you do when you get activated? In other words, what do you do when you feel stressed or emotionally charged? What you do will tell you whether or not you've really turned transformation into a lifestyle. If you're still honoring your addictive behaviors like they're your lifelines, that's not transformation as a lifestyle. That's addiction as a lifestyle. These could be addictions to sugar, alcohol, some activity like gambling or compulsive shopping, or even being addicted to becoming too negative or too focused on the negative. That is it controlling us. We are not in control of it.

If you are serious about rising up into your Greater Destiny, it's time to start exploring these things. Begin to examine what's really going on inside of yourself. Where are you really at? Has something in your life been falling away lately? Has something in your life been collapsing, but there you are, trying to hold onto it so tightly?

That's not transformation as a lifestyle. That's not somebody who is strong. That's someone who is weak. Now, is there anything wrong with that? Of course not. A person can stay weak for however long they wish, as this, too, is a choice. Or, a person might choose to start getting strong upon realizing that they don't want to live their life in this old way any longer.

3. LET GO OF WHAT NO LONGER SERVES YOU

Many of us will cling tightly to things we know are no longer serving us or simply are no longer working for us. This is because they are familiar and seemingly comfortable—though they may be slowly destroying us. Intellectually, we may know it would be best if we let this thing go, but emotionally and experientially, we have our heels dug into the ground. We're not ready, as in we are declaring that we are not ready.

What is beneficial for anyone holding on is to simply acknowledge that this is happening—acknowledge that the collapse is occurring and that we really don't want to have it be this way. Acknowledge that we're afraid and that we're not quite ready to let go of this thing. Inside we know it is this way, and it needs to be this way, but that it is bringing up a lot of fear.

Then, the collapse can continue. The collapse will happen at the rate we are letting it go, so if we hold on, it slows the process, though the process is inevitable.

Once we acknowledge our personal truth, letting go becomes easier. It's easier for us to loosen our grip on this thing if we choose to not remain in denial.

Your soul has already chosen to transform its destiny through you, but you are blocking it when you resist letting go of the things that no longer serve you, or just downright are no longer working for you. Talk about creating unnecessary suffering! So why suffer any longer? Let's roll up our sleeves and get to work on this together!

There are likely some things that are collapsing, crumbling, or are in the process of falling away that you've been holding tightly onto for far too long. Maybe something just came to mind while reading this. If so, make a note of it so you can add it to the exercises section at the end of this chapter.

Let's say we have a secret that we've been keeping to ourselves, and that could be what's knocking on our door. Or maybe we've got an addiction that's been ruling our roost, running our life, or even ruining our life. Maybe it's a serious addiction to sugar, sex, gambling, compulsive shopping, negativity, or whatever. Or maybe there's a person in our life who just feeds us with drama or with too much struggle, and we're addicted to this person. We complain about them all the time, but we also can't get enough of them. We've got to get our fix, right? We've got to get that adrenaline rush. In the simplest of terms, we have become addicted to the drama.

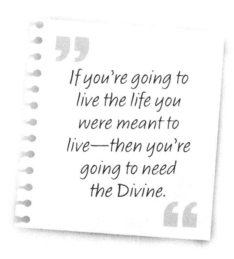

If you're going to live the life you were meant to live—then you're going to need the Divine.

Whatever it is, it would be beneficial for us to pose the question: "Do I think this is helping me to move the needle forward in my life?" If the answer is no, then consider a new strategy. Instead of continuing to stay focused on the addiction or the distraction, perhaps we shift our focus to getting connected to what is going on inside of us that we might be afraid of confronting that is likely contributing to the addiction or distraction.

Some of us are hanging onto old dreams from twenty years ago or old relationships that expired seven years ago. Some of us are hanging onto old ways of life and thinking, "Oh, when I used to be this or that, I was so successful. Everything was working so well. My life was so amazing." That might not even be the truth, but now it's been so long ago that the story has been exaggerated around this fantasy.

But your guides, angels, your Higher Self, and the Universe are saying, "Let it collapse. Stop trying to keep this thing in your life. It doesn't work anymore." And if you aren't willing to let go, you might simply need another round of suffering around this thing that's no longer serving you.

When you are simply unwilling to let go of that which is not serving you, eventually, the Divine will step in and co-create a wakeup call on your behalf. This generally will be louder or more painful than anything you've ever experienced before. It will finally get your attention though because if you don't let go of this thing that is up for you to be letting go of, it has the potential to take you down. Therefore, you need the help of the Divine to snap you out of it—at any cost.

Maybe we decided that we were done and we were going to leave a situation that was no longer serving us. But then we did not follow through on what we said we were going to do. We instead began to justify why we decided to not let this go. Even though we knew we really were to be letting it go. Think about the last time you justified something going on in your world. How recently was it? As soon as you start justifying, that ought to be the gauge telling you that something is off. And, if you continue justifying, chances are this part of your life will get louder as a way to, once again, get your attention.

The Universe loves you. The Divine loves you—let's be clear on this. So, when you can't see something for whatever your reason—or you possibly don't want to see because of what it will imply—at any point, the Universe or the Divine can step in and say, "I've got your back. I'm going to help you see it." If you need a loud wake up call, it will produce just that for you. Say, for example, you're on the verge of breaking a bone, it'll make sure you break that bone. Or you're on the verge of having a car accident, it'll make sure you have that car accident.

> *Many will cling tightly to things that are no longer working because they are familiar.*

It's actually working in tandem with you to help you learn by making something in your life difficult since you couldn't get it the easy way. You didn't notice the little feathers being dropped along your path. Instead, you had to have the Mack truck experience of something crashing down in your world. You might want to check out where I write in greater detail about the Mack truck experience in book one of the Transformation Trilogy. This experience is telling you that something's coming—and it's going to be loud. It's going to be shocking—it's going to jolt your system. Something's going to happen, and you're not going to see it coming. Even though you might have somebody in your corner alerting you that something's coming, you can't even hear that from whoever this is. It is not pleasant when this happens, but it certainly gets our attention—which is exactly what it was designed to do.

Have you seen somebody show up this way, where something's clearly collapsing in their life—something's clearly dismantling itself—and that person is hanging on so tightly to whatever that is? Where they're in a deep fight with this thing that's got to happen no matter what?

If we could all get this down, it would be a huge gift to humanity. If we could all be a walking embodiment of this principle, it would help other people let go of what's no longer serving them and avoid these catastrophic wake-up calls. If you were to embody this practice of letting go before things grew to the need for a painful wake-up call, think about how huge that would be for everyone you interact with.

THE COLLAPSE BEFORE SHIFTING TO A HIGHER FREQUENCY

When we shift to a higher frequency, it changes everything in the biggest, best, and the brightest of ways every single time. However, what you might not be aware of just yet is that as you're coming into this shift, something in your life will crumble, collapse, or be dismantled. When this collapse comes upon you, you're going to feel it to some degree in your bones.

Externally, this could be an old business, relationship, friendship, or partnership. It could be an addictive behavior or a lower-energy pattern that's been running your life for who knows how long. Maybe you've been working through a health issue and you're getting ready to shift your inner frequency to a higher place. This is going to directly affect your physical body in the best of ways.

If you haven't yet made peace with this—if you're still in your own internal fight, hanging on to what's not working because you've got all these justifications—then you're going to be bounced around; you might even think you're being controlled, that you're being manipulated, that you're being done to, that you're being hurt, and so on.

To transform our destiny we're going to need to understand this. Every time we go through another cycle in which our frequency is being raised to a higher place, we experience a change within our own field of perception. An example of this might be that instead of seeing ourselves as being done to, we see ourselves as being done for.

EXERCISES

Write down your responses to the following questions in your notebook:

1. When was the last time that the Divine or your Higher Self spoke to you and you answered? Did you listen and follow through on what it said to you? Explain.

2. Can you recall a time in your life when you didn't follow through on a message the Divine gave you? What happened as a result?

3. Describe your relationship with the Divine, if you are aware of it. If so, what does it look like? How could it be improved?

4. Are your addictions controlling you, or are you able to control them? Take a moment to list some of the things you know you are addicted to currently. This will help you see your growth when you reflect back on this later.

5. What have you been holding onto for too long and too tightly? There are likely some things that are collapsing, crumbling, or are in the process of falling away that you've been holding tightly to for far too long. Maybe something just came to mind while reading this. If so, make a note of it now.

6. Think about the last time you justified something going on in your world. How recently was it? What happened after that?

7. When was the last time you gave yourself permission to wake up to your present moment? Has this become a habit for you yet? If not and you were to choose to turn this into a habit, what is the first thing you would now do?

   And if you haven't done so yet, create an affirmative command for yourself, such as: "I give myself permission to wake up to the present moment today."

   Lastly, ask yourself: "How do I want to show up tomorrow?"

CHAPTER 3

DIVINE BIRTHRIGHTS

At soul level, we only want those things, those experiences, that truly belong to us. We want to live our lives in a way that we were destined to from the very beginning. We want to become who we are divinely meant to be.

Our guides, angels, and our Higher Self already know who that is. We already know what that is as well, though we don't have access to that information and the full truth just yet. So, the Divine is here to prompt us, nudge us, and point us in the right direction when we genuinely need guidance in order to fully and completely manifest our soul's highest purpose and transform our destiny.

Every soul born into this world, into this third-dimensional reality, has a specific set of divine birthrights. I'm going to speak on behalf of the three common birthrights that every soul born into this world has access to. There are other birthrights that vary from person to person, but they don't apply in this context.

Now, if these three general birthrights haven't manifested for us yet, it's not because we're being punished—it's not because the Divine is holding back. Quite frankly, it's because we've got at least one foot on the brake pedal. In other words, we've been holding ourselves back from physically manifesting these birthrights that we are intended at soul level to bring our life into alignment with.

DIVINE BIRTHRIGHT: FREEDOM

The first divine birthright is *Freedom*. We all are born into this life with it. We are to be free to express ourselves genuinely. We are to be free to accomplish what we've come here to accomplish. And yet, you need to figure out what freedom means to you because it very well could be different from what freedom means to me. This guide map I'm giving you will hopefully help you remember the truth that's actually encoded inside of you.

What would it be like for us to literally be able to say that no one or nothing controls us anymore? Think about this for a moment. The truth is we, in our true selves, wherever it is our true self is residing within us, are sovereign. We, as our true selves, are not to be controlled by anyone or anything outside of us. We're not even to be controlled by our own circumstances. How many people in our society, as it is at this present time, feel like they're being controlled by someone or something? As a whole, many have forgotten how to embody this birthright.

In order to start to access this birthright, you've got to get real with your own life when looking at this concept. How much freedom do you currently have in your life right now? This could be in relation to your family. Maybe you have a lot of freedom to express yourself with family members. And then again, maybe you don't. This might also look like freedom in your finances. Maybe you're free financially, or maybe you're not. Are you free to stand up for yourself? Are you free to stand up for your own rights?

And so, you need to define what freedom means to you. I've given you a couple of areas you might be free or restricted in, but this is where you must roll up your sleeves and really start looking for yourself. You've got to start meditating. You've got to start going a little deeper inside yourself. What does freedom mean when you're in a relationship? Freedom isn't just about how much you're experiencing this birthright but also how much you're embodying it. How do you bring freedom into a relationship? Or do you embody the complete opposite? Do you bring control into the relationship and try to dominate your partner? Do you try to make sure things always go your way?

Every soul born into this world has a specific set of divine birthrights.

There is no freedom in domination. That is being in denial of someone else's divine birthrights or in denial of your own. Say, for example, you have a seventeen-year-old child, and you haven't nurtured their freedom yet. Rather, your parental style is all about controlling them to make sure you feel nice and safe; you try to make sure that they never fall down so that you don't have to feel the hurt of them falling, or you don't have to experience your fear of them falling.

That's not nurturing, teaching, or empowering freedom. In this situation, you, as the parent, haven't accessed your own divine birthright and haven't embodied freedom in your own life.

If, in this situation, you do access your own divine birthright and fully embrace the process of embodying it, then there's going to be an awareness that you will have around your parenting style. You'll likely think: "Holy cow! What I'm doing right now is not helping my child to experience the freedom of making a mistake, the freedom of falling down and hurting themselves and actually learning something from that experience of falling down.

I'm blocking them from their own divine birthright. But I've been doing that because I've been blocking my own divine birthright of freedom. I haven't yet been accessing it, utilizing it, experimenting with it, and then ultimately embodying it."

Again, you've got to define this for yourself depending on what your areas of focus are in your life. Some people are further along than others when it comes to embodying this, and everyone has different priorities. Some are really family driven, so they need to bring freedom into their family dynamic. Others are more financially driven, and others are more entrepreneurial. You get the idea here. This birthright is unique to us as individuals and is something we all have and something we all progress towards.

Transforming yourself or transforming your Lower Destiny into your Higher Destiny means that over time, you become the embodiment of this birthright.

DIVINE BIRTHRIGHT: HAPPINESS

The second of these birthrights is *Happiness.* Happiness is a really big deal because if a person doesn't have genuine happiness at some point in their life, this in itself could cause them to unconsciously say, "I don't want to be here anymore. I want to leave. I want to exit the premises. I'll just go ahead and get sick. My sickness will turn into an illness, and then the illness will take over my body." Of course, in order for this to happen, we would have to drop into a deep state of unconsciousness. Which is something we do not want to do.

Transforming your Lower Destiny into your Higher Destiny means that over time, you become the embodiment of your Divine Birthrights.

Happiness is a divine birthright. In fact, happiness is actually a purpose. You can see it all around you because the people struggling to find their purpose can be some of the most miserable people on Planet Earth. It's because they haven't achieved this yet. You've got to come clean with this; you've got to connect with this conscious light and dial into it; you've got to start to embrace it in your world.

Now there's going to be some work involved here—some transformational work, that is. You're going to have to roll up your sleeves in order to sustain this. So, it starts off with having the recognition that this is a divine birthright for everybody. For example, as a parent, we all want the best for our children, right? We all want them to be what? What do we want them to be? Happy!

Perhaps you haven't yet fully embodied this divine birthright, yet you recognize its value when it comes to those you care about. Now, does this mean you need to be happy every day? Of course not. You are still going to have your challenges, obstacles, and problems to solve, but when you embody happiness as one of these birthrights, it becomes an energetic tone in your world. In fact, all of these birthrights are energetically encoded like a keyboard—like the key of C or the key of D.

All you have to do is push the key of freedom, and you start resonating. Or just push the key of happiness, and you start resonating. If you allow this key of happiness to really begin to penetrate your physical cells, what that means is, as an energetic tone, happiness is an undertone in everything you do. This doesn't mean you're always "Mr. or Mrs. Enthusiasm." It means that underneath everything, there's a constant current of happiness. It never leaves you.

These energetic undertones are either in your physical cells, or they're not. If they're not in your physical cells yet, you're always *trying* to be free—and if you keep on trying, you'll become desperate for freedom, and you may do some crazy or even stupid things for that freedom. Or maybe you're *trying* desperately to become happy; the same thing will happen—you'll do some frantic or idiotic things all because you're so desperate for happiness. And you're only desperate because you have not physically embodied it yet. It's inside of you, but it's deep inside of you. Again, you've got to do some work here. You've got to uncover these birthrights; you've got to embody them; you've got to become them; and in doing so they will become you and become noteworthy in your life.

DIVINE BIRTHRIGHT: GRACE

The third divine birthright is *Grace*. I am absolutely flabbergasted at how many people say they lack grace in their world—everywhere I go. I constantly hear things like, "Well, you know, Dale, you seem to be lucky all the time." Or some might say, "You know you're really special, right?" Or some that have known me for a while may say, "You seem to be graced all the time," implying that they do not share the same blessings that I do.

To them, I reply, "Yes, I am. No doubt." But then I say, "You know what? You can be too."

That's the best part of this whole thing. How do I know that? Because I know that you have the same divine birthrights inside of you that I have inside of me. The only difference is that one of us has fully embodied them.

One of my friends, a fellow spiritual healer who lives up in the Pacific Northwest, recently said, "Dale, I just have to tell you something. The amount of activity, angels, and guides around you—it's like you've got a whole army!"

I said, "How do you know that?"

She replied, "Because I can see it every time we're on the telephone. I get these flashes of all these beings that are around you. You've got to be one of the most protected people I think I've ever come across."

I just smiled because I knew she was speaking the truth. Why? Because I know what the undertone is. And I'm a walking embodiment of it. Grace is like the most beautiful cloud. It just hovers around you, and everywhere you go, it just follows you. And within that energy of grace comes things like divine protection—you're protected twenty-four seven.

Heck, I sometimes even forget to lock my doors. I just don't have that concern anymore. Now, when I was a kid and a younger man, I sure did—but I didn't have grace embodied just yet.

Now I'm not better than anybody, and I'm not less than anybody either. But because I have embodied these birthrights, I am a reflector for people who are close to embodying them themselves. You see, my friend up in the Pacific Northwest saw this coming brightly from me, because she is close to embodying grace too. That's what really allows her to see it.

Grace is like the most beautiful cloud that hovers around you, and everywhere you go, it just follows you.

To really embody grace, we've also got to develop the habit of getting better at doing the right things. For example, is it right to be partnered up with a certain person? Is it right for you to be working with this company? If it is, then you want to get better at really embracing that person. You want to get better at embracing that company. If these aren't right, they might be some of those things that no longer serve you.

If it turns out something is not right, and you still try to make it happen, then now you're in pushing and controlling mode. You're actually pushing the divine birthright of grace away. Remember, it lives inside of you. But in this case, you're pushing it down deeper. Within you, you're creating a separation because now you're doing things or hanging out with those that are not truly right for you.

With grace, when it comes to letting go, you just simply let go. You don't hang onto anything anymore. You don't go into a big internal fight. When you're living under grace, you show up graceful. If you're still doing the "jerky" thing—constantly pulling on people, constantly trying to control other people—that's not grace.

So, if you want your divine birthright of grace to be front and center, then you've got to start showing up gracefully. If you're not willing to do the right thing in a graceful way, then how can you be graced? They go hand in hand. If you embody grace, when moving from point A to point B, you do it transitionally instead of abruptly. Grace is a transition.

When we witness a physical death, there's a real difference when you're around somebody who has a graceful transition versus somebody who has a bumpy transition. And quite frankly, most people's transitions are, you guessed it–bumpy. Why? Because they've lived their lives in these abrupt ways, and more specifically, they've done things they really had no business doing—but they kept on doing them anyway.

They had extremely different experiences, which serve as a great reflector for this concept. Again, grace is found in how much of what we are doing in our lives is the right thing for us to be doing.

When somebody has a lot of grace, just watch how they live. They'll give it away every single time. They exude grace in everything they do. You might notice that what they're doing is the right thing for them to be doing. They do it transitionally and honorably. They're the walking embodiment of grace, so, of course, they have a huge cloud, energetically speaking, of grace around them—everywhere they go, they're always protected.

The forces protecting us sense what's coming at us long before it makes an arrival. That's why those of us who are the walking embodiment of grace can spot something coming. And when it comes, we just embrace it elegantly and surrender to it without the fight or the conflict.

So, these are our three most common divine birthrights: happiness, freedom, and grace. And they exist for each and every one of us. It doesn't matter what our circumstances are. In my own life, I had some tough circumstances to navigate through—and yet, all along, these birthrights were inside of me. And now, years later, they have become me, and I've become them. So once again, if I can do this, then absolutely anyone can do it too.

EXERCISES

Write out your responses to the following questions in your notebook:

1. Examine different areas of your life. Which areas do you feel you have the most freedom? And which do you feel you have the most restriction?
   a. Finances: Freedom _____ Restriction _____
   b. Love Relationship: Freedom _____ Restriction _____
   c. Family Relationships:
      Mother – Freedom _____ Restriction _____
      Father – Freedom _____ Restriction _____
   d. Career: Freedom _____ Restriction _____
   e. Other: Freedom _____ Restriction _____

2. Now give your overall level of freedom a rating from 1 to 10. 10 being a lot, 1 being a little. _____
   Why did you give yourself this score?

3. How much of that energetic tone of happiness do you currently feel in your life? Give that tone of happiness a rating from 1 to 10. _____ Why did you give yourself this score?

4. How much do you presently embody and experience grace in your life? Give it a rating from 1 to 10. _____ Why did you give yourself this score?

5. After answering the above questions, write a descriptive statement on how you could improve the embodying of these three divine birthrights in your life starting right now?

CHAPTER 4

FREEDOM OF CHOICE

In the last chapter we learned about our first divine birthright, freedom. One of those freedoms is the freedom to choose. We've all been given free will, and there are two parts of you that have access to it. One is your Lower Self, your ego or personality, and the other is your Higher Self, or soul. In fact, your soul started exercising its freedom to choose before you took your first breath. Your soul chose where it was going next when it came time to incarnate.

If we're not yet the full embodiment of our soul, then our ego can interfere by tricking us with our personal free will, which will generally contradict that of our soul's preferences. Now, I suppose the question is, which one will ultimately win out? Is it going to be the self-centered ego that lives under the influence of the personal agenda? Or is it going to be our soul, the one that is interested in our greater good and highest potential?

Some people don't want to exercise their free will at all—they want someone else to choose for them. I'm sure you've met somebody like this. This could be your mother, father, husband, wife, ex-lover, best friend, next-door neighbor, or one of your coworkers. This is the person who's avoiding personal responsibility big time because what comes with this gift, the freedom to choose, are consequences.

But before we get to the consequences comes responsibility. If we go out and make a choice that results in something unpleasant, but then we blame it on somebody else, then that's us exercising our free will. What we might not be aware of is that we're avoiding responsibility for our own free will when we do this. If we were to continue to do so, we could lose our free will for a period of time.

Examples of someone losing their free will could be a child who has been grounded by their parent for a choice they made, or a prisoner who is now serving jailtime, or an employee facing consequences from their employer. Maybe the employee begins to make choices that are not good for business. They choose to procrastinate on what it is that they agreed they would do. And they choose to do this, say, three or four different times over a period of time.

Now, due to this, the employer is seeing the employee in a different way. The employer is now perceiving his or her employee as someone who cannot be trusted at their word. Maybe the employer was originally thinking, even hoping, that they could promote their employee to a greater level of responsibility in their organization, with a greater amount of freedom. And now that opportunity is not there anymore; the employee has taken the opportunity off the table with their own personal choices. There may be a consequence where this employee has to have more supervision and less freedom to choose what they do with their time at work.

We should think of free will as a gift. The power of choice was one of the first gifts that you and I were given—both at the level of basic human as well as the level of divine human. We might ask ourselves, "Do we want to give the gift back? Or do we want to learn how to utilize it properly as a way to authentically empower ourselves in creating a more enriching life?"

Most of us are not taught how to utilize the gift of free will, how to really embrace it, how to really step up to the plate and take responsibility for this wonderful and sacred blessing we've been given. More specifically, we haven't learned to use it in a way that brings us into alignment with our soul and in a way that brings us into direct partnership with the Divine.

Your soul started exercising its freedom to choose before you took your first breath.

Do you know what happens when you start to align your free will with the Divine? What awaits us is the alignment of our personal agenda with our Divine Agenda.

Prior to that alignment, an individual might think and believe that they're on their own island and that whatever it is that they're dealing with, experiencing, or moving towards in their life, they're doing it all by themselves. Sometimes you'll hear them speak out loud in that way, for example, "If you want something done, you'll have to do it all by yourself."

This would be somebody that's operating within their own personal agenda. While that's going on, they do have access, however, whether they're in alignment with it yet or not, to that Divine Agenda. This would be at the level of their Higher Self or their soul. Even though we might not be aware of it yet, the higher, greater part of us is always living from this Divine Agenda.

So, if this person chooses to exercise their free will and access this higher part that lives from this place of the Divine Agenda, all of a sudden, they begin to realize how supported they are. They begin to see the whole network that surrounds them, both in the physical world and the world beyond the physical—which is filled with our guides and angels that are literally working in service to our greater journey.

When we're operating from that Divine Agenda, a significant part of it has to do with this level of support that is there to make life a little easier for us. When we're encountering a serious choice or a major decision, and we're living in alignment with the agenda of the Divine, it's not just us making the decision anymore. We ultimately make the decision with the support of the Divine because now we're working in conscious partnership with it by understanding that it can offer us insight into the choice we're about to make. The Divine can give us guidance on whether or not this decision is really right for us. The Divine can bring in extra help, not only from the realm beyond the physical but from the physical world as well.

That help could come in the form of a dear friend that we haven't heard from for some time. Next thing you know, we're on the phone with that dear friend or in a meeting with them and somehow, some way, he or she gives us the answer that we've been looking for. And that answer helps us to make the best choice possible.

In the physical world, we can have other forms of support, people that are there for us, like a coach or a mentor, people who we really respect and look up to and who maybe have a stronger connection with the Divine than we do.

These people in our lives can be of great assistance when it comes to helping us make the right choices. They don't make the choices for us; ultimately, we are to be making our own choices.

The Divine is simply waiting for us to come to it, to become aware of it, and to embrace a partnership with it. Once we embrace this partnership and it becomes active in our lives, whatever we're experiencing just becomes a little easier. The Divine is there to help smooth out the edges. The Divine is there to bring grace upon us and do its part to support us in a way that helps us succeed in having a happier, richer, and more fulfilling life. This is available to each and every one of us. All we have to do is become aware of its existence, its presence, its essence in our lives, and then simply choose it.

FREE WILL AND YOUR GREATER DESTINY

In Chapter 2, we learned that there are two levels of destiny—the Greater Destiny, also known as our Higher Destiny, and then there is our Lower Destiny. At the level of our Lower Destiny, we are generally unaware that the quality of our choices determines our ultimate fate. As we upgrade the quality of our choices as a basic human in the energy of our Lower Self, we're now rising up to our Greater Destiny. But that's because we're choosing it.

Reflect upon these questions for a moment. Do you know of anyone who literally came into this life and, shortly thereafter, appeared to completely be in alignment with their Greater Destiny? Or do you know anyone who seemed to come into this life, with the seed of their Greater Destiny buried somewhere within them, who quickly dropped into their human destiny and stayed there? And if you do, how long did they remain there?

More than likely, the majority of people that you know are still in their human destinies. They've likely completely forgotten that there's a Greater Destiny that awaits them. How did that happen? Take it a step further and consider that this same group of people probably thinks that their Lower Destiny *is* their Greater Destiny. And maybe you were right there with them before you started reading this book.

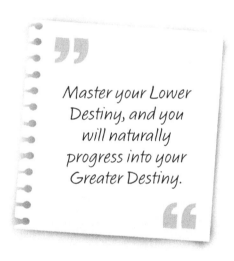

> *Master your Lower Destiny, and you will naturally progress into your Greater Destiny.*

What's happened there? Well, there's a serious misunderstanding of what destiny is—and more specifically, what their destiny is, and the breakdown between the human part and their greater part.

Here's the short answer: Master your Lower Destiny, and you will naturally progress into your Greater Destiny. Before we start this process to embody and ultimately sustain this greater, higher world of our Higher Selves in physical form, we've got to get our act together in the here and now. We've got to know ourselves fairly well on a deeper level. Change to:

Remember in the Chapter 1 Exercise when you answered the question: "How well do you know yourself?" Well, how well do you know that you know yourself? How strong are you in that knowing? How non-wavering have you become in that greater knowledge of yourself? Is it still easy to rattle your cage? How easy would it be for you to get upset—to be knocked off your path? What words or actions really put you in a tizzy, which then takes you looping in your mind? If that's what you're still doing, then your Greater Destiny would be way too much power for you. If you're still doing those things to yourself, you would literally short-circuit or burn your brain cells out if you had access to this level of power at this time.

You might remember years ago that the real powerful engines in our automobiles sometimes had governors installed in them so that we didn't burn them out. It's the same principle here. There's a governor that gets installed energetically in our subconscious. This is there for our own protection—it's there to serve us.

And so, the real simple version of this is to master your Lower Destiny, master your Lower Self, master your basic human status. As you do, this will naturally open the inner doorway into your Greater Destiny. Because you are now becoming worthy and prepared to wield this greater power.

THE POWER OF CHOICE

Every time we make a choice, every time we make a decision, it naturally puts something into motion. So, as the great philosopher Aristotle said, "Choice, not chance, determines our destiny."

There was an awesome movie that came out in the early nineties called *Mr. Destiny*, starring Jim Belushi and Michael Caine. Jim Belushi's character was a guy who was a walking example of the average person who thinks he has it all together—talk about a perfect example of a basic human, the Lower Self in his own Lower Destiny, who was completely unconscious of it.

He eventually finds himself meeting with Michael Caine, who plays the guardian angel—which is representative of his Higher Self. Ultimately, the experiences the main character is having are being given to him by his Higher Self so that he can, over time, begin to make these connections consciously.

In one particular part of the movie, he gets into this place inside himself where he thinks that maybe he picked the wrong woman to marry. Then, it goes back further to when he was a baseball player as a little boy, and he ended up striking out. Because he took that failure on personally at such a deep subconscious level, it influenced him in not getting the woman of his dreams later in life. He becomes tormented with this idea that had he just hit the ball that day and knocked it out of the park, then he would've gotten the woman of his dreams and his whole life would be different.

The whole purpose of his guardian angel, played by Michael Caine, is to come in and educate Jim's character on the power of choice. They have some altered-state experiences together in different scenes throughout the movie. In one scene, Jim Belushi is perplexed. He got his wish—he got the woman of his dreams, so to speak—but he is uncertain that this is what he really wanted.

The angel takes him back to when he was a little boy and says, "Do you remember when you were on the baseball field? You had the bat in your hands, you were at the plate, and the bases were loaded. You were the last one up, and you'd either strike out or you'd become the hero—and you struck out."

So, the angel brings him back to this moment, and as he does, he says, "Now that's the point. We're going to start right here. When you struck out, what did you do? You made a choice based on your action that told you that this is who you are, and this is what you should now expect.

"And, as soon as you chose that, it automatically put a series of events into motion. And that series of events led to this event—and now you're in a conundrum. Now, in this alternate reality, you got the woman of your dreams—so you thought. But, in getting the woman of your dreams, you realized the woman you originally married was the right woman all along.

> Every time we make a choice, every time we make a decision, it naturally puts something into motion.

"But now, she's hit it off with somebody else because she too went on to make other choices. Every choice she made produced another event, and now she's in a different place. It just happens to be, there's all this space in between you, and now there are other people involved."

Like I said, your choices can alter your destiny. You started making choices when you were a kid, and every time you made a choice, especially the significant ones, it put a series of events into motion. That's why once someone lives their life in a certain way and then realizes they don't want to be there, say that by then they've got two kids or they own three properties with another person, that's when things become complex. Or maybe that person is having an affair because they're so desperate and unhappy in this thing that they've chosen. Even at this point, they're certain of this choice they've made to have the affair because they have justified it in their own mind. And nobody can tell them otherwise.

They might've even had a few friends or family members come along and say, "You know what? I don't think you should be doing this."

And then they might respond, "I don't care. It's not hurting anybody else as far as I can see. And furthermore, my wife/husband deserves it because of such and such." And so, this produces another event, and another event, and another event—you get the idea. Now they're in this messy, difficult situation.

Was that their Greater Destiny? No, that was their Lower Destiny that they chose. And, if they're not aware of this, they might be trying to make it about somebody else. They might be trying to blame somebody else—to get somebody else to take the hit for their choices. But they are the one that made the choice. And, once someone makes a choice, a series of events follows it—no matter what.

Now, if you want to get in there and reroute a series of events that stems from a choice you've made, you can do that—but you've got to stand up and be super authentic. You've got to be real and courageous but also gentle. You've got to be all these things. You might say, "But people might not approve of me if I do that. They might reject me." Well, yes—they might. But choosing that authenticity is a step towards your Higher Destiny path, no matter how difficult it may seem as you begin cleaning up the messes that you made in your Lower Destiny.

When we're living our lives at the level of Lower Destiny, for the most part, our soul doesn't even get a say. It pretty much has to sit on the sidelines and just watch this thing play out. Now, the great news is that your soul is more patient and more accommodating than you are. So, it'll let you have this experience and it will wait and wait, since you're the one who gets to choose whether or not your soul gets to come into your life and ultimately take over.

CHOICE IS FOLLOWED BY A NEGATIVE CONSEQUENCE OR A BLESSING

When you or I make a choice, or a series of choices, the effect of that choice or choices becomes one of two things. One, it becomes a negative consequence—a negative consequence is usually painful, it's most certainly uncomfortable, and sometimes it's downright heavy. These negative consequences might be the effects of the choices that we made a week ago, a year ago, five years ago, etc.

Or two, it becomes a blessing. However, to get the effect of a blessing, you've got to make the right choice, whatever that is—and sometimes you've got to make a series of right choices. And when you do, you'll get the blessing. As this happens it will be rather natural for you to recognize it and want more of it.

There's a constant relationship going on between these two worlds of blessing and consequence. Nobody can stop it. You can, however, delay the negative consequence of a choice. And when the negative consequence comes upon you, it's going to come upon you with a little more intensity and be a little more painful since you tried to delay it.

One of the strategies I highlight in book number one of the Transformation Trilogy, *Being Called to Change*, is the "Worship Strategy."

This is when we take our activated energy and begin to worship it. We worship our emotions. We start acting like our emotions are our God and we live at the mercy of them. That, too, is a choice, and if that's the choice we're making when it comes to our emotions, there are going to be effects. You get to decide what the effect is going to be. Is the effect going to be a negative consequence? Or is it going to be a blessing?

> There's a constant relationship going on between these two worlds of blessing and consequence.

What happens if I act out my activated energy on my nine-year-old daughter or son? Is that going to lead to a negative consequence or a blessing? What happens if I choose to be adulterous when I made a promise to be faithful to someone? Do I get a blessing? Or do I get a negative consequence? What happens if I choose to steal a little bit of money from my employer? Maybe I justify it in my head, "But you know, I've been working really hard for them. I deserve this." Well, if you deserve it, then why don't you go tell them that's what you're doing? "Oh, I don't want to tell them." Why don't you want to tell them? "Because they'll take it away from me right away." So, you've now made the choice. You go in and you steal from the business bank account. It's only $200, and the account has $100,000. What's $200 when they have $100,000? No big deal, right? Or is it a big deal? You just made a choice to take someone else's money without asking them.

When we do things like this, there must be an effect—not because we're a bad person, but because it's the Universal Law of Cause and Effect. Choice becomes the cause; the effect becomes the consequence. In this case, every choice (also known as the cause) must be followed by an effect (also known as the consequence) or a series of effects. Whether we believe in this or not, it doesn't matter because universal laws are absolute and unwavering 100 percent of the time.

So, as we go back to this example, we've now committed to the choice. The $200 is gone. It's now being used for our own personal agenda. We've justified it in our head that it's okay because our employer doesn't recognize our worth anyway. So, let's now take a look at the question once again: Would this choice be followed by a negative consequence or a blessing? Pretty obvious, isn't it?

Let's say instead that we chose to treat that business bank account like it's our own. We exercise integrity, responsibility, and honesty. That, too, is a choice. What does that produce? Does that produce a negative consequence, or possibly a blessing somewhere down the way?

It's all about the quality of our choices as to where our path in life leads us. And even the smallest seeming choice can turn the rudder that one degree that takes our ship in a completely different direction. So, as you go forward, try to have the conscious awareness that even the smallest choice is best made with care and an intention for the best outcome possible.

HOW WILL YOU CHOOSE?

The moment you act out a choice, it then becomes locked in. Whether you like it or not, you then get to go for the ride—whatever and for however long the ride is going to be. The ride could be another month, six months, or six years. Each situation is going to be a little different.

These effects are nothing more than direct reflections of the quality of choices that we made. The higher the choice I make, the more blessings I end up with. If I'm making my choices from the human-destiny standpoint, this means I'm making choices for my own personal agenda versus the choices that are truly in my highest and best interest to make with an awareness of how this might affect others in my life, then negative consequences will result.

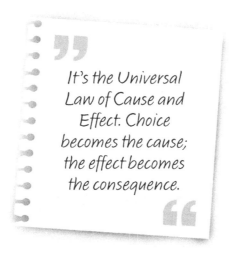

It's the Universal Law of Cause and Effect. Choice becomes the cause; the effect becomes the consequence.

The Divine considers everything. It never considers just one person. The ego, or personality, is the part of you that only considers one person, and it is what drives your Lower Destiny. What will you do next time something comes into your world, tempting you? Will you go for the temptation? Will you step into the doo-doo? While you're stepping in it, will you justify it to yourself?

Remember, when you're justifying and defending an action in your head, you can rest assured that something is off. But when you're acting from your Greater Destiny, you don't show up this way anymore. You don't have to justify anything. You get the message around what to do when you do it, and that's it. There's no more drama.

Why? Because the choice that you're now making is of a higher frequency. It's causing something to happen that's naturally of a more positive nature, without you even trying. You're not expecting anything to happen. But those types of blessings happen because the choices you are making are truly in alignment with your own integrity—with your own Higher Self.

TAKING ON OTHERS' CONSEQUENCES

If you're a parent and your way of parenting is to block your child from dealing with the consequences of his or her poor choices, then you as the parent take on their karma. You take on the consequences. You're going to take the hit. Someone's going to get the consequences—they're not just going to dissolve once they've been created. Of course, we see this a lot, right? The parents get in there and interfere because of their own unhealed issues, and they will not let their child have the consequence—they refuse.

But this doesn't just extend to parents. This can happen with siblings, spouses, friends, co-workers, business associates, etc. This is almost like a sickness within humanity. Taking on the consequences of others for the choices they've made is clearly one of the things we can do that makes our lives really complex and very heavy.

By taking on the consequence of someone else's choice, it might take you a month to clear up that consequence. Heck, it might even take you a year. In fact, in the process of clearing up the results of that consequence you took on, you could potentially destroy yourself financially, creating an even larger mess for yourself. Let's say, for example, that you chose a particular business partner and the partner that you chose ended up being incorrect for your business.

Next thing you know, you are in a bitter fight with this partner. It requires you to go to court, and the attorney fees alone end up surpassing $300,000. Then, maybe you have to pay even more to this business partner by the time all is said and done. You've burned out your finances and drained your bank account. So now you have very little money left. Or maybe you're even in debt—maybe you actually had to borrow money to cover this.

The consequence continues because now you have to change the way you've been living your life. You and your family are now living your lives differently due to the fact that your finances have been depleted.

In some of these types of cases, the individual will say, "You know, the funniest or saddest part of this entire experience I just went through is that I had a sense at the very beginning that this was the wrong person, but I went ahead and did it anyway."

Another example could be the enabler who gets in there and protects someone from having their consequences as a result of the choices they made over a period of time. Let's say there's a married couple. One person has a drinking problem, and the other does not, but the person who doesn't have a problem enables the drinker. They provide an extra shield of protection around their partner, keeping the problem from being discovered by family or friends and constantly sticking up for the drinker.

The enabler is possibly terrified to stand up to the drinker and put it on the line because they're afraid that the drinker might leave them—either out of anger or because if they became sober, they might start to view the enabler differently. They might find that they're no longer attracted to their enabling partner and want to end the relationship.

And so, the enabler's going to become heavy energetically—and clearly, a part of their life is going to jam up on them. They're going to pay dearly for this because again, they're meddling in someone else's choices and the experience they are to be having as a result of those choices.

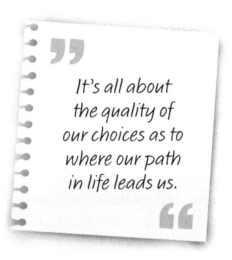

> It's all about the quality of our choices as to where our path in life leads us.

Let's look at the example of the individual who's the overprotector. They could be the person that just can't bear the thought of someone getting harsh consequences for their actions because they're so terrified of change. They're afraid of letting go of this other person. When people take on others' consequences, it can seem selfless at face value, but it is really all about a personal agenda. "Oh, don't you worry about it. I'll take it on. I can't bear the thought of losing you. There'd be nobody in my life to approve of me. There'd be nobody in my life who would make me feel safe."

Another example could be the controller. This person gets in there and monitors every single move, never letting the other person take a fall. You know who these people are; they're riding shotgun all the time.

This person is super needy. They find themselves interfering with the process of someone who has clearly made a couple of choices with negative consequences coming down the pike. But, because this person is so busy controlling everything, the process of the other person receiving their consequence temporarily gets sabotaged. The controller is constantly in there, trying to divert the natural order of things. But the Universal Law, the Law of Cause and Effect, always prevails, and even these acts of controlling have consequences.

In every one of these examples, the person interfering is not only taking on someone else's consequence, but in that process, they are also creating negative karma for themselves. We will take a dive into the positive and negative themes of karma later in the book. These choices they are making are also keeping them in their Lower Destiny. By taking personal responsibility for what they've been doing, however, they can begin to rise into their Greater Destiny. Now they are also going to have to clean up the messes that they've created as a result of these types of choices in order to do so.

THE BLESSING OF THE CONSEQUENCE

Once a negative consequence has been put into place, you are now destined to learn through the experience of the consequence. This in itself becomes another blessing, though it's a tough way to obtain a blessing and it doesn't always feel like a blessing, until you can reflect back on it later and see the growth that came from it.

In order to obtain the blessing from a negative consequence, you've got to take the consequence on as your teacher. In other words, no more resisting the consequence.

Here's a two-step strategy for you:

Step 1: Once you know you've created a negative consequence, just embrace it. Save yourself a lot of time and a lot of heartache. Make the choice in advance that if a negative consequence has been created as a result of one of your choices, you'll just surrender to it. Stop the fight. If you resist your own consequence, you're resisting what you're to be learning about yourself—and more specifically, you're resisting what you're to be learning about your own free will that you were given as one of your divine birthrights. The consequence isn't going anywhere, so the quicker you can get to embracing it, the better off you're going to be. It's just that simple.

Step 2: The moment you step into embracing the consequence is the moment when the retracing of it begins, from the time in which you made the first choice that was then followed by a series of choices leading up to the current embracing of the consequence.

You'll start to see the lesson that is within the consequence. This is where we can become fascinated by what we're discovering about ourselves at an even deeper level. I do hope that by now you have embraced the practice of journaling your insights and discoveries, as this will help the blessing reveal itself to you as we continue this journey together throughout the book.

LEARNING HOW TO CHOOSE WISELY

Consequence will always follow choice, and it's either a positive or negative choice and then a corresponding positive or negative consequence. On the Greater-Destiny level, it's so simple and easy to see it in full living color. On the Lower-Destiny level, it's almost impossible to see it because we can get so caught up in our own personal agenda.

When you're caught up in that personal agenda, you're not accessing the larger perspective at play. You're down there in the small perspective, thinking it's the bigger perspective—but it's not. It's like you're looking through a small lens, thinking you're seeing the whole thing when you're only seeing a part of the picture. That's why you're not able to see the complete process at play: that once you make the choice, it produces a result.

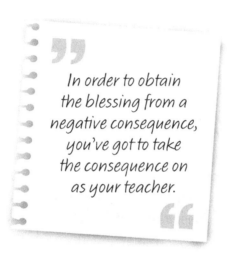

In order to obtain the blessing from a negative consequence, you've got to take the consequence on as your teacher.

The mark of a really wise person is somebody who knows the consequence of the choice they're about to make before they make it. But when you're in the presence of somebody like that, you're in the presence of somebody who's had a lot of experience, someone who's been down and out. You're in the presence of somebody who's probably been beaten up, who knows how many times, because of their choices.

Some of us have become so afraid to make a big choice in our lives. Why? Because we're afraid we're going to make a mistake since we haven't yet learned how to choose properly or wisely. And with some people, being afraid to make choices is killing their dreams, hopes, and aspirations. But not making choices is also a choice.

Choices are governed by laws that are changeless, such as the Law of Cause and Effect or the Law of Choice. We may not be able to change those choices, but what we can change is the way we feel about those choices and learn whatever there is for us to learn from them.

TWO AREAS CHOICES CAN BE MADE FROM

There are two areas where choices can be made from. The first area, which is the most obvious one, is your conscious self. This is the part of you that you're aware of. This is the part of you that decides to run a red light when you're driving down the road. You're making the choice to do that, even though you recognize there might be a risk—meaning there might be a police officer sitting nearby when you run through that red light, and they're probably going to put on their lights, and next thing you know, you're going to see them in the rear-view mirror. You chose to run the red light, and now you're getting a direct consequence right away called a speeding ticket.

When you wake up in the morning, you're choosing what clothes to wear. You're choosing what to do with your hair, your makeup, and how you're going to present yourself. Those are all conscious choices.

The conscious is your outer voice. Maybe something happened at your office, and somebody's really upset you—and you're literally fuming. At night you have a hard time falling asleep because you're thinking about what you're going to say to them the following day. You're going to walk in there and you're going to give them a piece of your mind. That's a conscious choice. That's you choosing to use your outer voice in a way that's going to produce an effect.

You might also choose to use your outer voice in a way to compliment, praise, empower, or to inspire somebody. That, too, is going to produce an effect. It's going to produce a positive consequence, even if the consequence is simply them returning a wonderful smile that makes you feel good because you know you just said something that impacted them in the best of ways.

The conscious choices are pretty easy to figure out. Whereas the unconscious choices aren't. The unconscious or subconscious is the part of you that you're unaware of, that can direct you to do something anytime it wishes. Your ego is part of your unconscious mind, and it has the ability to merge with somebody else's ego and get them to do something on its behalf, though it has to have a certain amount of your power to do so. Remember the example mentioned previously of the alcoholic and the enabler? These two figures are really working together subconsciously for the same goal—which is to keep this dynamic in place for whatever their reason. For the alcoholic and the enabler, the reason might be that they're not even a good match because neither of them wants to be in the relationship. So they're keeping it hidden by continuing on with this dance of unconsciously supporting each other's egos while one partner maintains the addiction to the alcohol and the other partner maintains the addiction to the enabling. What this does is it keeps both of them away from the possible truth that they are not even a good match. If this is what's really been going on, this is because at least one of them wants to possibly end the relationship. Usually, they stay because deep down they're afraid of something, such as possibly being alone for the rest of their life—thus, never being in a relationship again. When that choice is being made on behalf of your ego, you are likely completely unconscious of it.

When that unconscious choice produces its effect, which it will, even though that choice was subconscious, you might go ahead and create a second choice that produces another event. You might even blame it on another person and completely miss the mark that you, on an unconscious level, actually put all this into motion. That's why the unconscious is very tricky.

Carl Jung, the great legendary psychologist, said, "Until you make the unconscious conscious, it will direct your life and you will call it fate." And, if that's what you call it, then that becomes your destiny.

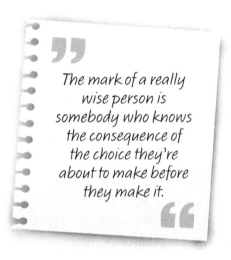

> *The mark of a really wise person is somebody who knows the consequence of the choice they're about to make before they make it.*

For example, say you fell down a flight of stairs and broke your ankle, then you blamed it on God. What happened? You've got something going on at an unconscious level that you're not addressing yet. Whatever that unconscious dynamic is has now been triggered, but your way of dealing with it in that particular state of consciousness is to then put it on someone or something else. In this case, God. But was this God, or fate, or the universe directing this and wanting this to happen? Probably not.

In this example, an unconscious choice was made to do something —and now that something's been done, which by Universal Law has to produce an effect, there is a consequence. And the consequences, either positive or negative, are nothing more than a direct reflection of the quality of choices that were made in preparation of the effect.

So, if the choice was negative, even if you were completely uncon-scious of that choice, then a negative consequence will show up on your doorstep. You might be thinking, "Where the heck did this come from? Oh, this came from so and so. I know it came from them. So therefore, I'm going to go after them." The moment you do that, you've now made another choice, which produces another consequence, versus the choice of recognizing the fact that this effect showing up on your doorstep strongly suggests that you had something to do with it.

Now if you are consciously aware of your choice, you'll know exactly what you did to create the consequence. But, if you're not conscious of it, it becomes very tricky. You can use the rule that if it shows up on your doorstep and it's a negative consequence, then at the very least, go inward. Trace it back. Do some self-examination. Ask for a clarifying dream that might reveal what choice you made that brought this effect to your doorstep. If you don't want to take it to your dream space, then take it to your meditation space. If you're not willing to do this, or not even willing to take a look or take any responsibility for a situation that's literally on your doorstep, it will simply create more doo-doo for you. Why let that happen when we can start owning what our part is with the knowledge and hope of a happier life? We can choose to own it and course correct with consciousness.

CHOICE CORRECTION

When you make a choice—and more specifically, when you make an incorrect choice, whether conscious or not, you are able to correct it. If you're a pilot on an airplane, and you've filed your flight plan, and you're now 2000 miles into your journey and realize that the plane has gone off course, then what are you going to do as the pilot? You're going to course correct. So, when you recognize you've made an incorrect choice, and it was a significant incorrect choice, you want to go in and clean that up.

You can course correct at any time, and it's not dependent upon others being involved. Even if they were involved in the choice. What it is dependent upon is you being aware that you've veered off course and you have the willingness to correct it. Then you've got to actually make a new choice to correct the course. I invite you to step into the captain's chair of your own life and steer your ship.

If you have to go in and clean something up, embrace it. Go clear it up. Don't preoccupy yourself with what others will think of you or if you feel that you might make a fool out of yourself. In the bigger scheme of things, who really cares? Do you think the larger selves of other people really care about you choosing to go in and clean everything up? Do you think their larger selves are going to make fun of you? Their smaller selves might make fun of you, but so what? You know what you're doing. You're cleaning something up from your past that you chose incorrectly. You're coming clean with your own soul and your partnership with the Divine. You're coming clean with your own Lower Destiny so that it will help you to rise up into your Greater Destiny.

TEMPTATION VS. OPPORTUNITY

When we make a choice, there are two things that happen. The first thing is that an opportunity for something that is real for us to experience comes knocking on our door. It's an opportunity—but we must be able to recognize it correctly.

The second is what happens when we're at the Lower-Destiny level: we're going to get a temptation. Now, the temptation is something that's 100 percent false—it only looks real. It looks like, "Whoa, this is going to change my life." It looks like, "This is the person of my dreams." It looks like, "This is the opportunity of my dreams." It looks like, "This is the solution to my current problem." But it's not—it's 100 percent false.

If there's an opportunity knocking on your door, it will lead you to something that's real. In other words, it belongs to you. It's of your soul. It could be a professional career that's custom made just for you that your soul has been involved in the creation of from the very beginning.

> You can course correct at any time, and it's not dependent upon others being involved.

Then, there's the temptation. A temptation could be a money deal, an investment, a love relationship, or a new business partnership that's coming in—and it's false. Temptation is under the rule of your ego, your personality, your shadow side, or your inner child. So, what happens then?

The temptation comes in, disguised as an opportunity that only appears to be real. But, come the end of the day, the end of the month, the end of the year, it's not. Obviously, when you're tempted, you could be convinced that it's real at first. You might be convinced that this is the opportunity of a lifetime, as in this amazing business opportunity or this amazing soul mate relationship, and nobody can convince you otherwise.

Now if this is the real opportunity that you feel and think it is, then it's going to play out that way and turn out to be a beautiful thing. But if it turns out to be nothing more than a temptation disguised as a real opportunity, then you're on your way for a detour towards a consequence.

For most people, once they get on a mission, that's it—we can't stop them. They're making unconscious choices, and now they've become almost hell-bent. They're going to do this because they're now convinced this is the opportunity of a lifetime. In other words, it's not what they think it is, but they're not ready to see it just yet because they haven't learned this lesson. They haven't learned how to discern between opportunity and temptation. If someone hasn't learned how to discern this difference yet, then you can be assured that temptations are coming before opportunities are going to come. They might get four temptations to one opportunity.

One of the ways to tell whether it's a real opportunity or a temptation disguised as an opportunity is to notice how you're showing up. Let's say you've told all your friends about this great opportunity, and they start giving you feedback that they're not seeing it in the same way that you're seeing it. You can use this feedback as a gauge. It's letting you know that something might be off here. In other words, it might not be what you think it is, especially since you're getting this feedback from multiple people.

Or maybe there are some real obvious roadblocks in the way or tough hurdles to overcome, and all of a sudden, this so-called opportunity is coming with real tough moments and things aren't moving that gracefully or easily. That's another gauge that can let us know that something might be off. This isn't always the case, but it's something to pay attention to. One of the ways to spot it is that your life becomes more complex. And as it becomes more complex, that should tip you off.

But when it's a genuine opportunity, at its very core there's that divine birthright of grace. That's not to say that this experience won't be void of challenges. But it means that as you feel into it, you feel the grace behind this experience, which is letting you know that this opportunity is truly meant to be.

In learning how to choose wisely, we've got to learn how to better discern between the two. Because a temptation can disguise itself as an opportunity to the point where we can become so convinced that we'll literally end friendships, or we'll end a relationship with our coach, our teacher, or mentor who says it's not what we think it is. But we're hell-bent, so they'll get out of our way partly because we pushed them out of the way and partially because they're willing to go. Why would they want to stand in front of us when we're so hell-bent on doing something no matter what? So, they get out of the way—and nine months later, or two years later, if it really was a temptation, we're going to start coming into a painful realization or awareness.

It's going to start off like, "Oh my gosh, what's going on here? Is this what I thought it was, or is this something else? I don't like what I'm feeling right now. In fact, I'm getting kind of shaky. My knees are starting to tremble a little bit. What have I done here? How did I even get here?" But now we're already nineteen months into the experience. We've invested a lot of money, time, and energy. If the temptation was a relationship, maybe we've even gone ahead and conceived a child.

We got sucked into a temptation that was disguising itself as an opportunity, and we bought into it. Now, what starts to come upon us? The blessing or the consequence? Is it positive, or might it be negative? Is it pleasant, or might it be unpleasant? And, by the way, when we buy into temptations, what happens to the real opportunities? They go and find someone else because we're unavailable. Three years down the way, we may realize, "Oh gosh, what have I done? Gosh, I wish I would've listened to some of my friends. They saw it, and I just couldn't listen. Holy cow, now I'm down $48,000 and I've got this problem going on." And now, how long will it take us to wind out of this thing? Are we going to be able to say to whoever or whatever this temptation is, "That's it. I'm done. I'm going to cut you out of my life right now because now I know what my real opportunity is"?

> To transform your world into a world of opportunity, you've got to heal and recognize all temptation.

Is that how it works? No, because now this temptation has created a huge distraction from the real opportunities—the opportunities that were ready to bring something real into our lives, whether that's pro-fessionally, personally, spiritually, financially, or relationally.

Now, here's where it really becomes interesting. So, we now painfully realize, "Ah—what have I done? Oh my gosh." And we're recognizing that these choices we've made now have some consequences—we've got some stuff to clean up, and as we're going through this internal process we might ask ourselves: "Well, what am I going to do here? How am I going to do it? How long is it going to take? What am I going to need?"

We start to clean it up, and as we're cleaning it up, another temptation shows up and we think it's a what? An opportunity. And we're still in cleanup mode. Are we in alignment with our Greater Destiny or our Lower Destiny? Which level are we operating at then? The Lower Destiny—as we're under the rule of our personal agenda. We're so desperate for the opportunity that all someone or something has to do is just come in and give a little gentle knock. They might say: "Hey, I'll take your problems away. I think that other person you're leaving sucks. Anyway, I agree with you. I'll be your best friend." But we haven't cleaned up our current mess yet.

And, of course, we're pretty convinced now that the opportunity has landed on our doorstep and it's 100 percent real. Now if we were to choose at this point to be objective and just slow it down, as in slow ourselves down, and look within, this is where we increase the odds of beginning to see what this really is and what's actually about to happen.

THE LESSON OF DISCERNMENT

Remember, there's a huge lesson for us to learn here, and it is the lesson of discernment. We are learning how to better discern between opportunity and temptation because when it comes to transforming our destiny, first and foremost, we must recognize that this third-dimensional world is the world of temptation. In this world, it's so easy to be tempted. It's only when we get into the higher dimensions that the temptation dissolves.

We as souls contracted ourselves to learn one of the most valuable lessons in life, which is to get really good at discerning—in fact, to get so good that we become masters at discernment. This is the marker that authentically empowers the individual to be able to make true and wise choices for themselves—especially the significant choices like the life mates, big financial decisions, or big career moves.

This lesson is going to keep on showing up until you can recognize when temptation is knocking on your door. And when you do, then you may laugh at it and think, "Well, this is funny. How did I not see that all those times before? But now I see it!" At this point you can see crystal clear, which means you can no longer be fooled by it. You're getting better at recognizing temptation and then choosing to turn away from it versus getting entangled again. This is you now learning how to choose wisely. You're doing it and you're getting better at it.

Perhaps you've learned to discern between temptation and opportunity because you've already been through the consequences three times—and you paid a big price for it. You're not complaining. You're recognizing this was the Universe or life helping you to learn this valuable and significant lesson—how to discern at the level of mastery. Then you can just recognize it and make a choice: "I'm not interested. This is not my path. This is not right for me and my life path; therefore, I'm choosing to turn away from it."

Remember, grace comes upon us when we are willing to show up gracefully—when we are willing to show up and do the right thing in the intensity of the moment in which we're being most challenged. When you embody grace, you're going to recognize opportunity just like you recognize temptation. And, next thing you know, your life is going to be in alignment with opportunity. Your life will become filled with opportunity that's designed to help you grow, to get you to stretch, to have you love more, to have you receive more love, to have you experience more in the best of ways, the biggest of ways, and the brightest of ways.

HEALING AND TRANSFORMING TEMPTATION

To transform your world into a world of opportunity, you've got to heal and recognize all temptation. You've got to transform yourself in this dimension where temptation rules the roost. You've got to navigate through this to the point where you can no longer be fooled again by anyone or anything.

That's the marker, or at least one of the markers, of the individual who has truly transformed his or her destiny. They can no longer be fooled, meaning their lives are rich in opportunity. If they are in a relationship with their true love, then they get the opportunity to go to a deeper, higher, and greater level in their love with each other. If it's a career that they're pursuing, their career becomes richer and better because they're getting better at it. They also become more connected to it. They feel lighter, freer, and happier.

At some point, everything starts to light up like a Christmas tree for these individuals. They start getting rewards. They start getting bonuses. The start getting blessings of all kinds. Cool things start to happen in their lives. Each area of their life can be enriched with opportunity because they've worked through the world of temptation. They can now recognize it from a mile away and they're no longer in judgment of it—not at all. And now that they can see it, they're choosing opportunities instead.

THE QUICK ROUTE

When we attempt the quick route, it often doesn't work out. The finer things in life, much like a great bottle of wine, take time to mature. So, when we attempt to rush and move things along in a hurry, they don't end up as sweet as they do when we take our time.

Your Higher Self is not connected to timeframes. It is extremely patient and is very connected to something that's real for you versus something that's false for you. Something that's real for you is generally going to take some time.

> *If it's a real opportunity, you don't have to sew up the deal because the deal's already been sewn up.*

So, here's another clue: When we're in a big hurry, we're off. We're desperately trying to make something happen, which means we're pushing on someone or something, which really means we're now the perfect candidate for the world of temptation. The world of temptation will suck us in so fast, it'll make our head spin. As I have often said in my seminars throughout the years, "If we can still get sucked in, we're going to get sucked in." You see, when we're pushing, we're being needy. And as always, when we're needy, we go into a pushing mode whether we're aware of it or not.

When we're needy, we temporarily disconnect from our Higher Self. We temporarily forget we even have a Higher Self. We're absorbed in our own personal agenda, trying to make sure our need is going to get met. We're going to take the fast route to get this thing done.

The Higher Self, on the other hand, moves slowly, wisely, and graciously. It's not in a big hurry for anything because it's already in recognition that it has everything. Why would you be in a hurry if you already have everything?

Once again, when you're at the level of Lower Destiny, when you're operating under the influence of personal agenda, you'll forget all this temporarily because you're disconnected and not thinking clearly. You're in a hurry to get something done and to close a gap. You're in a hurry to fill a void. A person under this influence might say, "Well, I've been alone for all these years, so I should get into this relationship right away."

But what's the big hurry? Take your time. Let the real one come along instead of the false one.

If you really are in a place where you've got some money to invest, let the real investment come to you. It'll come to you somehow; you don't need to constantly search for it. This constant seeking, this hurrying, has become like a disease for so many people versus letting that which is real, that which is a true opportunity, show up on their doorstep.

Remember that when you start doing the right things and you stay true to doing the right things, grace is going to come upon you—and this grace, if you recall, is one of your divine birthrights. With grace, opportunity will come in as well. It will be personalized to you—but more specifically, it'll be real.

Of course, this is not easy to master. If there's something in your life that you've truly mastered, you clearly didn't master it in a matter of a few months. In fact, you didn't even master it in the matter of a year. Yet, some of us are in this big hurry. The moment you catch yourself showing up this way, just apply the brakes right there. Recognize that you're moving too quickly. You're trying too hard to lock something in. You're desperate to make that choice or to sew up that deal.

From the Higher-Self perspective, you want to take a little bit more time because when you choose, you want to choose well in all aspects of your life. If you really have a higher aspiration that's in line with your Greater Destiny for financial success, then you'll get financial success. You'll get it in a way that's real, sustainable, and doesn't come with anxiety. You'll get it in a way that comes with peace, comfort, and with a settling in.

Now you will have to let go of all the neediness, of course. It's our neediness that hooks us into the world of temptation. Remember, until you fully transcend this 3-D world, as long as you have needy energy, there's a real good chance that your ego is going to trick you with one of those needs that hooks you into the temptation.

And what's that going to look like? Like an opportunity. And then, it's going to get you to move quickly to lock it in. You are not going to want to take the slow path. You'll want to speed it all up, and that ought to be another gauge. Just pull yourself back. Pull in the reins and ask yourself, "What am I doing? Why the big hurry? If this really belongs to me, now that it's found me, is it going to go anywhere?" If it's right and meant to be, it is not going anywhere. Savor each step. Allow each part of its natural process to simply unfold.

If you've bought into a temptation that's disguised itself as an opportunity, as soon as you get closer to sewing up the deal, it'll become all about how fast you can move. You'll see the temptations of others as you start to see it inside yourself, and you'll be literally flabbergasted. You might try to get in there and stop them from going for that temptation in their own lives because you care about them. But they'll shut you down so fast, it'll make your head spin. They may not even take your calls. You'll realize they've already made the choice. It's already locked into place. That's the path they're going on. They're convinced that this is an opportunity of a lifetime. So, it's all about moving quickly. They've got to get it done. That's how they get swallowed up in the temptation. And then the choice is locked into place, and they're on the ride, whatever the ride is going to be for the next few months, or the next couple of years, or maybe the rest of their life. Unless the choice is made to course correct.

> To transform your world into a world of opportunity, you've got to heal and recognize all temptation.

So, when it comes to transforming our destiny, we're learning how to recognize the temptation. We're getting better at recognizing a temptation so that instead of rushing into a choice, we recognize when it's time to pull out of that choice.

When we recognize an opportunity is coming, we can say, "You know what? I can work towards it. I can wait for it. I don't have to have it today. Rather, what I can do is go inside myself and find the part of me that already knows that I have this. I can locate the part of me that's already connected to it and choose to develop a relationship with that, first and foremost. I can start drawing peace from that relationship so I don't have to be in this needy place or this hurried place of desperately trying to sew up the deal that I believe is an opportunity."

Remember, if it's a real opportunity, you don't have to sew up the deal because the deal's already been sewn up. You know it's truly real because you're no longer pushing on anything at all.

EXERCISES

1. As a learning exercise in better understanding the restriction of someone's free will, find somebody whose power of choice has been taken away from them, or they have pushed it away, and have a conversation with them. See what their life is like as a result of their free will being restricted. Afterwards, reflect and journal on your experience and thoughts.

2. Think of a time when you made a choice that was followed by a negative consequence. Then describe what happened.

   Now think of a time when you made a choice that was followed by a positive consequence. Describe what happened.

3. What percentage of time do you believe you currently make choices that are followed by negative consequences?

   Now write down one thing you could do differently, starting today, that would up-level your choices to produce more positive consequences.

4. We learn more about ourselves at a deeper level when we can embrace consequences, so let's practice. Think of a consequence that you can fully embrace in your life. Now if there was a lesson you were to be learning as a result of this consequence what would it be? Describe the consequence and/or its lessons, giving it as much detail as you can.

5. Can you think of a time that a temptation came upon you, but you recognized what it was and didn't go for it? Please explain. What did you notice? How did that make you feel?

6. Now think of a time an opportunity came to you. Did you act on it, or did you not recognize it until it was too late? Whatever your answer, write it down. If there were 3 things you now could do differently as a result of what you've learned in this chapter, what are they?

Applying what you've learned in this chapter, write down three things that you now could do differently.

CHAPTER 5

SELF-CENTERED OR CENTERED SELF?

There are two voices that are constantly speaking to us inside. Picture an angel on one shoulder and a devil on your other shoulder—now you've got a basis of comparison for the place these two voices are coming from and the suggestions they give us.

THE TWO VOICES WITHIN: EGO-SELF AND SOUL-SELF

The first voice within us is the voice of the ego-self. Wherever our ego is at in current time, we can spot it by looking into our personality. Say we are being aggressive or pushing hard on someone or something, or say we are being really loud and talking over someone, which is another form of aggressive energy—this is our ego influencing our personality.

Our ego is also our Lower Self. It is the smaller version of us. Within this Lower Self is where we find the ego, the inner child, and our shadow side. All of which are components of our personality. We will learn more about these later in the book.

Now, what's so interesting here is that most people think this is their Higher Self, that this is the bigger version of them, because one of the tricks of the ego is to get you to attach, identify, and associate with it so much that you start to think that's who you are.

You see, you're not your personality. Your personality belongs to you and is a part of you, but that's not who you are. You are not your ego. The ego is the part of you that you have to maneuver through in order to ultimately become your Highest, Greatest Self, also known as your Divine Self. But therein lies probably our greatest challenge on the planet. How many people do you know, or who do you know, right now that are becoming their Highest Self in physical form?

> Part of your highest destiny is to become your true soul self in physical form.

The other voice within us is our soul, our Divine Soul-Self, which is our true self. This is the part of us that's real and authentic; this is the part of us that's already developed. In other words, it doesn't need any personal development. This is also the part of us that the majority of people separated from earlier in this life, for whatever the reason—and most likely are not aware of, at least just yet.

When this separation happens, you start this identification—you start this association. For example, if you think of your parents, without judging them, are they the walking embodiment of their soul, their true self? Or is it possible that they're the walking embodiment of their ego, their personality self, the smaller version of themselves? If your parents are still with us, who are they in current time here in the physical realm? That's a very good question to contemplate since your parents were your first reflectors when you came into this life.

So, wherever your parents were at the time when you were born, they were reflecting something back to you. And, more specifically, they were reflecting something back to you that you are to be learning about in this life. Now, whether you learned it or not, that's another story. But one of the roles of our parents is to reflect something back, whether positive or negative, shadow or light, that we're to be examining inside ourselves. Especially once we start to go into the separation from our true self. This separation most often happens by our mid-adolescent years. It is not usually until later in our lives that we become conscious again of this separation and then are able to look at what those reflections are there to tell us. This happens so that we can work towards integrating them and begin to continue moving forward on our soul's journey.

The soul-self is the Higher Self, which we could say is angelic. Your Higher Self acts as your angel until such time that you embody it. Whether you embody it in this life, or in a life thereafter, has to do with choice—not just choice on behalf of you as a personality but choice on behalf of your soul as well. The reality is, eventually you will embody your soul self as your Higher Self. This is your truest self.

Part of your highest destiny is to become your true soul self in physical form. Your soul is the larger version of you. It hovers just above the body. The reason for this is that the body is not ready for its entry yet; it would literally short circuit the nervous system if it entered before it was time.

When you stand in front of a mirror, what do you see? Do you see yourself as a soul, or do you only see your body? Your body plays off the personality, or the ego, and vice versa. So, when you stand in front of the mirror, it looks like you're looking at yourself. It looks like you're looking at the whole of who you are, but it's a trick—it's a big illusion. You are only seeing the personality, the ego—the Lower Self.

The true self has yet to be revealed. So, what is seen on the outside is only the fabricated shell that, with work, of course, will be discreated over time to reveal the true self that has been dormant within, in its waiting to be discovered.

Now, during this period of transition in having our true self reveal itself to us, we may have periods of judging ourselves, depending on how much judgment we've taken on in this life.

But with continued diligence and intention, we'll come into recognition of our true self once again. There will be many times along the way, as we're discreating the fabricated shell, where we will uncover unpleasant truths. There will also be some nice surprises along the way as well. You see, the fabricated shell was created by us when we got hurt at different points in our life. It was created with the honest intention of protecting us from further pain. In this process, it also added to the separation from that of our true self.

In order for us to discover the true self, we must break through those protective layers of fabrication by getting to our truth around whatever it is that comes up in our day-to-day life. By choosing to embrace it and no longer stuff it down or run away from it, this process will naturally happen over time.

If someone nears the end of their life without doing this work, then it might go something like this: they have become judgmental in the context of their life, and now they're leaving their body. Once they start to transition and realize themselves once again as a soul, through the act of letting go of their personality, they might carry their judgment over and literally judge themselves for missing the mark in their life.

> The fabricated shell was created by us when we got hurt at different points in our life.

So, that might then impede their transition. In other words, it just doesn't go away. It goes somewhere, but it does not go away because they didn't get to it in the context of their physical life. For anyone who has studied near-death experiences, one of the things you may have noticed is that often when a person is in this near-death experience, their life flashes before them. Significant events flash before them like they're experiencing a review of how they'd been living their life. And during this review, sometimes they think something like, "Oh my gosh, I never saw it that way." In other words, they potentially missed the mark. Their soul wanted them to do something, whatever that was that they were being inspired to do, but they either didn't feel the inspiration or didn't follow through on it. Through this near-death experience, this person will likely learn something of value that they bring back into their physical form. The near-death experience ends up being profound or life-altering.

So the idea here, whether you get it now, or in a near-death experience or after you've left this body, is to have an awareness that you're not just an ego and a personality; you're a soul that was living in a body. It's important to remember there's a true self somewhere inside of you, and it is the larger version of you. Let's hope that since you found this book you are getting it now and won't have to wait till your next lifetime to make progress on your soul's journey in this regard.

THE EGO-SELF IS THE TRICKSTER

The ego-self can be a masterful trickster, meaning with some it's going to be masterful and with others not so much. It is also the part of us that creates the fabricated shell that I was referring to earlier. In addition to creating this fabricated shell of a false self, it can also set up a trick in advance, and you might not even be aware of it. And then, you go for the trick, thinking that's the right thing for you to do. You move forward, and two weeks later, two months later, two years later, it's like, "Oops. How did I get here?" Suddenly, you find yourself in a mess. You've got something really intense and uncomfortable going on and you didn't see it coming.

Say, for example, you end up with a health issue that you had no idea was coming on. All of a sudden, you wake up one morning, and there it is, just out of the blue. Well, it's not really out of the blue. The health issue had been forming, it had been manifesting, and you just weren't aware of it.

Or maybe there's a big financial issue coming, or a big relationship change that's coming—better yet, a new relationship coming in. But it's not really a new relationship—it's a copy of all the others you've previously had. And it winds up leading you to frustration, depression, negativity, or unhappiness. Most people can really relate to that one.

Have you had a few of those? Do you know what that's like? That's the ego. That's the personality. That is not the soul.

If anything, the soul is allowing it to happen, but the soul is not prompting it to happen. It's the personality, or the ego, that's prompting it to happen because it's doing what it knows how to do. Some egos are tricksters at an expert level. Many people are outwitted by the intelligence and the smarts of their own egos.

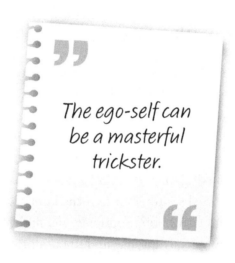

The ego-self can
be a masterful
trickster.

Why does the ego trick us? Because everything has a purpose. The ego has a couple different purposes, and one of them is to keep itself "safe." When we transcend the ego, it, as it knows itself to be, ceases to exist. And it doesn't want to cease to exist. However, in this process of transcending, the best parts of the ego will ultimately become one with your soul.

The ego can go to great lengths to create a distraction in your life so you don't get any forward movement. Depending on how strong it is, it can actually hook up with somebody else's ego, merge, and get that person to participate in the distraction. Never underestimate the craftiness of the ego!

An example of this might be two people that are together and their egos have taken center stage with each of them having a strong need to be right. If both have a strong need to be right, then these two can't be happy together. This is because both egos are in a needy energy of having to be right simultaneously. So these two will come to a standstill and in that, both parties are going to feel justified and right. Maybe one gets their way, then the other party might go off into the corner because they feel somewhat deflated since they didn't get their way, or they didn't get their need to be right met in that exchange. Then, this might reverse on the next go round, and the other ends up in the corner unhappy and deflated. And so, the bottom line to this type of relationship is that they both walk away unhappy or they're not able to be happy together.

So, what happens once we've been distracted? We're clearly not paying attention to the resonance of our soul at this point. And therefore, we've now disconnected from that resonance. But now if we're well into the distraction, the distraction can and more than likely will grow. This is where there will also be the creation of some additional consequences. If we continue from here, the distraction can get thicker and even more complex—where it can involve other people or other areas of our life, which could then cause an even greater distraction.

THE SOUL-SELF IS THE TRUTH ANGEL

The soul is also a truth angel. As you go deeper in your own transformation, you're going to need to be able to discern between when your ego is speaking to you through tricks versus when your soul is speaking to you through truth. Your soul, your Higher Self, is angelic. It's your guardian angel. If you're disconnected from it and not listening to it or if you're not listening to the Divine because of what it implies, you likely are not going to do the right thing.

For example, let's say you're in a situation that's going to get ugly. You'll start getting aspects of the truth from your truth angel, dropping feathers on your pathway that whatever this is that's coming is probably not going to be very pleasant. It's highlighting this for you so that you can start to prepare and adjust yourself in order to embrace whatever this is instead of going into a big fight with it.

The other thing that truth angel does for you is that when it's time for you to reroute or take a different course, it makes sure that the truth is always there. This part of us never, ever forsakes us, even when we slap it in the face, deny it, or pretend like it doesn't exist.

Once you know about this and start learning how to work with this properly, your truth angel can enrich your life like nothing on the planet. It watches out for you all the time. Your truth angel can literally spot a danger that's coming and warn you—if you learn how to listen, that is.

Our truth angel works through a resonance, meaning if you just slow down for a moment, it will ring true in your body. It's able to push a button, so to speak, and get you to see whatever it wants you to see.

Now, if you're all drugged up with candy, ice cream, cigarettes, pot, alcohol, etc., then all of this gets missed. In order to access these truth chords, you've got to be somewhat sensitized to your physical vessel. If you're constantly numbing yourself out, it's going to be almost impossible for you to be aware when the truth button has been pushed. There it is, vibrating inside your body, but you can't feel it because you've temporarily lost your sensitivity as a result of how you've been living your life.

The truth angel works by inspiring or prompting change. One of the reasons you have the truth angel is because your soul knew before you took your first breath that you were going to go through a lot of changes.

What that means for each individual, of course, is different. Obviously, some souls go through a tremendous amount of change in the context of their lives, and other souls go through much less.

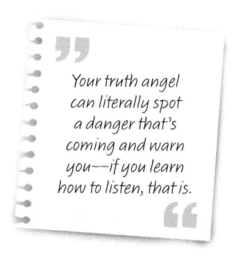

Your truth angel can literally spot a danger that's coming and warn you—if you learn how to listen, that is.

But all souls are going to experience change on some level, and there's a good chance they're going to fight it and go into conflict with it before they finally come into a state of surrendering to it. You, as a soul, already knew this before you moved into your mother's womb.

For example, someone may be twenty-eight years into their life, and their soul, as in that truth angel, is inspiring and/or prompting them to do something to create change. Their trickster, on the other hand, as in their ego-self, also does something to keep itself safe by creating a distraction. If the ego can get us engaged in the distraction, then there will be no forward movement, thus no change. Someone cannot change for the better when they're still distracted, and when they're distracted, they are making choices that can cause undesirable consequences, which, no matter what they do, come the end of the day, they'll have to go back in and clean it all up.

THE EGO IS SELF-CENTERED

The ego, within the Lower Self, is pretty much always focused on itself. All egos, to some degree, are narcissistic because at the core of narcissism is 100 percent self-centeredness. And, when we still have an ego that we have not yet tamed, trained, and transcended, we still have aspects of self-centeredness and narcissism within us, at the level of that Lower Self. Now we might not be willing to look at or confront it just yet because it can get pretty ugly when we do.

The ego, if left alone, or if we're still choosing to not being conscious of it, is going to keep the focus on us. We might be able to make it look like we're focused on everybody else, and we might even feel like we're focusing on everybody else, but we're not. We're really focused on ourself, as this is one of the many tricks of the ego.

Say you've got a big distraction going on in your world right now, which is keeping you away from your soul. It's keeping you away from your truth. Therefore, you're not even listening to your truth angel. And while that's all going on, you're focused completely on your own personality, on yourself—and you might not even be aware of it.

When you're in self-centeredness, you'll always operate from a lower perspective. The problem is, when you're being self-centered, you think it's the highest perspective—but nothing could be further from the truth. The ego can create a blind spot, a scotoma, where you really can't see your own self-centered personality. Therefore, you're operating through the lens of a lower perspective, but you think you're getting the higher picture. Remember, it's the trickster. You're being fooled into believing that what you're seeing is the only way.

You'll also start to discover that the person who's being self-centered— looking at their life or some part of their life through this place of the

116

lower perspective—is always being "done to." They might say, "He did this to me; she did this to me; they are doing this to me; etc." This failure to take responsibility is 100 percent ego and has nothing to do with the soul whatsoever.

THE SOUL IS THE CENTERED SELF

As written about in depth in my first book of the Transformation Trilogy, *Being Called to Change*, our soul-self is not self-centered at all. It is the "centered self," meaning whenever you are in alignment with it, you come from a place of center and operate from a higher perspective. You don't just see yourself anymore—you see others as well. You'll know when you're here because when you're at this place, you notice that you're making better decisions—and more specifically, your decisions do not create more distractions.

Remember, when we're in the result of what the distraction has created, this is 100 percent from ego. Now, if someone has a high degree of narcissism, they're going to have a difficult time being able to even admit that this is of their own doing because they're still stuck on the idea of what's been done to them. They're operating from a victim consciousness. When someone is in the centered self, however, instead of seeing things as being done "to them," they literally see and come to know something as being done "for them."

Louise Hay, author of the best-selling book *You Can Heal Your Life*, said, "When you can see the perfection in anything and everything, you will be the happiest person on Planet Earth." What she meant by that is that she eventually got to a place where she could see everything as it was being done *for her*—she could see the perfection of everything. When you're looking through this higher perspective, everything lights up around you and you see clearly; therefore, you don't get caught up in another distraction. It's almost impossible for your ego to trick you when you are sitting in the centered self.

This is how the angels live. Angels don't say, "Look what he's doing to me again. Look at what she's doing to me again. Let's go ahead and crucify them in the most negative of ways and the most hurtful of ways to make sure they get what they deserve." Angels see the truth; they see how everything is connected; they see it from a higher perspective. They say, "This is all being done for me. This is all being done for my betterment."

The truth angel works by inspiring or prompting change.

Wouldn't it be wonderful to be an Earth angel and operate from this higher perspective? Heck, from this place we might even find that we are actually capable of transforming our life into a heavenly experience here on Earth. Talk about transforming our destiny!

SELF-CENTERED LIVING VS. LIVING IN THE CENTERED SELF

When you veer off into the self-centered state, you're now in the process of misusing your power; and you're definitely not using your divine power. Your ego has you fooled into believing you've got it all figured out. Or it might be that you're desperately trying to figure everything out. In either case you can easily become stuck.

What's interesting is that when you're in the centered self, you'll never have it all figured out, and you're okay with that. You're not trying to figure anything out. Instead, you're letting it come to you. You're letting it be revealed to you, and you recognize there's a lot more to discover. And if anything, you're excited about it. In the centered self, you get to have moments where you're just at peace. There's no more wanting. You become filled with so much gratitude just for existing. You can sit on your couch or lay on your bed and just savor what's happening without trying to do anything—without wanting more—enjoying every second of it and feeling it in your body. That's somebody who's the embodiment of the centered self.

In contrast, the person who is self-centered may have a hard time even sleeping at night. Maybe they can't take an afternoon nap or can't sleep in because they live in their head a lot, thinking that makes them safe. That's the trickster at work. It's all about safety. It's not living in the body or in the heart. It's not living in the now. It's living out into the future— concerned about what's going to happen three months from now. Or it's living in the past—concerned about what happened a month ago.

When you're in the centered self, you realize that the greatest thing is just to be able to be in the moment. The power is in the present moment. This sounds like a great concept, doesn't it? But many people have no idea how to live in the moment. Why? Because they're still being tricked. And they aren't ready or willing to confront their trickster. Not yet anyway.

Once we reach a point of finally having enough, this is where we often become willing to confront this part of ourselves. As this morphs into a lifestyle, our resolve in confronting this part of ourselves becomes unwavering. But before that time comes, things might have to get louder and more painful in our world.

If you find yourself feeling miserable with your life or feeling miserable with a situation going on in your life, remember that what led you to this place is not the work of your soul; it is the work of your ego. The soul, on the other hand, is the source of all fulfillment. You'll know whether or not your soul is in the process of being embodied because you'll find yourself feeling more fulfilled. You'll have moments where you'll feel completely trusting of yourself—where there's no part of you that's trying to do anything anymore or trying to be something that you're not anymore. You just really are in a state of pure being in that moment. And everything that's right just happens for you, with you, and around you.

> When you're in your centered self, you realize the greatest thing is to be able to be in the moment.

When this happens, you might realize, "Wow, this thing is so easy—and for so long I was in this fight, for 28 years of my life, where I had to have everything be so hard. I was always in this struggle for something. And now I feel so fulfilled. Now when I leave my body, whether I want to meditate, or go off into an altered state, or just fall asleep and drop into a deep state of REM, it all happens naturally. Now I don't need a drug.

I don't need any stimulant. It happens because my soul, my centered self, is the source of all fulfillment. I become fulfilled just by being in this moment."

Many people who reach this point end up going to live in the mountains, away from civilization. They have everything they need inside. And who knows—at some point, I might do that too. Why? Because I've had a taste of it. I know what it's like. Oh, and by the way, even when removed from civilization, you can be of great service to humanity because you're still a part of it. When you're in a state of pure being, your energy is constantly broadcasting—it's coming from you and through you. It's touching humanity from anywhere you are.

CONFRONTING YOUR TRICKSTER

In order to confront your trickster, you've got to get real with yourself and recognize you've been the missing piece in this equation. Many people will say, "It's my kids; it's my husband; it's my wife; it's my boyfriend; it's my girlfriend; it's my mom, my dad, my past lover from 10 years ago—whoever. It's not me; it's them." It's everything outside—it's all external.

If this is resonating with you, and if you want that truth angel to be alive and well inside of you, to serve you 24/7, then you've got to get in there and live your life from the centered self. You've got to start connecting with your soul and your truth. You've got to start facing the music and do it in a conscious, responsible way.

We're going to have to confront this trickster, and not just once. It's not going down without a fight. Some have given this trickster—their ego, their personality—so much of their power over a long period of time, and as a result, it's gotten smarter, which means it has more tricks.

If you think you've seen the best magician on stage, you haven't seen anything yet. You've got the best magician inside of you. It can create an illusion so quick and even get you to buy into it as if it's your truth angel speaking to you.

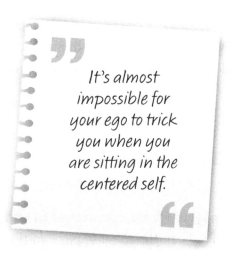

> It's almost impossible for your ego to trick you when you are sitting in the centered self.

To some, this is probably going to look ugly. Some of this might even disgust you or cause you to feel nauseous because you're going to have a moment like, "God, how long has this been going on? Talk about narcissism. I've been so narcissistic. My ego has been so self-centered—so focused on itself constantly." Someone who's really dedicated to their own transformational journey might get excited about hearing this information because it will empower them to see themselves how they are, warts and all. There'll be a real, genuine interest in what they just discovered about themselves. Once that occurs, some serious momentum can really kick in.

THE NEEDY SELF: AN EXTENSION OF THE EGO

The needy self is nothing more than an extension of the ego. Now remember, the ego can never be satisfied—it's impossible. There's no way you or I could ultimately satisfy anybody's ego.

Maybe you have a very specific need for safety. If that's true for you and that need is strong enough, then your ego will put you in a situation with someone or something where you'll start pushing on or trying, and possibly even trying hard to get this need for safety met. There is a good possibility that you won't even be aware that you are doing this.

This is going to cause a distraction because at some point, whoever it is that you've hooked your need for safety into is going to get tired of it. This happens because no matter what they do, they can't make you feel safe, and thus they're going to start pushing back on you. When they do, there's going to be a consequence, possibly a battle or power struggle, which is exactly what the ego wanted all along. Your ego loves it when you struggle, or have a confrontation with someone where the struggle becomes a theme of the confrontation and nothing gets resolved but keeps us engaged. When this happens, your ego gets stronger because it gets fed.

Another need could be the need for attention. This could be somebody who puts themselves into dangerous or vulnerable situations, all for the sake of getting attention. The ego uses this neediness to maintain its self-centered status. There's a good chance it'll create a distraction because the person may then find themselves with somebody they've hooked their need for attention into. That person may give them attention, but it's never enough. And when it's never enough, at some point, there's going to be a breaking point and it's going to turn itself around. Next thing you know, they're going into a consequential effect—another distraction.

Another need could be the need for importance. This could be somebody who has a certain role in life, and the whole purpose for that role is to make sure that everybody knows how important they are. That's not to say we shouldn't be important because most of us are important to somebody. When we make a difference in somebody's life, we become important to them. There's nothing wrong with that—just like there's nothing wrong with us feeling safe or receiving attention.

It's when we're needy for the importance, when we're needy for attention, when we're needy for safety—this is what causes the undesirable consequence. This is what feeds the ego and causes it to become stronger, in turn having us live a more self-centered life.

Someone might have a need for love. This seems to be a big one across the board, so here's where the trick comes in. If it turns out that you have a deep-seated need for love, what's going to happen? You're going to find yourself in a relationship with somebody where the love that you're experiencing is going to be false. You're thinking it's real, but it's false. And false love always complicates life—always.

In other words, if I have a deep-seated need to be loved, then I more than likely am going to find myself with someone that can't fill that need. No matter how hard I try, they won't be able to give it to me. Or at least not in the way I'd like to have it. Why? Perhaps it's because they haven't learned to love themselves. Or perhaps they don't have that love inside of themselves to be able to give to me just yet. As in we can only give to someone else that which we have to give.

By the way, this is not just referring to a romantic relationship. This could be a business partnership or this could be a friendship. There's a real difference between true love and false love.

So, if you find yourself in a situation that's becoming more complex, that is not true but false love. And it's 100 percent ruled by the needy self, under the guise of the ego.

Now what's so fascinating about true love? First, you no longer question anything. Second, you're always elated. Third, whatever was complicated becomes uncomplicated. You sleep better—you do better. It's even been proven that your heart, your physical heart, does better when you're in the energy of true love. But how many people have love going on in their lives that's not true? They're constantly in this struggle to try to get more love from whoever the other person is. That's the ego using the needy self to create the distraction as a way to keep us in that of our Lower Destiny.

We can only give to someone else that which we have to give.

Someone might have a need for certainty. If you have this need, one of the ways you'll know is that you're always doubting. It's like a sickness—it never leaves you alone. This is the person who gets in their head and starts overthinking, then they overthink some more. They have a deep need for certainty. There's something going on in their life that they don't feel certain about, and because their need for certainty is so strong, it takes center stage. The ego uses it to create a distraction from them actually connecting with and ultimately embodying their higher, Greater Self as their true soul self.

Another is a need for approval. This is a biggie. This is one that a lot of us learn in our childhoods. Early on, our ego starts to develop a need for approval from Mom and Dad. The problem is, Mom and Dad have not yet approved of themselves—and do you know what happens when we hook our need for approval into somebody who hasn't approved of themselves just yet? It becomes very complex because we're now hooking into somebody who can't give us what we so desperately need. So, we then try even harder.

This was the case for me. When I was a boy in my early childhood, I attempted to get the approval of my father. And as I moved into my adolescent years, I had my first conscious awareness that I was trying desperately to win him over, to have him approve of me, have him notice me and acknowledge me for something that I thought I was doing correctly. But it never happened. In fact, I went on for a number of years in the earlier part of this life never being able to get my father's approval on pretty much anything that I did. And even though, as I entered into my late teens and early twenties, I was starting to experience a decent amount of success, it was never enough from his perspective. It didn't mean anything to him, or at least that's what he portrayed.

Therefore, I never got that pat on the back—that "Great job!" or "Way to go!" I never heard that in the first thirty years of my life. Then, when I found myself in a relationship with my sweetie, next thing you know, I'm playing out what I played out as a child in relation to my father. I'm desperately trying to win her approval for whatever it is I'm accomplishing or achieving. But she can't see it, or if she can, she's unwilling to acknowledge it.

All the while, my confidence in myself is becoming weaker. It's starting to have an effect on me—my world is changing, and not for the better. This was my Lower Destiny. I just wasn't aware of it yet. It wasn't until I began to realize that neither my father nor my significant other were capable of approving of me. I learned later this was due to their own unresolves issues from their pasts. They were not able to give to me what they could not give to themselves. Eventually, over time, I was able to correct this by learning how to approve of myself.

I needed to learn how to connect with myself in a way where when I would accomplish something that appeared to be good, it would be good enough for me just to be able to acknowledge it and be able to give myself approval. As I learned how to do this, everything began to change for the better. I was able to not only move into a better relationship with a new girlfriend but also move into a new type of relationship with a business partner.

Upon doing this, it was easier for a new group of people to show up in my life that could approve of me. They could acknowledge me. And I didn't have to ask for it. All because I eventually got to what it was that I was to be learning—to give this approval to myself first and foremost. This is where I am beginning the rise into my Greater Destiny.

What happens when we try so hard to get something we desperately need is that we are our of alignment with universal law–the Universal Law of Harmony. Under the Universal Law of Harmony, we are coming back together in a harmonious way from the inside out. So, I put myself back together on the inside, and my external world changed to match. Our outer world is a reflection of what's going on inside of us.

This also corresponds to the Universal Law of One, meaning I was becoming one with myself. When I was desperate to win somebody else's approval, I was not one with myself. I wasn't in that state of having already approved of myself that I'm in now.

When our self-worth goes down, our self-confidence takes a beating. What do you suppose happens to our relationship with our soul then? We might lose ourselves. What about our partnership with the Divine? Does it strengthen it, or might it weaken it? Might we even disconnect from the Divine? Might we disconnect from our souls?

When we are with someone and have hooked our needy energy into them, we are basically with somebody that's never going to give us what we want. This is not because we're bad and not because we're undeserving of it; it's because they don't have it to give us. It's like hanging out with somebody because we think they're going to give us $100,000, but they don't have $100,000 to give. And we're still hanging around two years later for the $100,000 that they don't have. That's nonsense! We might say, "Oh, but I know they're going to get it one day." We're literally banking our life on the idea that one day they're going to get it.

But in the process, we're possibly losing ourselves. We're possibly disconnecting from our true selves further. We're possibly disconnecting from our relationship with the Divine. We're now pushing away all of these awesome things that are here to support us along our journey—all because of our needy energy.

Now you've got the contrast and can see the two forces that are going on within you until you bring them into union. The only way this inner battle is going to get resolved is when we get involved. We must decide to step in and take full responsibility for our own consciousness—and really put our hands on the steering wheel and learn how to start making better, healthier, wiser, tougher choices. The choices that are going to challenge us—the choices that are going to activate us. But remember, grace comes when we start doing the right things on a regular basis.

If this person who I'm so desperate to get one of my needs met from hasn't been able to give me that need, then I've got to change course and more specifically shift my focus from them to me. I've got to do something different. I've got to identify what would be right for me to do. Otherwise, I'm possibly going to go down with my own ship, drowning in the negativity, dysfunction, and complexity that's being created under the influence of the ego.

> *The biggest battle you and I will ever experience is within us.*

If you feel like you've got a complex life or that you're stuck in a place of constantly needing, now you've got a deeper insight into where that's coming from. It's coming from within you—not from someone outside. It's not your next-door neighbor or your ex. It's you.

You've got to confront your own ego, your own personality—your needy self. But this confrontation has to be consistent. It's got to become a lifestyle because if it's not a lifestyle, then you're giving your ego all kinds of wiggle room. And what happens when you give wiggle room to somebody who really wants to control you? They're going to manipulate you. Remember that. Consistency is the key.

DR. PHIL AND THE FOURTEEN-YEAR-OLD GIRL

I watched a great *Dr. Phil* episode. He'd taken on a mission to work with families with dysfunctional children where the roles of parent and child had become reversed and the child, most often a teenager, ruled the roost. Dr. Phil pointed out that in cases like these, the parents generally become afraid of the child, and they constantly give more power to the child.

The child continues making destructive choices that cause the entire family to become more dysfunctional. Sometimes these choices cause the family to go down, with the parents often losing large amounts of money in the process.

I found myself admiring the way Dr. Phil handled himself. One of these episodes featured a fourteen-year-old girl who definitely ruled the roost of her family. Her entire family was frustrated, angry, and at their wits' end. They didn't know what to do anymore. She would go out and do things that caused all kinds of undesirable consequences. She didn't have any money, so the parents came in and bailed her out over and over again. Meanwhile, at this young age of fourteen, she was heavily into drugs, sex, and belonged to a gang. Talk about complex, right?

Her parents were now at odds with themselves. You can just imagine the amount of pressure because of the dysfunction going on. She went missing for a couple days and came home after stealing their car. The car was all banged up, and they had to replace it. This drove their insurance rates through the roof since she had no driver's license. Of course, she had every excuse in the book as to why the car was banged up, which had nothing to do with her at all—she was taking zero responsibility at this stage.

She then announced to her parents that she was pregnant by one of the leaders of the gang—who she then said wanted to kill her parents.

Dr. Phil had a pretty good feel for the situation since he has a team that does a lot of research leading up to the show, and he was prepared for this experience they were about to have together. He further interviewed the parents to validate a few things to make sure they were on the same page.

While that was going on, the TV crew had their daughter on a stretcher in another room to conceal her identity from the gang she was part of. Her arms and hands were handcuffed to her body, and they had her covered up so that only her eyes, lips, and a little bit of her fingers were visible.

As Dr. Phil began getting ready to go into the room and confront the daughter, he made it very clear to the parents that the only way he was going to do this was if they gave him power of attorney. If they got in his way, he would shut the whole thing down and the parents and daughter would be on their own again. The parents agreed.

Dr. Phil walked into the room where the girl was being held and started the conversation by introducing himself and explaining why he was there. He said, "All I need to know from you is, are you willing to talk to me? Because if you're not, I'm not even going to try. I'm going to walk back out of this room."

The girl wouldn't talk to him. He gave her one warning after another. Then he said, "You've got fifteen minutes because there's something that's about to happen in your life fifteen minutes from now. And if you don't want to talk to me, that's fine. But what you need to know is the clock is ticking, and once we get to that fifteen-minute mark, what

I'm now talking about is going to happen and there's nothing you can do about it."

She started whining and trying to manipulate him. He called her bluff, saying, "You're not going to manipulate me. Here's the deal, you've now got ten minutes left to start answering my questions—and if you're not prepared to do that, I'm going to walk out of this room."

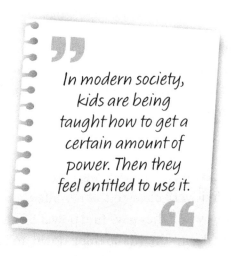

> In modern society, kids are being taught how to get a certain amount of power. Then they feel entitled to use it.

It took about five minutes, and eventually the girl was willing to listen to him. He then started asking questions. She wouldn't answer him right away. It took another four to five minutes for her to begin giving him vague answers. It was obvious that she was just trying to manipulate her way through this.

But Dr. Phil couldn't be manipulated, as he was very clear on what his role was. He didn't raise his voice, although he did speak firmly a couple of times to her. On about the twelfth minute of the fifteen minutes he had given her, she started to answer his questions.

Eventually, he got to the question, "I understand you're pregnant?"

She nodded her head.

Then he said, "Well, before we go any further, we need a pregnancy test."

She said, "Not going to happen."

He replied, "Two more minutes left. You're going to have a pregnancy test. I've got my team out in the hallway. They're going to take you into the clinic, and we're going to administer that pregnancy test." She fought and tried to manipulate, but he just held strong.

Eventually, they got her to go into the other room, and she sat on the concrete floor with her knees up towards her chest, refusing to let anybody give her the test. Dr. Phil went back out to be with her parents in front of the live audience, and he started to gauge where they were at. "Are you really willing to go the distance here, or are you going to cower down and cave in?"

The father assured him, "No, this needs to happen. We're at our wits' end and we don't know what to do anymore." The cameras were on the daughter, and every now and again, they'd switch back to the parents to show their reactions. She said she was thirsty, so they brought in a bottle of water.

She finally agreed to do the pregnancy test, but before they could even get to it, she spilled the bottled water on the test and destroyed it. She did the same thing again with a second test. They got a nurse to hold her down for the third one.

At this point, he made it very clear, "I'll stay here until midnight if I have to, but you need to know you're not going to manipulate me. You're going to break before I ever do." They got the third pregnancy test done, and it turned out she was not even pregnant.

So, for four months, she was using the pregnancy lie to manipulate her parents. They were terrified that she had a baby growing inside of her, and all along she didn't have a baby at all. At that point, it was all exposed.

The girl then switched to acting very charming and sweet. You can always tell a manipulator, right? A manipulator is like a Jekyll and Hyde. When they realize they can't manipulate you, they'll go into charm mode.

By this time, everyone was in the same room together: the daughter, the two parents, Dr. Phil, and his staff. He told her that the time had come, and he gave her three options. Option number one was to put her in jail with no bail. For option number two, he listed a series of consequences for her behavior. Option number three was to remove her from the situation completely—to remove her from her parents, her home city, and from the gang for at least three months. Then, they would reevaluate in the third month if this removal needed to be extended. The only way for her to come home was for her to be on the other side of all this.

After giving the parents three options, Dr. Phil said, "Now, if it was my child, here's the option, I would pick," which was option number three. Both parents nodded their heads and signed a legal contract where they could not back out.

She then turned on the charm about how she was going to change and be different, how it was going to be so much easier for her at home to be with her parents, that she wanted to be with them, and on and on.

At some point, Dr. Phil called her bluff and said, "You know what, just stop. I don't believe you at all. In fact, I don't think your parents believe you. How about that, Mom and Dad? Do you believe her?"

The father said no.

The mother hesitated a little bit, and at this point, you could see that she probably always gave in, which contributed to the problem. The father was more on the disciplinary side. You could see the imbalance between Mom and Dad in that regard. But the mom went for it, and she looked right into her child's eyes and said, "I've decided alongside your dad that this is what's going to happen."

The girl refused to go, so Dr. Phil's head guy said, "This is not negotiable. You've got exactly sixty seconds to say goodbye to your parents... fifty-nine, fifty-eight, fifty-seven, fifty-six..." She still wouldn't get up.

At the minute mark, the parents came behind her and whispered so that she could hear them, "We're doing this for you." As soon as they walked out of the room, the crew came in and grabbed her. She didn't fight them once her parents were out of sight.

At the young age of fourteen, this girl's ego, her needy self and the personality self, had enough strength to literally overpower her parents to the point of their lives being turned upside down on a financial and an emotional level. Though the complications had been becoming greater by the week, Mom and Dad couldn't do anything about it until one of them had the idea to reach out to Dr. Phil.

Now that's an extreme situation, but what's interesting is Dr. Phil gave a statistic about the families that are being ruled by this very thing across the country right now. It's these kids who are literally being taught how to strengthen their own egos—their own personalities. This is coming from their environment, which includes their friends, the culture of the school they attend, their teachers, relatives, and usually the main contributors being the parents. In all fairness to the parents, this is more than likely being done unconsciously rather than consciously.

The kids are being taught how to get a certain amount of power, and then they feel entitled to use that power.

TAKING CHARGE OF YOUR OWN LIFE

You must remember who's in charge of your life. Is it you, or is someone outside of yourself, like the parents who let their fourteen-year-old daughter take control?

Have you been letting somebody take charge of you, rule over you, or influence you somewhere in your external world? Maybe it's one of your children, or your husband, wife, or a close friend. Or it might be an overbearing neighbor, a controlling business associate, or a demanding boss.

If you do have a child or children, have you stepped into the driver's seat as the parent? As parents we want our children to know who runs the household. If, for some reason, your children believe they run the household, you're doing the exact same thing to yourself as the parents in the Dr. Phil story. You're letting somebody else run your life. And you're in denial in the greatest of ways. You're denying your highest responsibility to yourself and to that of your children.

You're the one who's to oversee your household. You're the one who's to be in charge of your field of consciousness and subconsciousness. You're the one who is to be taming your ego. You're also responsible for your inner child and your shadow side, two areas we will explore in the next chapter.

But here's the deal—if you're still letting other people run your life externally, you're doing the exact same thing internally. You can begin to correct this by starting the process of connecting on the inside. Again, you've got to get real with yourself. In order to rise up from your Lower Destiny to your Greater Destiny, you've got to get onto your ego, your personality, and this smaller version of you—and then you've got to accept, even if it takes you some time, 100 percent responsibility for you and the way you've been showing up in your life.

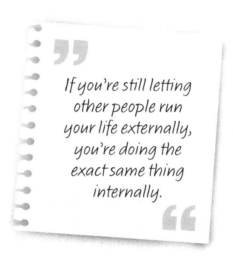

If you're still letting other people run your life externally, you're doing the exact same thing internally.

Just as with Dr. Phil and that fourteen-year-old girl, there are times when you've got to regain control of a situation. Dr. Phil did this girl and her family a huge favor. This is why he's got a lineup of families waiting to get on his show. Now, did the fourteen-year-old girl see it that way? Not at the time, but hopefully on the other side of it she finally did. That is the ideal outcome.

Remember, the ego within the Lower Self is self-centered. It only sees things through a lower perspective. It sees things as being "done to me." So, that's how the fourteen-year-old saw it—as being done to her. But does that mean to say we should listen to her? No. And this is where we've really been messing up. We've been living and operating within our Lower Destiny for perhaps far too long. Because we're letting these lower parts of us rule our roost. They're like that fourteen-year-old girl—they're spinning out of control. It's time to take charge of these parts and take charge of our life. And it can be done. When we take charge of our lives, this builds that inner muscle. It helps us move towards our next victory. And each victory becomes a little easier than the last.

THE BATTLE BETWEEN YOUR EGO AND YOUR SOUL

You're enrolled in a much bigger and more significant process than most realize. First and foremost, if you really do want to have access to your greater purpose, then you've got to get right with your soul. You've got to connect with your soul. And then, ultimately, you've got to be in the process of embodying your soul—which means you've also got to be in the process of taming, teaching, and transcending your ego.

As long as your ego is in charge, your soul cannot enter. You can connect with it in the higher realms, but it cannot enter. The ego won't allow it. That's why the biggest battle you and I will ever experience is not on the outside. It's the battle that's going on within us. And we can narrow it down very specifically to that of the ego and the soul. That's why the soul will say "enough" when we've crossed a line.

When we've crossed a line, we're literally hurting ourselves. We're creating more negative karma. We're elongating our soul's journey, and the soul doesn't look at just one lifetime; your soul looks at a lifetime as a part of its overall journey. Your ego, however, looks at this lifetime as this is the only one you'll ever live.

Remember, the soul has free will too. You don't just have free will at the level of Lower Destiny; your soul can make a choice anytime it wishes. And if it does, it's now non-negotiable once the line gets crossed. The soul is often very patient, at least to an extent—as long as it knows that there is some kind of positive forward movement happening.

138

Let's say a person is destined to have an eighty-three-year lifespan, and now this person's at their forty-seventh year and it's not going well from the soul's perspective. This is somebody who not only hasn't cleared out any of their unresolved karma that they came in with, but they've created more karma on top of that. On a practical level, this is like somebody staying in a financial investment when the financial investment is clearly going south.

The soul has the unique ability to see the future. It can see certain choices that have been made and the effects those choices have now accumulated. So, if you were the soul, as that soul, what would you do? Would you say, "Oh no, we're going to give them one more chance." Are you kidding? Has this person proven worthy to get one more chance? It's like how some of us deal with love, right? If we have been abused, taken advantage of, and betrayed time after time, at a certain point, we're a fool to go back to that person. We're just asking for more betrayal. The soul can also get to a point where it finally says, "Nope—no more. It's over."

When we've crossed a line, there is generally no coming back from it. This is why we want to get better at catching things before a line is crossed. The soul can also create an intervention when we are about to cross a line, so long as we have reached a point where we want to make a change.

Say there's a relationship that's gone real toxic and even abusive. Two or more souls can actually communicate with each other and set something up so that the person who is having a difficult time getting out of the abusive relationship can do so—as long as that person has a clear intention to leave. A while back, their soul declared, "That's it. This is over now. No more," and their soul has been setting up the end of the relationship with the other soul for some time.

Their partner, who they need to get away from, may go out and find somebody new to go in a relationship with. If something like that were to happen, then the abusive partner would be okay with the idea of getting out of the relationship. Even though the partner who was being abused might complain for a while about being left, because it happened in a way that they didn't see coming and were hurt by it, they will, once they get past the trauma, start to see that they were blessed.

We want to get better at catching things before a line is crossed.

They will eventually begin to realize: "It was a blessing that my partner ended up leaving me because I couldn't leave them. I was the one who was stuck. When somebody else came along and grabbed their attention, they began to shift their focus off me and onto that new person. And when that happened, this is when they were willing to let go of our old relationship together, which is exactly what needed to happen. Because I couldn't do it—I couldn't let go on my own."

THREE STEPS TO DEALING WITH THE EGO

You've got to be willing to get to the part of you that's been running you. This means learning to face and tame your ego. This isn't going to happen overnight, especially if your ego holds a large chunk of your power or if it has become incredibly smart or even spiritualized. Meaning it has learned about spiritual concepts and can imitate your Higher Self in order to make you believe something is for your greater good when, in fact, it's for the ego's own agenda.

Facing the part of you that's been overpowering you requires examining your personality through the results that are showing up in your life. The results never lie, even when there is a trickster inside of us.

Begin by examining your life. Look to see if there is a part of it that has been spinning out of control lately. Is there any area of your life that rules you, controls you, or has power over you? Is there any part of your life that consumes a great deal of your time or energy? If you aren't sure, then maybe you've convinced yourself that you're living in a bed of roses and everything's just fine. Well, that might not be the case at all, but maybe you haven't been willing to admit it to yourself just yet. It's time to come face to face with some of your ugly truths and quit this Pollyanna nonsense that everything is hunky dory when it isn't. This is the only way to make continued progress in your quest for a Greater Destiny.

Maybe you have a pretty good handle on this, and you don't have any areas that are spinning out of control, but as you read this chapter, you will likely spot some areas where you could better tame your ego.

Either way, it's time to get very real with yourself in order to transform your destiny. Every one of us can transform our destiny. And not only can we transform it, but it's in our Greater Destiny to transform our destiny.

There are three steps that you must become clear on and become pro-active with when it comes to the ego and personality. I've often referred to this as the 3 T's—taming, teaching, and transcending.

Step 1: Taming—Start taming your ego. This means you've got to pull in the reins—just like Dr. Phil did with the fourteen-year-old girl. He knew exactly what needed to happen. Somebody needed to step in and take charge. She was spinning out of control, and by the age of sixteen or seventeen, she could very well have been found dead in a ditch somewhere. Yet, the parents, left on their own, couldn't do it. They needed help—and good for them for asking for help and then doing what was necessary to fully embrace that help.

Maybe you, the reader, are having an experience like this—where you feel like you're spinning out of control around something that's going on in your world, personally or professionally. And if so, just know that you too have a soul, you are a soul, and at any point at any time you can bring help to assist you in your situation just like Dr. Phil was brought to that couple for their daughter. As seen in the example of the person who found themselves in a toxic, abusive relationship, help can show up in a variety of ways. Sometimes it's obvious, and other times it is not as obvious, but it's there.

Once you get through an experience like this and you begin to reflect back, that's where most people can see the blessing in the experience of it all.

Step 2: Teaching—One of the ways we can work to teach our ego is to **be willing to learn some new things.** Dr. Phil sent the fourteen-year-old girl to a facility where she was set up to receive an incredible education and learn how to live a better life and to be taught some new things, such as how to work on herself. What a great gift for her to be given that opportunity—whether she thought so at first or not!

So just how important is education? It's incredibly important. We all need education, and more specifically, we need higher education, meaning we need the type of education that's designed to authentically empower us. Then, we need to use it to help us get better at teaching our ego.

Step 3: Transcending—Transcend your ego. Now, of the three steps, quite frankly, transcending is the toughest. But it can be done. And eventually, you will do this because your destiny calls for it. What's the real purpose of your ego? What's the real purpose of your personality? These are thee things that you're going to want to uncover because they're going to serve you impeccably well when it comes to this third "T" in the 3 T's.

It's our Greater Destiny to transform our destiny.

To transcend means to lift it up. You're going to need a lot more than a rehab program, but it can be done! When this is truly in motion, the ego is listening to you, and because it's listening to you now, you can guide it along. You can guide it to this place of lifting it up, because remember, at some point, to transcend the ego, that means the best parts of the ego will be integrated into that of your true soul self.

That's what we're up to here—to really, truly move the needle forward to turn this into a lifestyle. One where there's no more resistance. This is where we begin to see our ego with a level of fascination. It's important to not just see it as a jerk or a trickster and to hold it in constant judgment. That would only keep everything in motion the way it's been. When we make our ego wrong and blame it, this can really hinder our progress. Rather, become the observer and find that level of fascination in what you're now observing.

We've got to lighten it up and recognize what's really going on. We need that ego if we're going to transform our destiny. And that's why it's so important to learn how to tame it, teach it, and transcend it.

One of the biggest questions I've gotten over the years is, "Why do we even have this ego?" This doesn't make any sense to many people because of where they're seeing it from. Their ego has tricked them into seeing the limited perspective so that they will stay in the ego and at the level of self-centeredness. They'll be trying for who knows how long if that's their strategy. In other words, we need a new strategy that's designed to empower us to get to our ego. Creating a new strategy will be covered in further detail later in the book.

Just remember, this starts with our willingness and our readiness to stop this business of trying to make it about somebody else. This is all part of the lifting-up process that opens up the doorway to that Higher Destiny, to where you ultimately embody it and you begin to live it. This is going to empower and change everything in your life—and it will change it for the better forever.

I believe there will come a day when that fourteen-year-old girl on Dr. Phil will thank her mom and dad profusely. She's probably going to be very grateful to Dr. Phil, as well, for being as stern as he was because that's exactly what she needed. Similar to what the ego often needs from us in our work of transcending it.

Dr. Phil saw her, he saw the game, and he was not going to be affected by it. He also saw what was at stake—her life and possibly the demise of her family. He wasn't going to buy into her games.

That's the kind of attitude we need to develop when it comes to addressing our ego. If we don't have this attitude, then we're buying into the games our ego plays. Remember, the ego is a trickster. It's going to try and trick you into believing an illusion. It's the magician, and it's going to cast a spell in order to keep itself safe. It says it wants to keep you safe too, but it's only serving its own agenda. So, when we buy into something that was cast by our ego, we are distracted from what we are really supposed to be doing, becoming, or moving towards—which is our best self, living our best life.

Will you be courageous enough to stand in the heat, stand up to yourself, and do the right thing? If you are, you're that much closer to living in grace.

EXERCISES

Write down your responses to the following questions in your notebook.

1. Describe your ego? On a scale of 1-10 how well do you think you know it? 1 being very little and 10 being very well. And whatever the number you just gave yourself, why did you give yourself that number?

   What are some of the things your ego does to trick you? When was the last time it tricked you?

2. Who's in charge of your life? Is it you, or is it someone or something outside of yourself that you've given your power to? Be honest here and really reflect on this question before responding.

   If you have given your power over to someone or something else, who or what is it? Whatever or whoever your answer, why have you been giving your power away?

   What could you now begin doing to get your power back? When would you be willing to start doing this?

3. If you do have a child or children, have you stepped into the driver's seat as the parent, or is your child in control?

   As parents we want our children to know we run the household. If your child is in control, what are some things you now believe you could do to begin to regain a healthier, more positive position of control? When would you be willing to start doing this?

4. Think about a time in your life when you were spinning out of control. Describe what was happening. How did you regain control? Did you ask for help?

5. Describe a time that you were tricked by your ego, but you didn't see it coming. What kind of a mess did this possibly create?

   And how long did it take you to get out of that mess?

   Knowing what you know now, what could you specifically do differently to get better at recognizing a trick of your ego?

CHAPTER 6

BECOMING CONSCIOUS:
GETTING TO KNOW THE LOWER
PARTS OF OURSELVES

A re you aware that you could have a dream your Higher Self has created on your behalf to give you an advance warning around what you're about to choose to do? It's showing you a part of you that's about to pull the trigger on something; you're unconscious towards this part, but you're going to be left with the manifested consequence. When this happens, it is your Higher Self giving you a heads up in your dream space, so the potential outcome doesn't have to be so painful. The more we understand the unconscious parts of ourselves and bring them into the light, making them conscious, the clearer these messages from our Higher Selves will be. Becoming conscious, as wonderful and divine as it is, is a long, challenging process, but it's incredibly worthy of our time, energy, commitment, and devotion.

When Carl Jung first brought his idea of the unconscious mind into the world, people thought he was crazy. The majority of people in the emerging field of psychology just couldn't accept that there were unrecognized parts of themselves that were bringing about undesirable consequences in their lives. They would say, "No, this is God. This is my husband. This is my kids. This is my parents who are doing this to me." Fifty years later, Jung has become a legend. There's a whole group of psychologists who follow him, who respect and admire him and his work.

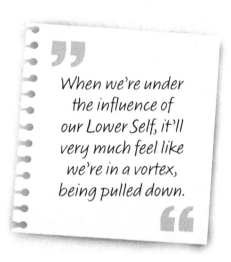

> When we're under the influence of our Lower Self, it'll very much feel like we're in a vortex, being pulled down.

When we get tired of the unnecessary pain, at some point, we will choose to get to know all aspects of ourselves—not just our Higher Self but also all parts of our Lower Self too: the ego, the inner child, and the shadow self. All of these aspects of us are influences on our subconscious minds and our choices, so it is important to get to know them. Yes, all of these parts of your Lower Self can and often will influence you, whether you like it or not, so you must get to the point where you are able to say, "I want to get to know all lower aspects of myself. I don't want to remain unconscious to the parts of myself that are making choices on my behalf. Because I'm the one who gets to deal with the consequences."

In the previous chapter's exercises, I presented the question: How well do you know your ego? So now I ask you, how well do you know your inner child? How well do you know your shadow side? The reason that it's important to get to know your Lower Self and all its parts is so that you can work with them and eventually come to know your Higher Self on a much deeper level. In this chapter we will be exploring the inner child and shadow in greater detail, just as we did for the ego in the previous chapter.

Maybe you have a part of you that likes to hold other people in judgment. Maybe you have another part of you that is a coward—it likes to live in secret. Maybe you have a part of you inside that's filled with rage, resentment, or hatred. We wonder why we live in so much conflict, why we are so depressed, and why we experience so much confusion. It's because we've got parts of ourselves inside that we're possibly still in denial of, and even though we're still unconscious of these aspects of ourselves, they can still make choices and create consequences in our world.

These behaviors are coming from our inner child or our shadow, under the influence of our ego, to act out and trip us up. For the ego, it is merely a self-serving way to distract us. But for our inner child and our shadow side, these are subconscious ways of getting our attention so we can truly help them heal and grow.

How do we know when we are operating from these aspects of our Lower Selves? Well, as the name implies, the Lower Self is down below. When we're under the influence of our Lower Self, it'll very much feel like we're in a vortex, being pulled down. In this place, we might find ourselves struggling or experiencing hardship. Or maybe we feel like we're in some pocket of inescapable darkness. Or maybe we're going into a meeting or conversation with someone that's important to us, and somewhere it takes a turn, and we're on this downward spiral, and all of a sudden, everything seems to be getting heavier.

These are all experiences that we might find ourselves having that suggest we're operating from one of these aspects of our Lower Self.

Which brings us back to what I mentioned earlier—the more we heal our past of unresolved issues, the less we experience the Lower Self, and the less likely it is to influence us in these ways that feel like struggle, darkness, or heaviness.

THE INNER CHILD

Have you ever been in a relationship with somebody and after you had been with them for maybe a year or so, you started to see them a little differently—and more specifically, you started to see that bratty, dysfunctional, unhealed little boy or girl inside of them? That is their inner child.

What happened next? Did their child heal or raise up to adult status? Did this person become a genuinely powerful person? Or is it possible that their inner child, perhaps in conjunction with your inner child, took center stage in your relationship and, over time, destroyed it? And even though you might still be with this person, it's destroyed the passion. It's destroyed the sexual connection you had. It's destroyed the idea of you working together towards your bigger dreams. This is two people who continuously make unconscious decisions from the inner child parts of themselves and are not yet willing to become conscious and ultimately responsible for their choices.

It's important to know that the unhealed child inside of you that hasn't been raised up to adult status yet can take center stage in your life at any point in time. You could be in a work environment, and next thing you know, you become the brat of all brats. You could be in a love relationship, as mentioned previously, and next thing you know, you turn on a dime and start saying or doing things that are mean or hurtful. You'll know when your child has taken over when you become bratty, demanding, bossy, pouty, or needy when interacting with others.

If we remain unconscious to our inner child, we will most likely blame our behavior on somebody else, or we'll start justifying what we said or what we did. We'll justify our choices by saying something like, "I'm worth it," or "They are going to pay for what they did to me." And, of course, the piece that we forget is the other person involved. Nine times out of ten, there's going to be a pushback, or a consequence, and often we don't see it coming.

The unhealed child inside of you can take center stage in your life at any point in time.

Sometimes, that pushback can be downright intense or ugly, and generally, the person who's getting pushback from their choice they made from their inner child isn't aware of it. That's why it's so important to bring awareness to this part of ourselves.

Another name for the inner child would be your subconscious self. This is the part of you that, for the most part, is hidden until you become aware that it exists and then choose to learn how to access it, work with it, and assist it. By helping your inner child, your subconscious will begin to reveal parts of you that have been blocking you in achieving your most important goals and materializing your greatest dreams. As you resolve and heal these parts of yourself, these things become more tangible.

For the inner child to be strengthened, we must recognize where it is possibly stuck. If as a child or adolescent, you experienced trauma, there's a good possibility that it's still inside you and hasn't been healed. Childhood trauma is usually strong enough to literally put the growth and evolutionary expansion of the inner child or the subconscious into a stuck position—a holding pattern.

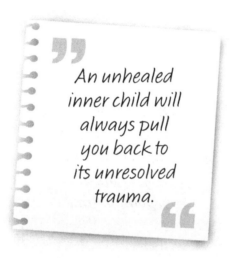

An unhealed inner child will always pull you back to its unresolved trauma.

So, if I wanted to strengthen my inner child, this is the first thing I need to check for: "Do I have unresolved issues from my past? Do I have wounds or traumas that I experienced when I was younger in this life that I have not yet resolved?" If the answer is yes to these last couple of questions, what that strongly suggests is that there is, at the very least, a pattern of holding back by that of our own inner child or subconscious. This is a good starting point to begin to assess what parts of our past we are to be healing and resolving.

Let's say we have three different parts of our past that are unresolved. In other words, there are three different places in our past timeline for us to heal those parts that we've identified. We can pick one of these areas and then begin to work towards healing this part and resolving that issue that was left unresolved from our past. As we do this, it starts to empower and strengthen our inner child. Then, as we heal the other two areas, the inner child continues to grow stronger.

In the process of strengthening this inner child and helping him or her become healthier, we will find that he or she is more willing to work with us. Our inner child will now be able to respond to our directives and let us take the lead, which will ultimately allow us to accomplish more, experience more, and achieve more in our personal and professional lives.

So the next question is how do you differentiate between an unhealed inner child and a healed inner child? An unhealed inner child will always pull you back to its unresolved trauma. And from that place it will potentially take over your life, even if it's just for the next hour or two. This is when we begin to act out. We act out whatever that unresolved issue is from our past. This is now where we can and often do act it out with someone or something in our life.

On the other hand, we have a very different experience when our inner child has been healed. This is a child that is willing to work with you. This is a child that will actually now help you. This is a child that is working in an energy of oneness with you. You can see this play out in an actual parent-child relationship. Let's say the child is eight years old and is really healthy—not just physically, but emotionally, mentally, and spiritually. This child is far easier to work with. In fact, you might even say this child is a joy to work with.

Why? Because the child is more receptive. The child is more present. And because of that, you end up having a more pleasant experience with this child. Now, if you and the eight-year-old child decided to go out and do something together, whatever you decided to do becomes more fun, possibly more productive, and a lot more enjoyable because of this synergistic working relationship between the parent and the child.

For even more information on healing the inner child, I invite you to check out The Game Changer course that I offer on my website at www. DaleHalaway.com.

THE EGO

We've already discussed the ego's impact on our choices quite extensively so far. The ego is also one of the lower parts of us. It's important to keep in mind that the ego is not "bad." It's just doing its job, until you teach it differently. Trying to blame the ego or to conceptualize it as "wrong" is a form of resistance that will, in fact, further strengthen it. Instead, begin to observe it. You may actually find yourself in awe of its craftiness. When the ego tricks you into letting your needy energy control you, you literally eject from the captain's chair of your ship and let your needy self control your life. Then, if you're really not paying close attention, you'll go and blame it on someone or something else. That's when you can drop into the "poor little unfortunate me" syndrome. Personal responsibility doesn't even exist in that moment because at that point, you're more committed to hanging on to your needy ego self and whatever or whoever it's hooked into.

Over time, you will begin to recognize the tricks and traps the ego is attempting to lay, in the subtlest of ways, and you will be able to sidestep them.

Becoming aware of the distractions of your ego is beneficial, but it is going to challenge you again and again. Sometimes you're going to stand up to the challenge and really embrace it, and then you're going to get a victory. Other times, you're probably going to cower down because of your needy energy. That neediness is what the ego uses—big time. However, don't be hard on yourself. Each time this happens, it's a step further into awareness and being able to prevent it from happening the next time. The more victories we have, the less likely it is that these tricks will show up, and the closer we will get to transcending our ego.

Throughout the book, the ego will be the most common aspect of the Lower Self that we'll be referring to. This is due to its relative position in the Lower Self and its opposition to the soul in the Greater Self.

THE SHADOW SELF

The third lower part is the shadow self. This aspect does exactly what it sounds like; it hides in the shadows. Its hidden aspects manifest through our behavioral patterns. Do you have aspects of yourself that other people don't know or secrets that you are reluctant to share with others? These are some of your shadow aspects, created by your shadow self.

> Do you have aspects of yourself that other people don't know or secrets that you are reluctant to share with others?

If you aren't sure, then here are some examples of what a shadow aspect might look like. Say someone has a gambling addiction. They are in a business partnership and have found a way to dip into the company's investment accounts. Or there's a relationship in which one partner begins to have a secret affair. Or this could be a person who smokes but doesn't want anyone to know. Addictions are common shadow behaviors. Maybe someone has an addiction to marijuana, or alcohol, or even sweets. It could be anything that is a hidden behavior. It might not be devious, but it is secretive, and most people have a very difficult time actually talking about their shadow behaviors.

Whatever the example, when we are showing up in a way in our life where the shadow side is influencing our behavior, we are not living with honesty, integrity, and authenticity.

In looking at our own behaviors, if something feels secretive or shameful, it can be helpful to ask, "Is this my shadow side? And if it is, what is it up to right now?" The most important to ask would be: "Why? Why does my shadow feel it has to do this?" Then, whatever the answer is to that question, now it becomes a question of: "Can I embrace this? Can I accept this? Can I learn from this? Can I begin to show up in a way where it is possible to give my shadow side what it truly needs to heal and transform from within me?"

Our goal in doing work on recognizing our shadow is to shine a light on these hidden aspects and bring them out into the open. This is where the transformational healing of our shadow can really begin. Ultimately, we want to live a life of openness without secrets, so it is important to get acquainted with the shadow in order to do that.

THE PRICE YOU PAY FOR YOUR UNCONSCIOUS CHOICES

Earlier, we explored unconscious choices, which are choices made from one of these lower aspects or areas of the Lower Self. Remember, when the choice is being made from one of these unconscious aspects, if it was given a voice and it could speak out loud right now, it would probably say, "This is my only way of getting your attention." Why? Because it needs our attention. In order for us to heal any unconscious part of ourselves, we have to bring consciousness and awareness to it.

Let's say you're unconsciously choosing to let your inner child basically run your life. This begs the question—where the heck have *you* gone when this happens? Do you vacate the premises, as in have you mentally or emotionally checked out? Do you go off into hiding and do the secretive thing? Where does the "conscious you" go when you make this unconscious choice to let your unhealed inner child take center stage?

I see this in relationships with people who say they really love each other, and next thing you know, the dysfunctional, unhealed child takes center stage, and all bets are off. You'd better have your helmet on because they're coming out swinging. I've watched people do some absolutely nasty things to each other. It's an unconscious choice to let your unhealed inner child run your relationships.

We've all heard stories of, or witnessed a parent abusing one of their children. Maybe not physically; perhaps it's emotionally or verbally. That's not them being an adult. That's them acting out from an unconscious part of themselves. They've unconsciously chosen to let this part of them run their life, and now, because one of their kids really upset them or because they disapprove of something that one of their kids has done, they are behaving in a way that is not only immature but abusive.

I knew a mom who was a former model, and she berated her daughter all the time to make herself feel better. It really did a number on the daughter's psyche because the mom wanted the daughter to model, but then she'd looked at the pictures and she'd say things like, "Oh gosh, we shouldn't have spent this money. I should have gotten her a nose job." The horrible things she would say were unbelievable.

The mother is under the influence of her ego, which means some of her choices are coming from the unconscious. It looks like it's about the daughter, but it's not about the daughter at all. It's about the mother.

> *Our goal in recognizing our shadow is to shine a light on our hidden aspects and bring them out into the open.*

Maybe there's a father who decides to put his child in a certain school, and he won't reconsider, even when the child isn't doing well in that environment. It doesn't matter because, again, it's not really about the child. It's about the parent. And more specifically, it's about the ego getting some kind of gratification, the ego getting some kind of a need met. Maybe it's that need for perfection, or maybe it's that need to be right. Or maybe it's that need for recognition. With both these examples, the ego is saying, "Look at me! Look at how great of a parent I am because my child is now at this amazing school/or is now a model."

Meanwhile, these children are under tremendous stress and pressure. They might even be doing something behind the parent's back that the parent isn't even aware of. All of a sudden, maybe they're into drugs or sex or partying or alcohol or whatever the consequence could be that was made both from the child's unconscious and from the influence of the parent's ego.

It's not uncommon that a parent cannot accept something about their own child. And so they're constantly making these choices that are likely more unconscious than conscious. They feel their child needs a nose job, or they feel their child needs to go to a certain school, or needs to get excellent grades, and then everything's going to be okay. No, in this scenario the only one that is going to be okay is the parent that is putting all of this into motion. Whereas the child often feels the stress of the unrealistic pressures and lower desires of the parent, which at some point causes the child to begin to believe they will never be good enough. This is all coming from the ego, and when the ego is at influence, its choices will be self-centered ones.

Let's go back to the business example where a partner is taking money from a shared business account or trust. Stealing is a shadow behavior. This person justifies their actions with entitlement, which is a function of the ego. Remember that wherever the shadow is expressing, the ego is always there influencing.

This person is taking money out for personal reasons, but they justify their actions; they reason with themselves that somehow this is okay; that somehow they deserve this; that somehow this is owed to them. They think they're entitled to do this and doubt their partner will even catch on to what's going on.

At some later point, their partner finds out that this is what they've been doing. And in that now comes the consequence. In this case, the company could be broken up, or the partner who has been stealing could be sued. It could mean bankruptcy for the business or jailtime for the thief. Whatever it is, there will be a negative consequence eventually.

Now please understand, if you've behaved in any of these manners, that's not the real you. That's the ego, the shadow, or the unhealed, dysfunctional inner child that you've unconsciously let take center stage in your life. It's like the parents on the *Dr. Phil* show who were allowing their fourteen-year-old to run things. It doesn't take a rocket scientist to figure this one out. You can see clearly that the parents could not stand up to the child, and somewhere along the way, the child took center stage. Under the influence of her ego along with the expression of her shadow, she had taken complete control of the situation. A fourteen-year-old brat was in charge of the household and running wild. Just think about that for a moment.

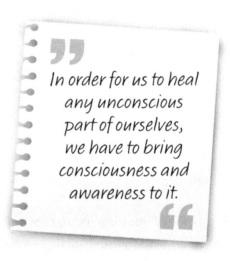

In order for us to heal any unconscious part of ourselves, we have to bring consciousness and awareness to it.

Where do we end up when we make these kinds of unconscious choices? Obviously, we'll keep on doing it if the choice remains unconscious. Makes sense, right? If you're not aware that you're the one who is choosing to allow this to happen, then that means two things. Number one, it's going to keep on happening. Right along with whatever you do afterwards, such as get upset with somebody, blame somebody, or give somebody a piece of your mind. And number two, if you continue down this path in this way, then it's going to get louder. In other words, it's a question of time before somebody is going to really get hurt. And when that happens, negative karma comes upon us. You'll know when it happens because when that level of karma strikes you, you might very well feel like you've been hit by a Mack truck—and in that moment, you can't change the outcome because the outcome has either happened or is now happening. At this juncture, we can no longer run away. We are going to have to accept and work with the consequence or consequences that have now manifested.

We will get further into the subject of karma later in the book, but as it relates to this example, now that your karma has come to visit you, and even though your choice that led up to that karma was unconscious, the Universe will not provide you with any leeway. The Universe doesn't say, "Well, you know what? They were so unconscious that we're going to give them a pass and let the karma go." That would be a personalized Universe. And quite frankly, if that were the case, we would all be doomed. Ultimately, if people were allowed a free pass, there would be no order. People would not learn anything and would repeat the same patterns. This lack of order would affect everyone involved in that person's life, such as kids, spouses, coworkers, employees, etc.

It's only when we're conscious this is where we can actually do something really constructive, positive, and productive.

The key here is to get better at recognizing a choice that is being made from or influenced by our unconscious, for as we do, we increase the odds dramatically of making a conscious choice instead and shifting a potentially negative consequence to a potentially positive one.

MY INVITATION TO YOU: CHOOSE TO BECOME CONSCIOUS

My invitation to you, my challenge for you, is for you to choose to become conscious of what you've chosen to do unconsciously. It's a big one—I get it. I've had my own path and traversed through my own stuff, and it was a tangled mess to navigate through. It's not easy. If this was easy, everybody on Planet Earth would have already done this. I'm sure if Carl Jung was among us right now, he would tell us it was tough for him as well.

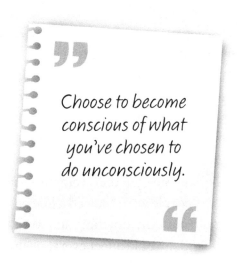

> Choose to become conscious of what you've chosen to do unconsciously.

You're ultimately going to have to look at the parts of yourself that have been unconsciously making choices on your behalf. And then you get to deal with the consequences, whether you like it or not. This is the only way out of this unnecessary pain and suffering—by going into these parts of yourself and getting acquainted with them. This is done through the conscious choice of fully embracing the consequence of the types of choices that were being made on our behalf from within the unconscious. That's what opens up the doorway for you to be able to know more about your Higher Self. Otherwise, knowing about your Higher Self is just one big intellectual exercise of fantasizing. And, come the end of the day, if you're not getting to know your Higher Self, your life's not changing—and your life could be changing in the biggest, brightest, and best of ways.

You must first consciously choose to connect with whatever part of you that's being shown to you—as in a lower part of you that hasn't healed yet, isn't resolved yet, might be downright dysfunctional, might be filled with judgment, might be filled with hatred, or might be filled with depressed energy—whatever it is, connect with it. Get to know it.

Intellectually, you might know that your Higher Self is big, beautiful, strong, and all these wonderful things, but it means diddly squat if it hasn't been embodied. The way to embody it is to connect with the lower parts of yourself, one by one. And then, you've got to go the distance with each one of them. And you can do it. If one could do it, we all can.

EXERCISES

Answer the following questions in your notebook.

1. For the next week, carry a small pad of paper and pen with you. Every time you say something negative or self-deprecating, write it down. This is a great way to start becoming aware of what is going on within your unconscious. It will also reveal where you are slipping into autopilot or having your ego, inner child, or shadow take over the wheel. This will give you a good road map of what is coming up first for you to begin working with.

   And then at the end of the week, journal what this exercise revealed to you.

2. How well do you know your inner child? Or did you even know you had one prior to picking up this book?

   And now with this next question, go with whatever you get as the answer comes to you.

   If your inner child had a specific age, what would that age be?

   Now sit with your minds eye and see your child at this age. Write out a detailed description as you pictured it.

If your child had something it wanted you to know right now what would it be?

If your child needed something from you right now what would it be?

Whatever your answer, could you give it that?

These descriptions and time stamp will serve you well later in tracking your inner child's healing and growth as you continue this journey of transforming your destiny.

3. Ask yourself: Do I have unresolved issues from my past? Do I have wounds or traumas that I experienced when I was younger in this life that I have not yet resolved? If some answers came up, then jot them down now. These are the ones you are consciously aware of. Committing them to paper will begin to jar the subconscious ones loose, as they are now ready to be revealed to you. Continue noting them when they do reveal themselves.

4. Have you ever been in a relationship that became ruled by your or the other person's inner child or both of your inner children? How did that affect your relationship?

5. When was the last time you justified one of your actions that you believe was influenced by your inner child? What was it? And what was the result?

6. How well do you know your shadow side?

Are you aware of any of your shadowy behaviors? If so, what are they? What are some of the things you keep in the shadows? Are you willing to get real with yourself and commit them to paper right now? If you can do this, then you are on your way to bringing your shadow into the light.

CHAPTER 7

A FEW KEYS TO PERSONAL TRANSFORMATION

W hen it comes to transforming ourselves, this chapter will focus on five essential keys to that process. Each key stands alone, but when you combine them, they become very powerful in transforming whatever it is you want to change inside yourself. You see, that's where the real transformation exists. It's on the inside—not the outside.

In many of my classes I bring to the attention of of my students the Law of Reflection. It states that our outer world is a reflection of our inner world. Another way of saying the same thing is that our outer landscape reflects our inner landscape. So, at some point, whatever is going on inside must begin to express itself on the outside. Transform the inside, and you'll naturally get a transformation on the outside. That's the beauty here. And not only will you get a transformation on the outside; you'll get to keep it forever. How about that? It's 100 percent sustainable.

When we're trying only to change something on the outside, it's not that it's bad, but it's difficult to sustain because when you really get what's going on—and more specifically, who you really are—you understand that everything that's happening in your outside world is a mirror to your internal universe. It's reflecting something back to you; whether it's positive or negative, shadow or light—it's doing that on purpose. This is one of the reasons why you as a soul have chosen to come here.

Now, before we move into the five keys, I want to take a moment to share about a healing modality that I created, which I will be referring to throughout the rest of this chapter. It is called the TransCovery Process®. It has helped thousands of people move their lives forward in profound and meaningful ways. That being said, let's begin to explore the keys to personal transformation.

FIVE ESSENTIAL KEYS TO PERSONAL TRANSFORMATION:

Key #1 – Identify It

First, you've got to identify the part of you that's up for healing, for transformation, or for some kind of a resolution or an integration. You've got to identify it, and you've got to identify it correctly. One of the ways we do this is through self-inquiry. This is where we ask the types of questions that specifically take us deeper into a part of ourselves, such as: "If what I'm feeling right now was given a voice and it could speak out loud to me, what would it say?" or "If this problem that I'm currently struggling with was reflecting something back to me about me, what would it be?" Self-inquiry, in my view, ought to become a daily practice for every single person on Planet Earth.

Another powerful practice for self-inquiry that you could become engaged in is to consciously choose to work with your dreams. You might think of your dream space as a powerful resource that is here to serve you along your journey in healing, maturing, and transforming yourself.

You can begin this process by simply getting into the habit of writing your dreams down. Dedicate a notebook that you will use exclusively for this purpose and get into the regular practice of writing down your dreams upon awakening. Sometimes, when you're in this stage of using the first key, it takes a little while to get into the routine. Dreams can be murky, confusing, and difficult to remember, so be patient. With continued intention and diligence, they will begin coming more easily.

Your dream space is here to serve you in healing, maturing, and transforming yourself.

This process is extremely valuable and can help you identify circumstances in your life that are ready for transformation for months to come. Say you have a profound dream. You might have somebody help translate it for you—when you do, you get great value out of that. It enriches you, and assuming that you wrote it down and journaled it properly, that dream could serve you again, months from now, to the point where it'll blow your mind. You might think, "Wait a minute. I thought this was translated four months ago." Yes—it was. But it was

TRANSFORM YOUR DESTINY

translated with the intent being that you would be ready to receive it somewhere in the future. And that future now come upon you.

You see, if you're not ready to receive whatever you're to be identifying, then what's the point of giving you the whole enchilada? That could really mess you up. Often our dreams reveal something to us incrementally. We might get multiple pieces of a message over a period of time.

This is one of the areas where I feel that people like some psychics or clairvoyants can make big mistakes. They're using their higher abilities of dialing into you. They're seeing all kinds of things and they choose to give it all to you. Now sometimes going to a psychic or clairvoyant is the best thing you can do. Some can really help you. But that is not the type of psychic or clairvoyant I am referring to here. I am specifically referring to the type that shares too much information that potentially can hinder rather than help.

So what happens if you're not ready to receive what they share? This can sometimes wreak havoc with people, as it's just too much, and perhaps this is a weakness on the psychic's part. Maybe this is one of their lower aspects, where they tell too much because they can. Just because I have access and I'm privy to your timeline, or to what's going on with you, doesn't always mean I should give it all to you, at least in this present exchange. Why? You might not be able to handle it just yet. It might be too much information right now.

Just because you can, does not always mean you should. That's the mark of a weak person. Just because I can give you money, doesn't mean that I should give you money. Just because I can give you a Christmas like you've never had before, doesn't always mean I should. Why? You might take advantage of it. It might screw you up. You might become one of the most entitled people on Planet Earth as a result of me going over the top. Can you see this? That, too, becomes a personal choice.

Get in the habit of asking yourself, "All right—so I can do this, but is it appropriate for me to do this?"

Someone may get a powerful dream, but right now they can only understand 35 percent of it. No matter how hard they try, they can only get a particular amount in present time. Therefore, it's important to have the practice of writing our dreams down. Many people neglect to do this because they think they've got it all worked out. They're missing the mark, only they don't know they're missing the mark. They don't realize that there's an extra benefit lurking in the ethers that they could access at some later point when they're ready to do so.

But they haven't been willing to do the practice on a regular basis, at least just yet. Why? Well, because they're busy, or they're depressed, or possibly angry at someone or something. Meanwhile, they're shooting themselves in the foot. If there's a part of you in your Lower Destiny that you've been ignoring for twenty-three years, do you really believe that if you start to connect with it today, for the first time, you're going to immediately know everything about it? Of course not.

Just because you connect with your inner child today doesn't mean you know everything about them. That's ridiculous and immature. And by the way, your inner child is going to pick up on this and hold back because it's hard to trust an immature person. Wouldn't you agree?

Can you trust somebody who starts to show themselves as being immature, who always wants to jump the gun, who always wants to get there as fast as they possibly can? Can you trust someone who is all about pushing on that result? If not, why don't you trust that type of person? Because they're unpredictable and inauthentic. And, what happens if, by chance, you decide to trust them? I'm sure you've done that at least once, right? At least once you've trusted someone like that. What was the result? Did they let you down? And what did that do for you? How did that make you feel? Did you lose money? Did it cause you stress or strife?

Remember, something's got to happen when we go down these pathways. When identifying what needs healing inside of you, you must ask yourself: "How deep is my knowledge of whatever this part of me is that is coming to the surface? How well do I really know this part of myself? And more importantly, does this part of me feel like I really know it?" Maybe it doesn't because you've been running away from it for, we'll say, ten years.

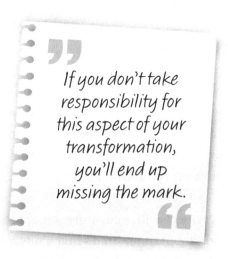

> If you don't take responsibility for this aspect of your transformation, you'll end up missing the mark.

Or perhaps you do the hit or miss thing, like, "Well, I'm in the mood today, so I'm going to work with you." But tomorrow you're not in the mood, so you show up like, "You're on your own, baby. Go do your own thing. I have no time for this." Does this sound like you?

There's a consequence that comes with choosing to show up like this, and the consequence is that this part of you doesn't believe in you. It doesn't trust you. It's says, "Okay, so today she's on, and then who knows? All bets are off for the next five days. I couldn't count on her if my life depended upon it." This can happen on the inside. Obviously, it can also happen on the outside, too, when people come into our lives, and at some point, we know we can't count on them anymore.

We end up saying, "You've told me 101 times in 101 different ways that you're going to do something for me, and then you don't do it. You don't follow through on your word. I don't believe you anymore. I can't trust you. I want to trust you and I want to believe in you. I like you. But I'm sorry—enough is enough." This same scenario can play out inside of us too. We may have a part or parts of ourselves that don't believe in us because we've let them down so many times in the past. We've been back and forth, in and out. One day we're on, and the next five days we're completely off.

Now we don't want to overlook this first key. We don't want to go to through this key too quickly. We don't want to bypass this because what I've come to greatly appreciate is that this key of identifying what is up for healing is sometimes the process in itself.

Set the intention when you go to bed that you are going to remember your dream. And then be prepared with that notebook by your bed for when you wake up. By going to bed with this intention in place, your subconscious mind can work on your behalf while sleeping.

If you're interested in learning to better connect or deepen your under-standing into that of what your dreams are trying to communicate to you, check out my Free Dream Master Class invitation at the back of the book.

Key #2 – Connect with It

Once you've identified the part of yourself that is up for transforma-tion, you have to connect with it. If you are writing down your dreams in an earnest attempt to identify the parts of yourself that are ready to transform, your dream space will know that you're willing to connect with it, and it will start giving you more dreams. But, if you don't habitually attempt to connect with this part of yourself, then it gets the message that it's just not important to you.

This is why we have people who have gone years without being able to remember a dream. They're not in the practice of connecting with them. Not only can they go years without remembering a dream, but at some point, their dreams could take a turn towards the dark. Their dreams could get really twisted and distorted because there's no one home to steer the ship.

Now be aware that identifying and connecting with parts of your personality will not happen overnight. You've got to get into the swing of uniting with them on a regular basis. You've got to prove to them that you're here and wanting to connect with them. Be patient and persistent, as there is no quick fix to do this. Don't let your ego trick you into thinking that you're going to have this all handled by the end of the coming week.

I'm sure you've heard someone say something like this to you: "You know what? I know I've been untrustworthy. I know that I've broken your trust with me, but I assure you that from this moment on, you can count on me—I promise you. Just give me your checkbook. I'll take really good care of it—I assure you."

Would you buy that as an opportunity or a temptation? This person has told you so many times in so many different ways that they're going to do something, and they don't do it. They've betrayed your trust. Maybe they've gone ahead and taken advantage of you. Maybe they've cheated on you, and now they're coming to you, on their knees, saying, "I know that in the past I lost your trust, but I promise you from this day on, you can trust me."

The results show that this person has a history of not following through on what they tell you they're going to do, and results don't lie. This person hasn't earned your trust. In fact, they've repeatedly broken it. This person would have to earn your trust before you could ever give it to them again.

In the same way, you've got to earn trust from your soul, your Higher Self, showing that you are the real deal and can be counted on now. And leading up to that, you're going to be tested through temptations from that of the ego.

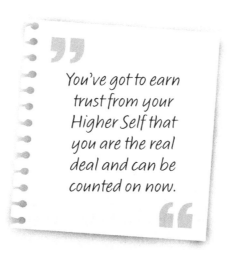

> You've got to earn trust from your Higher Self that you are the real deal and can be counted on now.

Do you think your Higher Self trusts you? And are you worthy of its trust? Can you really be counted on when your Higher Self speaks to you? Do you follow through without hesitation? Or do you start to question it and then go do something else that's completely different than what you're being encouraged to do, or being prompted to do, on behalf of your own Highest Self?

Identifying and connecting with your Higher Self is a process that takes time. There's no way you're going to go from A to Z overnight. It's like you're building something within yourself, and ultimately, with practice, it becomes phenomenal. It becomes great. It becomes the foundation of all foundations for you to truly live the life that you came here to live at soul level. That's what's really happening on the deepest of levels, and that takes time. You know that old saying "Rome wasn't built in a day"? We're in the process of building, in this case, that inner foundation. This is huge, especially in a world that, for the most part, hasn't really been taught how to do this yet.

So, we've got to be at a certain place along our journey where we've now convinced our soul that we're the real deal. Can you change this within yourself overnight? No, you can't. But you can change it. Absolutely, you can. Is this going to be a long process? Yes, it's going to go on for a while, but it's worth it.

Coming back to this second essential key—to connect with it—what does that really mean? You've got to be able to feel into it, which means you've got to stop the resisting. You've got to stop the avoiding. You've got to stop running away from this and going to your favorite numbing-out strategy. You've got to feel it. And then, what happens?

It's like when you're in a relationship with somebody—it could be one of your dearest friends or a sibling. Let's say you're having a cup of coffee or a glass of juice together, and you're really connecting. When we're connecting, we walk away with a feeling. We're allowing ourselves to feel into this person. We're allowing ourselves to feel into what we're conversing about. We're allowing ourselves to feel into whatever we're experiencing together. That's what connection really is.

I started off in my twentieth year of this life learning how to become a professional salesperson. I struggled a lot with it at first, but then, eventually, I punched through. When I did, my sales just climbed, and they kept on climbing because I had tapped in. I was connecting with my customers, and I was connecting with them in a way where they just couldn't say no. This is because they were filled with a positive feeling. I'd constantly have those who became customers as a direct result of my unique sales approach who would say to me, "This was so much fun. This was so engaging." I had no idea it was going to be like this.

It's the ability to connect, which means the ability to feel into that person, to really feel into their desires, to really feel into their genuine wants. When we're having a conversation, there are certain words that I'll literally feel into as they're coming out of my mouth. And when I do that, it's always amazing how quickly the other person feels exactly what I'm feeling in that moment. Not once did I tell them what to feel, and yet they start feeling exactly what I'm feeling. It's because when I'm connecting, what I'm really doing is feeling into it. There's no resistance here. There's no avoidance. I'm not thinking about what I'm going to say next. I'm very present. I'm listening attentively. I'm really with them. I'm connecting because I'm feeling into everything that's going on in that conversation, and it leaves that person feeling better. They just feel good. They feel on top of the world, and it's very authentic.

On the other hand, a person could have a conversation where they're going in intellectually. They have all the right words, but they're not feeling into the words. They're not feeling into the conversation. They're not feeling into the other person's wants or desires. The only connection that occurs is intellectual; this person hasn't felt into us and vice versa.

But, beyond a shadow of a doubt, when a person really feels something from us, it causes them to experience connection. And when that happens, they just want to hang out with us more. That's the bottom line. There are not many people who can do this just yet, including most salespeople, but this is a powerful and necessary key you must acquire when it comes to transformation.

If you're going to transform, heal, and resolve a longstanding issue that's been going on within you for a long period of time, you've got to get good at this. This is a significant part of the healing modality in the TransCovery Process®—really connecting. Some people will go through the TransCovery Process® too quickly. Sometimes in my live classes, I'll give specific directions, such as pausing in between the questions—to let a little silence go by for just a couple seconds. Then, I'll walk through the room like I normally do, and I'll hear someone speaking it as fast as they can get it out. They're not connecting. They're intellectualizing.

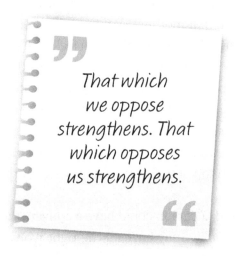

That which we oppose strengthens. That which opposes us strengthens.

Connecting is a very powerful thing. When this part of you that's unhealed, wounded, or dysfunctional starts to really feel you feeling into it, and you're now feeling exactly what this part of you has been feeling, the transformational magic can now happen. It always does. But so many people have a difficult time doing this, not just in transforming themselves but in relating daily in their external worlds too. They connect intellectually because it's safe and they can control the conversation and where it goes. It gives them security.

It's an absolute gold mine for you to learn this essential key of really connecting with these parts of you. Again, the key here is in choosing to feel into whatever you're feeling when one of these parts of you surfaces. If you've been traumatized and there's a lot of fear inside of you, which is common when we've been traumatized, you can use this essential key in the transformational process. Remember you're going to connect into that feeling. You're not just going to feel the trauma; you're also going to begin to allow yourself to feel the fear. This is not about acting out on the fear but rather feeling into the fear. For when you do, this fear that has been inside of you will start to jar loose in the overall process of transforming that fear.

Don't be alarmed should you start shaking physically. This is happening because you're completely feeling the feeling. In this process of feeling the feeling, many times, it only takes minutes for that feeling to move or transform.

There's a part of you that has been feeling this fear or this apprehension ever since the traumatization happened. Can you see it? Sometimes just seeing it opens the doorway into connecting with this part of you. And then, when that happens, the transformational magic comes into play. Now something magical is about to occur in that moment because this part of you, for the first time possibly in a long time, has a moment where it literally feels the connection with you.

Now you're willing to go there and feel what this part of you has been feeling for who knows how long. Now you can connect with it on a real and deep level so that you can begin to heal it. This is a beautiful and victorious moment. And once you experience it, you'll want more of it.

Key #3 – Accept It

After we've identified and connected with this part of us, the third key is to accept it—and more specifically, to accept it exactly the way it is without condition. So, if it has three warts on it, accept all the warts. Now here's a little golden nugget—your ego does not want you to accept it.

The ego wants you to think, "How could I possibly accept this thing, especially if it's got a wart on it? This belongs to somebody else. We've got to make him pay—the one who put the wart on this part of me." It's looking through the lens of a lower perspective. No matter how you cut it, the ego will have a difficult time seeing this properly. Or at least until you teach it how.

This is also where you might need to tame your ego. Then teach it, educate it, and let it know that you're in charge. We're talking about your life right now—your path. It's your larger destiny. We're talking about you, the real you, and the many parts of you that are possibly still suffering. You're the one who needs to get on board. You're the one who's got to get into the driver's seat. There is nobody, including Jesus, Buddha, Krishna, or any ascended master, that can do this for you. And, if you do have someone show up and say, "I'll take that on for you," then run for the hills because ultimately this type of assistance will not help you. You see, if you don't take responsibility for this aspect of your transformation, you'll end up missing the mark, and you'll be forced back to exactly where you were.

It's like when you're entering into a relationship with somebody. You're in the relationship, and right away you see all these red flags. Not that there's anything wrong with that, but what can really twist you up and make things complex is when you start judging what you see as wrong and then adopt this idea of believing we can change the person. Do you have any idea what you're signing yourself up for? Talk about egotistical.

So why do we do this? Well, it's for safety reasons. It's all to lock that person into place because deep down inside, we have a frightened little child we haven't yet acknowledged or become conscious of. That's all that's really going on here. So, we play this internal game and think, "I know I really don't like that, and I know I'm never going to like it, but I know I can change them. It might take me a year—but I know exactly how to do it." And then, a year later, we can't stand this other person. But see, the whole thing started off incorrectly. When we're operating this way, we're in direct opposition to this third key.

> We are exhausted and drained when we fight energetically with some part of ourselves all day long.

I've coached people in relationships throughout the years who will say to me, "No, I'm never going to accept this about him or her." I mean, that is a tough go. That's going to haunt them for all the months and years that they're in a relationship with this person. That's a heavy burden to take on, to say, "No, I cannot accept this but I also can't leave them either." That's heavy stuff.

What frees you is to be able to accept the other person just as they are. If you can't do that, then you've got a big problem because they're probably not going to change for you. And, as soon as they get wind that you're there to try and change them, they're going to push back on you. You'll have times where you'll feel like you've just been hit by a truck because you're in a no-win situation. It'll never work should you continue to show up this way.

It's the same concept when it comes to your internal transformation. The goal here is to get to a place of acceptance of whatever this part of you is in its current state—not in its future state when it's perfect. You're going to be waiting forever for perfection if that's what you're doing.

Rather, when you move in with complete and total acceptance of this arrogant part of you; or this part of you that's filled with hatred; or that's really judgmental and overly critical; or that just likes to live in your head all the time to the point where you suffer with headaches from too much pressure, you're finally choosing to get out of the unconscious fight with these parts of yourself.

The moment you're in a fight with a part of you because you can't accept something, that part of you is going to fight back. It, too, is governed by the Hidden Law of the Universe, also known as the Law of Opposition, which clearly states, "That which we oppose strengthens." It also says, "That which opposes us strengthens." This means that by resisting something, we literally make that something more powerful. This law also means "that which is opposing me can strengthen me."

Most people can't even see this; that's why it's been referred to as the Hidden Law of the Universe. In my first book *Being Called to Change*, I call this unconscious resistance. In fact, I even go as far as saying it is the silent killer, meaning it can kill your dreams, your aspirations, your most meaningful goals, or something that you really value in your life.

So an example of this might be, when I'm not accepting a specific part of me, I'm giving it more power. How? Because I'm resisting it. Now for those of you who have a pattern of giving your power to someone or something else, this is how you do it. There have probably been times in the past where you've gone ahead and blamed it on your partner, saying something like, "Well, he takes all my power." No, he doesn't take all your power; you've been giving it to him—and the reason you give him your power is because on the inside, this is exactly what you do with yourself, as in you're giving your power to this part of you that you've been in resistance of and, in turn, have had a challenging time accepting.

You've potentially been in a state of refusing to accept a part of you that you don't like—a part of you that you've been disapproving of. And, because you haven't accepted it, what that then means is unconsciously you've chosen to fight with it. You've chosen to resist it. You've chosen to continue to make it wrong. And when you do that, this part of you, operating in accordance with this Universal Law, must fight you back. And then, you might complain at the end of day, saying, "I don't know why the heck I keep on feeling so exhausted." If I went into a boxing ring and this was my strategy—to fight with my opponent all day long—this would leave me completely drained. This is why when we are in this situation, we are exhausted and drained, because we have been fighting energetically with some part of ourselves all day long.

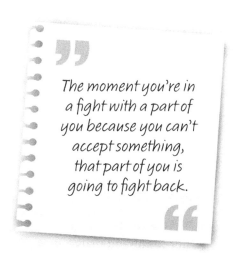

> The moment you're in a fight with a part of you because you can't accept something, that part of you is going to fight back.

Now let's recall the other definition of this Universal Law: "that which opposes me strengthens me." If we were to use this same example of the fighter in the boxing ring, and if we better understood what was happening here with our opponent giving us opposition, but we consciously took the time to learn to work with this opposition, then that is going to strengthen something within us. This would be a new and different strategy where we are literally working with this law as a way to gain a benefit or a victory by choosing to work with it.

This third essential transformational key comes into full effect as we choose to completely accept a part of us just as it is right now—no more of this business of, "I'll accept you when you heal. I'll accept you somewhere in the future." Instead, you can begin to acknowledge, "Right now, I'm really challenged. I'm really activated because I recognize this is a tough one for me. I have a big issue around acceptance." Just acknowledge it, once and for all. Go to it—choose to become and remain conscious of it.

If you're entering a new relationship with somebody and you really can't accept him or her, then get the heck out of the relationship, friendship, or partnership because you're going to torture yourself if you don't. You're going to torment yourself if you can't accept their faults. Just be honest. Stand up and stop cowering by taking the weaker path because you don't want to rock the boat or you're thinking somewhere down the way they're going to change for you—when, in fact, that might or might not be true.

Instead, you can stand up honorably and say something like, "I think you're a great person—just not the kind of person that I've been looking for in this way. How do I know that? Because there are these things you do that I know I can't accept. I'm being truthful with you right now. I know we've been together for six months, and I can see these things that happen with you that I know in my heart of hearts—I know in my bones—I'm not going to be able to accept. This is not because I don't like you. I know I just cannot accept it."

Therefore, within you, you achieve this point of resolution and you are able now to simply call an end to this relationship with love, respect, and gratitude, knowing that you are no longer willing to put yourself through this type of torment. You can end this relationship, even though you originally used to think "I'm going to try and change this person." Eventually, you realized, "If I go there, this person is going to push back on me and fight me."

Another example of this would be, say you have a potential new business partner. If whoever this person is or whatever this person does is simply not in alignment with your being-ness, at the level of your highest truth, you might get an intuitive sense that this just can't work long term. When you're in touch with your being, as in your soul or Higher Self, not your ego or Lower Self, you will realize this greater part of you would never allow you to completely accept this situation. Because if it did, then you might get hoodwinked by your ego and choose to become a business partner with this person. And next thing you know, you're sabotaging your business because you moved out of alignment with yourself.

So, from that higher perspective, your Higher Self is letting you know this. It doesn't mean that this person is bad. There's just a misalignment between you and this other person. There's a misalignment with the way you live your life, approach your life, and the way you build your business versus the way they do it. But it's significant enough that when you're really being honest with yourself, you just can't accept them in that position in your life in that way.

It could also be that you're not able to accept someone because you have a part of you that holds people in judgment when they're not living up to your standards. So, you might want to explore that as well. You want to explore to see if there might be a lower part of you, as in a part of your personality, that is judgmental.

You've got to go into self-inquiry on both the higher and lower levels to check and see if there's any part of your personality that possibly has a hang up and is attempting to show itself to you through this act of bringing this type of a person into your world on a regular basis. Whoever this person is, where do they fit into your life? Or where are you attempting to have them fit into your life? And then more importantly, do they fit? Are they in alignment with you and your state of being?

The lower perspective has more to do with discovering or uncovering a part of you that's in conflict with a particular type of person because it's ultimately in conflict with some part of you. So, the conflict is showing itself through the interaction with this person.

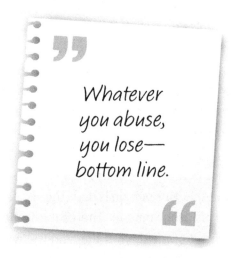

Whatever you abuse, you lose— bottom line.

Ideally, you want to be able to accept it if you're going to be partnered up in a way where you'll be spending more time together. You clearly don't want to walk around with this internal conflict on a regular basis because it's going to eat away at you. It can even make you start to dislike yourself. And when we don't like ourselves, that in itself can be detrimental. And if we end up going through a long period of time where we really don't like ourselves, this can be harmful as well.

One of my earlier mentors, who is no longer with us, Jack Addington, worked with a lot of different correctional facilities. He would often tell me that an inmate's ability to like themselves generally didn't exist. They'd been beaten down so much, and that usually started off with a parent. Eventually, the baton gets passed, and perhaps the parent who beat them down is no longer doing that anymore because now there's distance between the two of them.

But the child, who is now a young man or young woman, picks up the baton and starts doing the exact same thing, beating himself or herself down. The effect this has on them, Jack would say, is that they literally had not even an ounce of ability or opportunity to like themselves, which really means they hated themselves. And so, when they'd go out and commit these crimes, they were coming from a place of complete self-hatred inside. That reflected in their outer world, "I have no respect for your property whatsoever. I have no respect for the rules that are set forth for all of us to live a happier life. I have no respect at all."

When hatred is at play, people are capable of doing some of the ugliest, most destructive things that a man or a woman could actually do to somebody else. Jack saw this play out repeatedly, not just with one inmate but thousands of inmates, over a period of time.

Jack brought a lot of hope to these inmates, working with them on a clear mission to help them learn how to like themselves again and raise their self-esteem. He was very passionate about working with them and contributed to this part of society for a number of decades before he passed.

The point here is that it's all about accepting what is—accepting that you've got an issue, for example, around not liking yourself. And, accepting that you've got this issue because way back when, something traumatized some part of you. That's what you're to be in acceptance

185

of—once you go into complete acceptance of it, unconditionally, just as it is, that's where the transformational magic can happen. Then you can really start moving towards helping these parts of yourself truly heal, once and for all.

Key #4 – Own It

You've got to step into the driver's seat and take full responsibility for all parts of yourself. This might sound simple, and every now and then, it might be—yet there'll be other times when this is going to challenge you to the core, if it hasn't already. It will be a process that will likely go on for a little while, especially if you're dealing with a part of you that you've been in denial of for a long time.

All the great teachers have talked about this thing called "responsibility." You don't go from zero to a hundred overnight in accepting full responsibility for a part of you and for a part of your life—if that part has been dysfunctional and caused a lot of pain over a long period of time. Because for whatever reason, you unconsciously chose to avoid taking on the responsibility for the healing of this aspect of you and/or this area of your life. This process is not going to be a quick fix. You get to accept the responsibility for the whole enchilada, whatever that means and however twisted or distorted it might be, as it starts to unwind out of you. You might be able to pull this off in a week, but likely it will be more like a month, or quite frankly, it might take the whole next year to where you are in a complete state of full ownership of this part of you.

Taking ownership for something is one of the most powerful keys in transformation. Because when you take ownership for something, it releases an aspect of your authentic power. But you've got to be the real deal. It can't be the intellectual thing where you talk a good game, but then, when placed in the right environment, we can clearly see that it was just all talk and you're not embodying it yet. This fourth essential key is very powerful. Which means it's going to challenge you. But, as always, when you're moving into a greater state of power, you're always challenged multiple times. There's no easy, fast way of going about this.

So now let's reverse that by thinking of the person who doesn't take responsibility for themselves or for parts of their life. I'm sure you know of at least one person who will not take ownership. They won't take ownership for their addictions, for their patterns, or for what comes out of their mouth, no matter how negative or critical it might be. They won't take ownership for their mistakes or for when they mess something up. Does this person have any power? Does this person see life through what's being done *for* them or through what's being done *to* them? What might have happened to their power?

> When you're moving into a greater state of power, you're always challenged multiple times.

The more powerful we become, the more we're rising up to our Greater Destiny. By the same token, if we reverse that and if we're stuck in our Lower Destiny and dropping even lower, what's now happening? We're becoming powerless.

Think of a person you know who thinks like a victim, talks like a victim, and acts like a victim. They likely don't have much personal power. The more they stay on the victim train, the more powerless they become because whatever little bit of power they have, they're misusing it. And, as always, when you're misusing your power, you're abusing it. And whatever you abuse, you lose—bottom line. Abuse your power, and you lose it. Use your power properly, and you retain it, and it will grow. You choose. Both options are available to every one of us.

Taking responsibility for all parts of yourself is going to be challenging, especially since we've been living in a world that has taught us to do the exact opposite. When people are not taught to be responsible for themselves, they are taught to be powerless. All you have to do in order to slowly start stripping someone's power from them is to send the message, "You don't really have to be responsible. We'll do it for you. There's a savior coming to rescue you. Somebody will take it all from you. Somebody will take all of your mistakes and poor choices you've made away from you." Our world is filled with this message.

We have literally been programmed from the moment we took our first breath to move away from personal responsibility. It starts off with our parents because more than likely, they haven't taken full responsibility for all parts of themselves either. In fact, there's a good likelihood that when you were born, your mom and/or dad had a dysfunctional, wounded, unhealed inner child that they weren't even aware of—which really means their inner child was more than likely unconsciously choosing what was going to happen next in their life. I'm not blaming the parents—far from it. I, too, had to learn this—or rather, I chose to learn and rediscover this.

When you get this key right, it will change everything in your world in the best of ways because now you're going to get your power back where it belongs—and then, more importantly, you're going to be utilizing it properly. When you use power correctly, you get more of it.

In the first *Spiderman* movie, there was a really moving final scene with the line, "With great power comes great responsibility." How much personal responsibility have you taken for yourself and all areas of your life? There's no right or wrong answer here, but there is an answer that'll tell you how much power you actually have access to in current time.

Should you choose to do this and stay in the process of moving yourself towards a level of self-mastery, then you will become a responsible and powerful person, which would be great for the planet, the community, and your family. Everyone is truly destined for this. Whether or not they'll go for it anytime soon, that's where, once again, personal choice comes into play.

Now, how do you do put this fourth key into practice? Well, to own a part of yourself, to own a part of your life, you've got to learn how to be with this part of your life that you're in process of taking ownership of.

The active part is through observing. Everybody has an observer within them. This is proven repeatedly in your dream space. When you're in the dream state, you are in the dream, playing out a part in it, but there's also a you that you might not even be aware of. It's the you that's actually observing you while you're in the dream. Talk about soul aspects!

When you're in process of taking ownership for a part of yourself, the way to ultimately go the distance is not just to be with whatever that is but also to observe yourself while you're being with it. The observer allows you to go in, just like in your dream space in which you're dreaming and you're aware as the observer simultaneously. When you're aware of the part of yourself that you're playing in the dream—at any point from the observer's point of view—then you can go in and literally rewrite it, modify it, and massage it. You can do all kinds of phenomenal things. But with most people, this observer has remained hidden. Although it's an aspect of their soul, it's buried somewhere in their consciousness until, of course, they uncover it.

It can be empowering when you become aware of your observer in your waking life as well. This is where, once again, you are in the seat of your observer at soul level, simply observing yourself going through whatever it is you might be going through in your day-to-day world. But you are seeing it as if watching a movie, which gives you the ability to be more objective. What this does is it allows you to see from the higher, unattached perspective, which then provides you with more insight and guidance into the very thing that perhaps you could be doing next in whatever it is that you are currently going through.

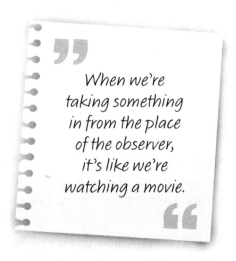

> When we're taking something in from the place of the observer, it's like we're watching a movie.

And so, in order for you to fully activate this essential key, you're going to need this observer. And more specifically, you're going to need to become aware of your observer. If it's in your awareness, it's a question of time, and you're going to have your first experience. It could happen tonight in your dream state, or it could happen while you're driving on the interstate or doing something else. Suddenly, you'll have an awareness. It might only last for a minute or two, but you'll realize, "Oh my gosh—I'm actually watching myself from this place of the observer doing this thing I'm doing right now! How could I be doing that?"

And next thing you know, you'll lose it because you'll start questioning it. That's all part of the process when you're learning how to do this and moving towards mastery of it.

When you do it, you're going to be amazed. You're going to be like, "I think this is what Dale was talking about. This is kind of freaky but exciting. I think I just struck something that's really cool." Yes—it is. It's a natural resource that resides within you, waiting for you to access it, and then to learn how to master it.

When you become aware that you have an observer and you learn how to activate it, reignite it, reawaken it, and then start using it, in your first experience, even if it only lasts for 30 seconds, you will feel more conscious of yourself than you ever have before. You'll be conscious of exactly what you're doing, and you'll be able to see it in the most minute of detail.

Again, it's very powerful and empowering. So, when you're in the process of taking ownership, at some point, your observer's going to activate— and you're going to need that observer because it's only through the lens of the observer that you can awaken this key.

It's going to help you to identify what needs to transform. The observer's going to help you to connect with whatever it is. The observer's going to help you see what you're not accepting completely or uncondition- ally. It's going to help you see where you're at in your own process with your natural ability to take full ownership. The observer's going to allow you to see what you're really to be learning from all of this and where you're at in the process.

The observer is completely unattached to what's going on, mind you. The observer is also not into drama. The observer is 100 percent neutral. It's completely objective. It's like the sharpest lens that allows you to investigate your life with complete clarity, even if it's only for 30 seconds. It is then that you see every single detail, all in a short period of time.

When you have your first couple experiences with this, you might think that you've been drugged. You might even think you're hallucinating, but you're not. It's that powerful because it opens up a channel inside of you. I'm making a big deal of it right now because it's exciting! And you're going to need this if you're going to go the distance in taking full responsibility for the parts of yourself that will come up to be healed and to ultimately be integrated into the whole of who you are. This is a significant part of your overall transformation.

This might be a part of your life where you made some poor choices, and you need to do some cleanup and resolve some things. Because the observer is your soul, it is not attached to anything. So, when I am accessing my soul from the seat of the observer, I'm able to get greater detail and clarity because I'm not vested in any particular outcome. I'm not personalizing what I'm observing. Instead, I'm unattached and free to fully see whatever it is that I am to be seeing or recognizing within myself.

Think, for example, of a time when you've found yourself engrossed in a movie, lost in it, and when something dramatic happens, you find yourself reacting to that part of the movie. On the other hand, if you were to watch that same movie from the seat of the observer within, unattached, not taking anything personally or connecting it to your own life, you would catch more of the subtle details of the movie. When I'm too vested in an experience, I'm not going to get as much detail as I would if I were detached. How do I know this? Because two months later, when you go back and watch the movie from the observer place the second time around, which I'm sure you've done at some point, you're somewhat surprised. You might ask yourself, "How did I not catch that the first time around?"

When we're taking something in from the place of the observer, it's like we're observing ourselves in our own movie, as previously mentioned. There's a part of us that's engaged—like the actor in the movie—as well as the viewe. We're doing both.

As you're moving towards a place of complete and total ownership of whatever it is, at some point, you are going to need this observer. You're going to need to learn how to observe while you're in gear because it's only through that lens that you pick up on all the detail. And you're going to need that detail in order to go in and start making the changes—to fully you embrace your own transformational work.

Key #5 – Learn from It

As you're going through the entire process of identifying it, connecting with it, accepting it, and taking ownership for it, what truly releases you in your own transformational process is when you have learned from it—and more specifically, to a point where you've now mastered it.

Some people might say, "Gosh, this takes a long time." But think about this: Why does it take four years to get a bachelor's degree? Why does it take six years to go to chiropractic school? Why does it take eight years to go to medical school? To think that this might not take some time is the equivalent of saying, "I want to resist this thing. I'm still in a fight with this thing. I haven't taken ownership for it. I'm just kidding myself. I've only taken ownership for it intellectually. Why does this have to take so long? This thing sucks. Who set up this process anyways? I want to speak to the director who created this."

That is somebody who clearly has not taken ownership yet; maybe they intellectualize it or speak the words and act like they've taken owner-ship. You've got to bring them from the intellect into your experience. As I've said, all these keys must be embodied.

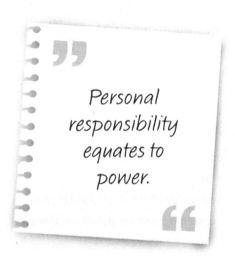

> *Personal responsibility equates to power.*

What it might look like to work with this key so it can be embodied is: while you're going through this process, whether it's embracing the con-sequence for a choice that was previously made, or taking responsibility for one of your issues, or transforming some part of yourself—at some point, ask the question, "If there was something I was to be learning here about myself or the way I've been living my life, what would that be?" Maybe it's learning how to be courageous, learning how to trust yourself or to trust others that are truly dear to you, learning how to make better choices, learning how to be kinder or more respectful, learning how to be more attentive or a better listener, learning how to put yourself in someone else's shoes to gain a deeper understanding of what it is they might be going through or where they're coming from, etc.

APPLYING THE 5 KEYS

Where are you at with living your life with these 5 keys? Is there an internal fight going on with one of them? Or is it pretty much smooth sailing? Maybe you're still in training and you're somewhere between wherever you started and where you ultimately want to land. The goal here is to become an expert, a master of your own transformation to where you're no longer in a fight with it at all—where you're no longer in a fight with any part of you that's been trying desperately to get your attention—or with any part of your life that's been knocking at your door because you made some poor choices that you're possibly trying to run away from.

Or maybe you've got something else going on in your life. Perhaps you've got a big decision that your Higher Self has been asking you to make for the last two and a half years, and you're still sitting on the fence, avoiding this decision because there's some part of you inside that's just so scared of what the choice implies for you. So, you're letting that indecision steer your ship.

This is another unconscious choice that you're to bring fully conscious so you can start getting a little more grace. How about that? Would you like to have more grace in your life? As I keep reminding, it's available to each and every one of us.

Someone who has mastered this has learned, probably through a tremendous amount of painful experience, how to utilize these keys. He or she now now has the discipline that they've found and then strengthened within themselves.

The only time they act on anything is when they get the message that it's the right thing for them to be doing. They've come to appreciate the significance of grace. How much might you appreciate grace in your day-to-day life? Could that make a big difference for you? What kind of a difference could that make for you? It would make things easier and more pleasant for you, wouldn't you agree?

You're now learning about a way that you can make things at least a little easier by literally calling forth your divine birthright, that of grace. Remember, you can claim it anytime you wish.

If you're interested in learning more about the proven healing modality, the TransCovery Process®, which we have been referencing throughout the 5 Keys in this chapter, I have included this process and how you can utilize it for your own personal transformation at the end of the book.

EXERCISES

1. On a scale of 1 to 10, up until now, how much personal responsibility have you taken for yourself and all parts of yourself? 1 being very little, 10 being a lot

   Yourself 1-10 _____ All Parts of Yourself 1-10 _____

   Why did you give yourself these numbers?

   There is a direct connection between the amount of personal power we get to utilize and the responsibility we have taken for ourselves and our lives. Meaning the more responsibility we've accepted for ourselves, the more prepared and empowered we are to wield even more of our own power.

   Can you think of someone who has been avoiding personal responsibility and as a direct result they have become more powerless in their life? If so, who? And what do you see?

   On the other hand, have you noticed someone who is accessing more of their personal power as a direct result of having become more responsible for themselves and their lives? If so, who? And what do you see?

2. We all have things waiting to be healed. What is at the surface for you to heal right now? How deep is your knowledge of whatever this part of you is that has come to the surface? And more importantly, does this part of you feel like you really know it? If this part of you wanted you to know something, what would it be? Depending on your answer you might want to consider doing some journaling now or as soon as the opportunity presents itself to do so.

If you want to work with it even more, you could use the TransCovery Process® (mentioned previously) or your own transformational modality to process it.

3. On a scale of 1-10, 1 being very little, 10 being a lot, how much do you trust in your own follow through? Why did you give yourself this number?

How much do you feel others trust your follow through? On a scale of 1-10, 1 being very little, 10 being a lot. Why did you give yourself thiat number?

Why did you give yourself these answers? What do you think you could do differently to have better follow through and trustworthiness?

4. You might recall when you were learning about the Hidden Law of the Universe, here's an exercise to help you understand it and see it even more:

If there was something or someone you've been opposing or resisting in your life, who or what might that be? And why have you been resisting this or them? (The key here is to recognize it. The sooner you can recognize it, the higher the odds are that you can actually do something really constructive about it.)

What would be a constructive next step to accept and ultimately not resist this person or thing any longer?

5. On a scale of 1-10, 10 being a lot and 1 being a little, how accepting of yourself are you?

   What parts of yourself are you in judgment of? (Be honest. These are the parts of you that are first up in learning to accept.)

   I invite you to really pay close attention—to really get connected to what's going on here for you right now. You see, there's a gateway that just opened up for you. Will you step through, or will you resist it one more time by hanging onto this disapproval, shame, or judgment that you had this part of yourself in? What are you feeling about yourself right now? Whatever your answer, document it.

   Bonus exercise: I invite you to listen to my meditation "The Reimagined Self." As an area of self-judgment comes up, this would be an opportunity to journal on what is revealed to you. This meditation was specifically designed to help us see and transform our feelings and energy towards parts of ourselves we don't like, whether physical, health-related, or something else.

   If you want to use this meditation, you can find it on my website: www.DaleHalaway.com

6. How well do you take ownership of your mistakes on a scale of 1-10, 1 being very little, 10 being a lot?

   Do you know someone who doesn't take ownership for their mistakes?

   If so, how would you describe this person when it comes to having or utilizing personal power?

   What is this person reflecting back to you about yourself?

CHAPTER 8

UNDERSTANDING KARMA

To understand karma is to immerse yourself in the reeducation of what you thought you knew about it, much like you have done with destiny.

Here are the dictionary definitions of karma, which reflects how we understand the concept of karma as a society.

From the Merriam-Webster.com dictionary:

Definition of *karma*
kar·ma| \ ˈkär-mə *also* ˈkər-\

Noun.

1. the force generated by a person's actions held in Hinduism and Buddhism to perpetuate transmigration and in its ethical consequences to determine the nature of the person's next existence
2. a characteristic emanation, aura, or spirit that infuses or vitalizes someone or something

From Dictionary.com

Karma, noun

1. *Hinduism, Buddhism.* action, seen as bringing upon oneself inevitable results, good or bad, either in this life or in a reincarnation: in Hinduism one of the means of reaching Brahman.
2. *Theosophy.* the cosmic principle according to which each person is rewarded or punished in one incarnation according to that person's deeds in the previous incarnation.
3. fate, destiny.
4. the good or bad emanations felt to be generated by someone or something: *Let's get out of here. This place has bad karma.*

Now these are hitting closer to the mark than the definitions of destiny did, but let's take a closer look and add in what these dictionary definitions left out or missed completely. What is not noted here in these definitions is that there is a program on the planet that says karma is a punishment or a curse. In reality, this is far from the truth.

> *"The universal law of karma...is that of action and reaction, cause and effect, sowing and reaping. In the course of natural righteousness, man, by his thoughts and actions, becomes the arbiter of his destiny."*
>
> – Paramahansa Yogananda

More often than not, when karma gets brought up, it's in a negative context. For example, maybe you're gossiping with a friend you're having a coffee with, and you end up spilling your coffee on yourself. You might say, "Well, that was karma." The truth is, there is both positive and negative karma, and both types are here to bless us, enrich us, and empower us. Both are here to support us in our transformation, healing, and growth.

When you're only thinking of karma in a negative, heavy way, it helps the ego run away from it, push it down, or deny its existence, but understanding and working with karma is essential to transforming your destiny.

Karma is not there to punish you. Yes, it can be heavy at times, but overall, its purpose is to set you free.

POSITIVE KARMA

Positive karma is the type of karma that we create for ourselves and that we're being blessed by as a result of something good that we've done— as in a good deed or an act that made a positive difference in someone else's life. Of course, there are other ways to go about creating positive karma, such as developing an attitude of giving selflessly, where we just give for the sake of giving. We don't look for anything in return, and we are true to that. We don't feel the need to post it on social media or tell anyone about it; we just do it from a genuine, caring place.

Another area that's often significant when it comes to creating positive karma is how we contribute to our family, our community, or to the company we represent. We can also create positive karma through the powerful act of fulfilling our deeper soul purpose.

When we're fulfilling our deeper or greater purpose, that in itself puts us in a higher state of being. And when we're living in that higher state of being, somehow, some way, other good things come upon us, whether it's a good friendship or a better, deeper, richer, more authentic experience with a loved one. Or maybe it's a new promotion with the company we represent.

Positive karma is very much like a blessing. It's something that just happens. It's one of those experiences where we're in the right place at the right time, doing all the right things. And then this beautiful thing happens that we didn't see expect.

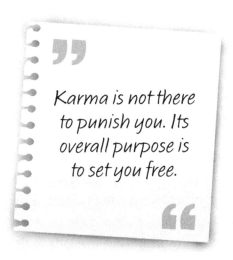

Karma is not there to punish you. Its overall purpose is to set you free.

That blessing could be what turns out to be one of the best relationships of your entire life. Or maybe it's your dream job, or maybe it's inheriting money that you didn't see coming. Or again, something that happens in our life where there's an element of ease. There's an element of grace, and there's an element of pleasant surprise. It's something that's being bestowed upon you.

This type of karma is what we've created as a result of showing up for someone else or towards something else in an act of 100 percent selflessness.

One thing to be aware of is that we can actually hold ourselves back from positive karma.

We can actually blow the positive karma that we've created and block it from making its way onto our doorstep. One of the biggest ways to block it is to refuse to resolve, heal, and transform our negative karma. It doesn't matter if this refusal is unconscious. Even if we're not aware of what we're doing, we can create a block that holds up the process of some aspect of our positive karma raining down on us or being bestowed upon us.

So opening ourselves up to resolving our negative karma is an important factor in keeping our positive karma flowing to us. When times get tough along the way of resolving it, this is something we will want to remember. The rewards are well worth the work!

NEGATIVE KARMA

Negative karma, when understood correctly, is not really even negative karma. I'm using the word negative karma as a way to create a contrast between these two types of karma, but ultimately, when we understand negative karma from a deeper perspective, we begin to see that when negative karma is understood properly and embraced correctly, it can bless us too.

Negative karma is always going to be about learning something of significance and value. I'm sure you've heard it said before that Planet Earth is one big school. Earth school is where you and I are to be learning specific lessons.

Now the lessons that you're to learn and the lessons that I'm to learn are probably going to be different; these lessons are unique to every soul.

Once the lesson is mastered or learned really well, it naturally turns into wisdom, which is a blessing, for as we become wiser, this naturally empowers us to be able to make better, greater, and healthier choices in our day-to-day lives.

This type of karma is also going to be about letting go of something, and it will be unique to us as an individual. This process of letting go is going to happen multiple times throughout our lives because not everything that we experience or create is meant to be in our lives forever.

When the timing becomes right for us to let go of karma, it's going to also be about identifying something or someone that we are supposed to be letting go of. Should we choose to continue to hang on to whatever or whoever this is that's no longer working for us, no longer serving us, then it's more than likely not serving the other person or situation either.

In addition, choosing to hold onto something we're supposed to be letting go of also increases the odds of us creating more negative karma in our lives. This could potentially hold us back or block us from being able to access some of the positive karma we've already created, at least temporarily.

What we need to let go of could be an old career, an old way of life, an old habit, or possibly an old friend, an old lover, an old business partner, or an old client, etc. This type of karma is about ending something or completing something, and it's probably the biggest reason why many individuals never really experience genuinely new things in their life; they become hell-bent on holding on to this thing, as in an old project, old way of behaving, a person, a friendship, a relationship—and they'll hold on to it for dear life. And while they're doing that, they're actually holding themselves back from experiencing a better, richer, and more meaningful life.

The Universe will continue to apply pressure in order to wake us up so we can stop creating more negative karma for ourselves. This could be gentle at first, but if we continue to not respond, then that pressure could amp up over time.

If we have a pattern of hooking into others (which many people do), the only way to change that pattern is to catch yourself in action when you're literally going for the next play in the cycle sequence of that pattern. And then, you've got to pull in the reins.

We can actually hold ourselves back from positive karma.

If you do, there's going to be a blessing for that—maybe not right away, but if you do it on a regular basis and turn that into a lifestyle, then the blessing is coming. You will be enriched from it because you'll be moving into greater alignment, first and foremost, with your own soul. And you'll also be moving into alignment with the soul of the other person that you're so hooked into. This changes everything for the better. It lifts everybody up.

But if you continue on with the negative pattern, you've just advertised to the Universe that you need more pain, that you need another gut punch. Remember, the Universe is impersonal. So, if you need a punch, you're going to get one. This is not because you're being punished. This is actually the Universe's way of loving you. Maybe you've dragged this out for five lifetimes and you're doing the exact same thing again. If that's the case, you bet you need a gut punch! And hopefully, it'll wake you up this time.

Remember we are at choice here. So, you could choose to really fight your growth for another couple years, and if so, you're entitled to that. That's you exercising your free will at the level of your ego—at the level of Lower Destiny. You're not accessing free will yet at Greater Destiny because your soul hasn't stepped in and given you a good kick in the butt yet. Oh, and by the way, if your soul, at any point, chooses to give you a good kick in the butt, it'll be like nothing you've ever experienced before.

A good butt-kicking could be where you come home one day and you learn that your wife or your husband has been cheating. You didn't even see it coming. Or maybe your health takes a turn for the worse without you seemingly getting any warning signs. And next thing you know, you're bedridden. Once again, you didn't see it coming.

Another example of this would be you're driving down the road, and you have somebody in the car with you, a good friend or your spouse. And you're laughing it up in the car. You're just having a real nice time together while driving responsibly down the roadway, and out of the blue, you end up in a car accident. You walk away from the vehicle ultimately, yet the accident shakes something up in your life. Whether it shakes up your health or shakes up your finances, it literally shakes up some part of your life. Once again, did you see it coming when these types of things happened? This is us causing something or at least co-causing something to come into motion as a way to get our attention. This is our soul attempting to shake us up and become more aware so that we can get on with clearing up our negative karma and move into creating positive karma.

Once our attention is gotten, then comes the process of uncovering the why, and asking ourself: "What is it that my soul is now bringing to my attention in this loud way? Am I finally going to get it and move into the clearing of my negative karma? Or am I going to choose to make more?"

Your soul works in conjunction with the Universe, which means it works with your guides and angels, and your soul may no longer be willing to wait and play this little game that you've been playing for the last three lifetimes at the level of your Lower Destiny.

> One of the first things we've got to do when it comes to negative karma is stop creating more of it.

Your soul is very patient, but at some point, it's time to stop participating in these games and dynamics because they're just repeating over and over again, and you're simply dragging it out. You're just elongating it and causing more pain and unnecessary suffering for yourself and possibly even others.

One of the first things we've got to do when it comes to negative karma is to stop creating more of it. You've got to catch it when you're in the action of creating negative karma, and then you've got to pull in the reins. This is going to require awareness, which you're now getting. It's going to require good choice making, which you're now learning. And, it's going to require discipline, which you're going to have to muster up inside yourself. Nobody can do this for you.

You've got to get in there and roll up your sleeves. I'm talking about an inner muscle of self-discipline. You've got to strengthen your discipline. Most people's inner discipline muscle has atrophied, but it's not dead. It's there. You've just got to wake it up.

So why not get on the path of consciously clearing your negative karma? And better yet, get on the path of creating positive karma for you and your loved ones.

THE KARMIC LAW OF RETURN

The Karmic Law of Return drives the creation of all karma. Over the next few chapters of this book, you're going to learn pretty much everything there is to learn about karma. What you're about to read could go one of two ways: either you may feel uncomfortable and question your prior choices, or you could very well be inspired by it because of how it will empower you to identify your own negative karma, and then go beyond that into the advanced level to learn how to resolve karma without creating any more of it. Hopefully, you do the latter and choose to see this information as an opportunity to begin course correcting and embarking on a path of creating more positive karma.

Now, resolving karma without creating more is an aspect of self-mastery, and it's not easy to do—as there is no quick fix here. So please don't get discouraged if it takes you a while to get this one figured out. Being hard on ourselves only slows our progress. This is going to be a major set of lessons that will impact your life for the next while because the subject of karma can go very deep. So just settle in and observe and marvel at the process of how this will challenge you and stretch you.

The most exciting part of this is that what you're about to learn is already inside of you. It's all been encoded—and more specifically, it's been encoded at the level of your Greater Destiny. It sits inside your Higher Self. So you are truly now in process of discovering and bringing forth something you already have—pretty cool, huh?

The simplest explanation of the Law of Karmic Return is that everything—not some things, not 99 percent of things, everything—you and I put out into our own personal universe must return back to us. This is not because we're bad people and not because we're good people. It's because it's an unchangeable law.

Another way in which we could explore this law is by better understanding the Law of Cause and Effect, which states that for every effect, there must be a cause, and every cause must be followed by an effect. So whether I put out something that is negative or positive, whether it is a choice, an intention, a directed thought or feeling, an act or deed, it must be returned back to me in a way that shows me what it is that I put out somewhere in my past, so that ultimately, I can learn from it.

You do not have to be conscious for the Law of Karmic Return to work. In fact, you could be completely unconscious, and this law still works like magic in your life. Everything you put out into the Universe must pass through this law. Every time we send something out, it must come back to us with equal measure.

If a person does this over a period of years or even lifetimes, then that measure grows in intensity. Next thing they know, they come into a life where they are seriously handicapped, and everybody feels sorry for them. Very few would understand why, and those few would be the true mystics who can read the past timelines and see that it has nothing to do with this life.

They can be severely handicapped because of previous lifetimes where they put out the kind of energy that was restricting, confining, paralyzing, and possibly even hurtful to others. And now, that energy is coming back with great intensity. Why? Not because they're a bad person, and not because they're a good person. It's because this energy they've been putting out, usually for more than one lifetime, has now returned, and now that person finds themselves in this current situation. They have been metaphorically hit by the Law of Karmic Return.

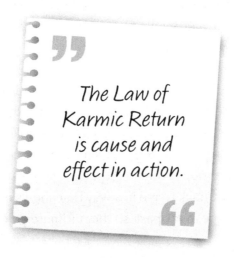

The Law of Karmic Return is cause and effect in action.

This can be avoided, mind you, but to avoid it we must get to resolving our karma and not carrying it from one lifetime to the next, which we will get to later in this chapter.

Remember, everybody has free will. Everybody's at choice. You can choose to get hard on yourself, on the Universe, or on God. You know what happens with your situation then? It intensifies and elongates—because the law says whatever we put out into the Universe must return to us. Maybe not right away and maybe not even in this life—because in this life, you might be on a mission to create as much karma as you possibly can.

This would be the unconscious person who has no clue of what they're up to, no clue of the implications—nor do they want a clue. In fact, any-time you go in to try to correct them, they often will intensely defend their position while being mad at you and attempt to shut you down. They might even hurt you or at least try to hurt you—thus creating more karma for themselves. They don't have a clue that they're setting themselves up for negative karma in this life and possibly the next.

With regard to the Karmic Law of Return, it doesn't matter what you send out or when. At some point, it must return to the sender. It must return to the sender to the exact degree in which he or she was send-ing it out. So, if I'm sending something out with deep hatred, burning anger, or with a tremendous amount of aggression, then it's going to come back at some future point in the same manner as how I've been sending it out. Now if I've been doing this for a long time, then what happens? It amps up times two, times four, times eight, times ten, etc.

It all comes back to choice—to free will. The person who's using their free will in such a way where they're literally hurting themselves—and while they're so busy hurting themselves, they can't even see the hurt they're causing in the lives of others—which ends up creating more karma for them at some future point.

That energy must return to them. Now, why is this? So that we can learn our lessons. When you and I are sending out energy, it's actually a blessing for it to come back. So, with that understanding, why keep doing this? It's like a boomerang with poison on it. Are you really going to throw it out knowing it's going to come back to you and affect some-thing in your life that you really value such as your health, your finances, or possibly the way you show up in a relationship? Most likely not. So next time you start sending hate daggers or projecting your hurt onto others, remember this. It just might be the thing that stops you from creating more negative karma for yourself.

THE PURPOSE OF THE KARMIC LAW OF RETURN

The Karmic Law of Return is not here to punish us; rather, it's here to help us learn something we are to be learning in this life. You see, it is here to help us grow. This is the soul's way of saying, "There's a law in place to govern that we're eventually going to grow," even though this person's probably going to fight it because they're at the level of their Lower Destiny and they're operating within their personal agenda.

But what this will eventually do is get them to grow as a soul. So, the soul is completely on board with the Karmic Law of Return. The ego resists it because it doesn't want anything to do with growth. Remember, we've got to tame our ego, educate it, and teach it how to get on board.

This law is set up so that we can come to a place of knowing who and all that we already really are—to never have to question again why we're here, what we're connected to, or what we're to be a part of that's much bigger than we are. Now, if we're unconscious towards this and we're still in our own fight because we're on lower ground in the Lower Destiny, then we're in violation of the Karmic Law of Return. Which means we're not resolving the karma that we already have. We're probably creating more negative karma. As in, this is where this type of karma is created from, when we've descended to that lower ground.

Now we're going to be tempted like we possibly can't imagine, until, of course, we master this. But once we master it, there's no longer a reason for the temptation to create more negative karma. We now can see the temptation that is coming from a distance; therefore, we are no longer buying into the temptation. We have mastered this part of our journey, which now will empower us to deepen our commitment to the resolving of our past karma. So, from this point on, we're conscious of the temptations that would lead to the creation of any more karma. Sounds pretty good, doesn't it? And it is possible. So don't let your ego trip you up into thinking it is not.

Moving forward now, let's remember the Law of Karmic Return is cause and effect in action. For every effect, there must be a cause—and for every cause, there is an effect. No one can escape this. Even though someone might try, but good luck. They're not going to get very far.

Every time we send something out, it must come back to us with equal measure.

Again, this law does not reflect punishment. How many people do you know who have a distorted perception that karma is here to punish them? They're not being punished. Rather, they're completely misunderstanding this law. Or maybe they've been refusing to understand. Maybe they just really want to believe that they're being punished because there's a story that comes along with that. Maybe that gets them a lot of sympathy from people. Maybe that's their deal. Maybe they're desperately trying to get people to feel sorry for them. But God didn't say they were being punished. The Universe doesn't punish. Spirit doesn't punish. That's a misalignment—a huge misunderstanding of the law. However, when we deepen our understanding of the law, we won't be tempted to even think that way.

A healthier way of seeing it would be in recognizing that this law is not about retribution; rather, it is simply an extended expression of the consequences of natural acts. That is all it is. If I choose to do something, it's going to put a consequential series of events into motion—be it positive or negative. It's all based on the quality of the choice that I made. An example of this might be if I choose to continue to stay in a toxic relationship, there's a chance that I may have a painful death. And that might be my karma.

Now, if I go ahead and blame it on somebody, then that means I haven't learned anything, which really means I'm coming back to repeat the whole thing all over again. Well, that's a bummer! Why would I want to repeat another toxic relationship all over again? Because I haven't learned my lessons yet—and if I haven't learned my lessons yet, that means that they all come back to me for a do over and I get a new opportunity at some later point to learn those lessons well. To learn a lesson well means growth. If the lesson hasn't been learned, there is no growth that we as a soul achieve, which means those lessons get put back into motion again. Why? Every time we learn one of our lessons fully, we naturally drop into a deeper level of knowing our true selves. This is one of the greater purposes of our soul—to come to know our true self.

So, taking personal responsibility and not blaming is one of the keys to clearing up and not creating more karma. In other words, the next time you want to play the blame game, stop and think. "Do I really want to go there? Can't I just own it and prevent further karma from building up?" It is easier to do this than you might think, and it's incredibly empowering. Give it a try and watch what happens!

KARMIC LINES

We are each born with karmic lines unless someone is a brand-new soul. If we have lived more than one lifetime, then we are going to have karmic lines. These are carryovers from a previous time. There are negative karmic lines and positive karmic lines.

THE NEGATIVE KARMIC LINE

A negative karmic line represents past choices that ended up hurting people and/or hurting one's own self. Our negative karmic line is the personal karma that we enter this life with. You're the one, and you're the only one, who can resolve it, and ultimately, you cannot escape it until you do.

If you have a negative karmic line, somewhere in your past timeline, as in another lifetime experience, something happened, and you created karma for yourself but didn't resolve it. Then, possibly on that same karmic line, you had one or more lifetimes after that one where you repeated the same thing. Every time you do the same thing, what does the karma do? It grows in intensity; it gets stronger. The karmic line gets thicker, goes deeper, and becomes longer.

Perhaps I come into this life with three very specific karmic lines, and each one of these lines dates back to a lifetime prior to this one. One of those karmic lines, depending on the age of my soul, might date back seven lifetimes ago.

Now let's remember the Hidden Law of the Universe again, which is the Law of Opposition. It states, "That which we oppose strengthens." If I were to continue avoiding the healing and resolving of my karma, then this karmic line becomes strengthened whether it's in this same lifetime or a subsequent one.

There are light karmic lines and heavy karmic lines. A heavy karmic line dates back further. For example, you might only be thirty years old, but you might be dealing with a karmic line from ten lifetimes ago or more. And maybe you've done the exact same thing in the last ten or more lifetimes that you're doing in this one. You've just been repeating your patterns, and the karmic line is growing in intensity. It's growing in weight and density.

Our negative karmic line is the personal karma that we entered this life with.

Some people come in with only one karmic line. Others, like me, have come in with more than three karmic lines—these are generally the very old souls. Regardless, it's going to be unique to you as a soul.

I was in my thirties when I discovered this through working with many different people. I hadn't awoken yet to my psychic and mystical abilities at that point, but I still had pretty good intuition, and I was very practical. It was a lot more work for me back then than it is today, but I was able to trace a person's karmic line back to the first twelve years of their life. I got good at identifying the different things that would happen to them during those years.

This means that we can learn about our own karma by really getting back into our childhood. We can learn about our karma once we know what to look for. We can spot this karmic line or the karmic lines that we came into this life with.

For example, let's say that in the past, I was a control freak. I was extremely controlling to the point where I enslaved people. When you're that controlling, you're creating negative karma because you're hurting people. You're shutting them down. You're helping to disconnect them from their soul-self and move them away from their own authenticity. You're possibly helping them turn to alcohol or to drugs. You may even be helping them become a murderer. And when you are doing this, it's creating karma because you're causing a lot of harm. Let's say I had a big controlling problem five lifetimes ago, and I still haven't resolved that since.

Now, it looks like I was getting away with it because here it is, five lifetimes later, and I'm still doing it. So, am I really getting away with this? No—all that's happened so far is the energy that I've been putting out hasn't yet come back. That's all—it just hasn't returned yet.

This will be unique to the sender. As I mentioned earlier, sometimes the energy comes back to you right away, partly because you have the help of somebody in your corner that will spin it back to you. Other times, it'll take months or even years before it fully comes back. Then there are times you can go in, look for it, and literally pull it up to clear it.

But what happens if you're not resolving your karma? Or what happens if you're creating more karma, but you just don't know that's what you're really doing?

Let's go back to the example where I was this control freak for five lifetimes. I'm now coming to this current life and bringing in this karmic line. So, what's going to happen in my first twelve years of life? I'm possibly going to have somebody in my life who's going to take control of me or be very controlling when around me. Heck, they might even enslave me or molest me. In this scenario I'm going to have somebody in my life who's going to take advantage of me, somehow, someway that quite frankly might turn your stomach. Why is that? Because I need to eventually see the karmic line. If I can't see it, then I can't identify it. If I can't identify it, then I cannot go to the next step of resolving it.

Now, I know you're probably saying, "Wait a minute! This doesn't sound very fair!" But who said it must be fair? We're talking about a law that's completely impersonal. It's precise—and more specifically, we're also talking about a person's soul.

If my soul decided before this life that this is the lifetime that I was going to clear out and resolve that karma, then I'm coming in with the karmic line. Which means that karmic line is going to set itself into motion somewhere in the first twelve years of my life. So, I'm going to have some level of abuse that goes on in the first twelve years of my life.

Now, it's going to look like I'm being done to, and perhaps I am on one level. But then, later in life, when it's time for me to really roll up my sleeves and start to resolve this, I'm going to realize I was blessed. I'm going to realize that I was being *done for*. I'm going to realize that I needed that so that eventually, years later in this life, I could start to see the karma that I as a soul chose to resolve in this life, once and for all. That's the greater purpose of the karmic line.

Does this happen for everybody? Of course not. This happens for maybe 5-10 percent of the people on this planet at this point in time, while 90-95 percent of people are unconscious. Until recently in human history, most people have not only gone unconscious but stayed there until their last breath.

It's easy to see this. Just look around; even in these circles of people who say they're becoming conscious; they're not really doing the work. Maybe they're building nice businesses on the internet, but put them in a love relationship and watch what happens next. You might see that they're great in business but not in close relationships. Or perhaps they can't take care of their bodies if their lives depended upon it. They've figured out a way to make a lot of money, but they're destroying themselves physically.

There's a TV show that focuses on business called *Back in the Game*, hosted by Alex Rodriguez. They follow celebrities who have made millions of dollars and are now broke, literally living paycheck to paycheck. They've been stripped. You see into these people's lives and witness how close they came to suicide or to complete and total self-destruction. And yet, when they were making those millions of dollars per year, they looked like they were a god or goddess.

Some of them were even in the spiritual community. They were meditating or praying. They were doing all these things that you think would be enough. And yet, they got wiped out. Now they're destroying themselves. Some even succeed in literally taking their own lives. That is somebody who is not correctly recognizing their karmic lines—somebody who is not even recognizing karma. Not only are they not clearing the unresolved karma they came in with, but they're now literally creating more karma on top of the karma that they were supposed be resolving in this life.

When most people die and become conscious of their Higher Selves and what has occurred, right away they say, "Oops!" But the good news is that they get to come back again, pick up where they left off, and take another shot at it. Thank God for that.

At some point, however, it's about remembering. It's about waking up.

I often hear people say, "I can't stand this life. Who set it up this way? This really pisses me off. I really don't like it here." People like this might try to kill themselves, maybe not as a direct suicide, but they'll go for an unconscious suicide.

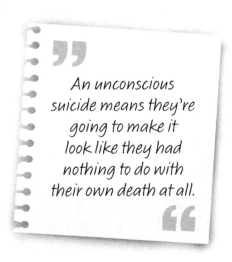

An unconscious suicide means they're going to make it look like they had nothing to do with their own death at all.

An unconscious suicide means they're going to make it look like they had nothing to do with their own death at all. But the soul knows they had everything to do with it. They used unconscious suicide as a way to get out of this so-called nasty place. That's somebody who's obviously got unresolved karma and who's now trying to escape the healing and resolving of that karma. They're forgetting that they're on the wheel of karma (which we'll be covering in the next chapter), and they can't get off until they do the right thing in working towards resolving their negative karma.

This negative karma is the past life errors that we've made. Our ego can definitely lead us into creating all kinds of karma for ourselves when it gets us to step away from consciously and responsibly steering our ship.

The big difference in personal karma and our negative karmic line is the negative karmic line is what has happened somewhere in our past timeline that we are now bringing forward into this lifetime to clear. We've got to choose to learn how to strengthen that inner discipline muscle because it's going to require discipline to really get into these negative karmic lines and ultimately resolve them.

THE POSITIVE KARMIC LINE

In addition to the negative karmic lines, we also have positive karmic lines. These positive karmic lines have our talents, gifts, or blessings encoded into them from previous lifetimes. So, if you come into this world with two negative karmic lines and one positive karmic line, then for the most part, you're not going to have a lot of access to your positive karmic line until you prove that you're serious about clearing out your negative karmic lines. You've got to prove you're the real deal. Once you do this, however, these dormant gifts and talents can come online.

If you were allowed the fullness of your positive karmic line right away, you likely wouldn't do any work on clearing your past negative karma. You might look at this as a reward that is simply waiting to be bestowed upon you for doing the work.

Again, these positive karmic lines include your abilities, talents, or gifts. For example, you might come into this life with a karmic line of being a great entrepreneur, but you've got three negative karmic lines. In other words, you're coming in to resolve a fair amount of negative karma. So, early in life, during those first twelve years, your karmic lines are all going to show up. They must—they're governed by universal law to do so.

Often by the time we are in our early teen years, the positive karmic lines have been buried. We have fallen asleep or are completely numbed out to them. Maybe you had a parent who didn't understand them, so they just shut them down, and they didn't want to talk about or acknowledge whatever gift or ability you might have been exhibiting at an early age. Or they possibly mocked it or put it down, causing you as a child to stuff it down.

Say you're discovering something about yourself as a child or young teen. You're beginning to sense or feel that you have had a previous life and something from that life is carrying over into this life. You attempt to share this with somebody else, like a parent or friend, who clearly does not believe any of this at all. They completely shut it down. Usually, you can't have a two-way conversation about things like this, so these thoughts get locked away and forgotten over time.

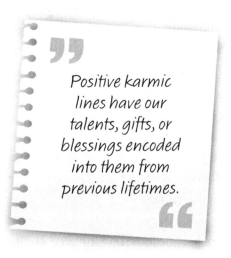

Positive karmic lines have our talents, gifts, or blessings encoded into them from previous lifetimes.

So, by the time you turn seventeen, you've completely forgotten about all of this. You have no conscious access to it, partly because you weren't able to talk openly about it when you did remember it.

It's not until you're twenty-seven, or thirty-five, or forty-three that something happens in your life where you're being opened up again. You're being brought onto a pathway where you start to remember again. You might realize your gift is that you're really skilled at entrepreneurialism—but in this life, you're not going to get full access to it just yet.

You're going to get partial access to it until you prove worthy; and that you truly are well on your way to resolving your negative karmic lines.

Or maybe you were a naturally gifted artist, but your father thought art was a waste of time. He completely shut you down, and you didn't discover until years later that you had amazing artistic abilities. Or maybe you had dreams that would come true, and this completely freaked your parents out when you were young. They shut this gift down because it scared them. And years later, you began to uncover this psychic ability that got shut down at that tender age.

Once it's proven that you're going to go the distance and you can resolve your negative karmic lines, then you'll get full access to your positive karmic lines. Full access means you're going to utilize them exactly the way your soul set into motion—and more importantly, at that juncture, you're no longer creating any more negative karma.

Once you get to the point where the Divine knows and your soul knows that you're on the path, there's no more turning back. Both of your feet are pointed forward in the exact same direction. Once spirit becomes convinced—once the Divine is convinced that you are the real deal— that's when you get more access to your positive karmic lines; your hidden gifts and abilities. And when you do, life becomes a lot more enriching, interesting, and exciting!

RISING FROM LOWER DESTINY INTO HIGHER DESTINY

Why would we want to resolve our karma? To rise into our Greater Destiny, that's why! The most meaningful part of one's Greater Destiny is: this is where the discovery of our soul's deepest purpose is made. This is where we get momentum working for us. This is where we feel free. Remember, freedom is one of our divine birthrights. Living our life from the birthright of freedom means we are able to genuinely express our most authentic self. Now, as we're making our way to this place, from our Lower Destiny to our Greater Destiny, it's important to recognize there are going to be blocks, and it's a really good idea to become aware of what these blocks are. There are four common blocks we're all going to have to deal with in our life experience.

Block #1

The first area that can block us is our unresolved negative karma. We've already been learning about this unresolved negative karma and will continue to go even deeper on this first block in the next few chapters that follow.

Block #2

The second block is in our unhealed, unforgiven past. Whatever has happened in our past timeline—where we got hurt, or we were violated, or somebody wronged us—his will affect us unless it is healed and forgiven. Whether we are aware of this or not, our unhealed, unforgiven past can pull us out of the present and back into that trauma over and over again. This alone can make us feel like we are being held back from being able to rise up to a better life.

If we have an unhealed, unforgiven past, we might be into taking drugs or we might have some other addiction that we find ourselves getting lost in. If we're escaping with addictive behaviors, we're probably not going to be super conscious about this unhealed, unforgiven past, and it is likely to keep us on the path of our Lower Destiny. So this is where many have gotten snagged—they're living much of their current life in their past. This is where they often think and speak a lot about their past in terms of "if only" or about what was done to them. This is not being present. This is being stuck in some pool of previous memories.

They're not healing their past; rather, they're living their lives in some part of the past and they're not super aware of it, at least not just yet. Or they don't know what the consequential effect has been and continues to be for making this choice of living in and from the past in their day-to-day reality.

Forgiveness is most certainly an instrumental part of completing our transformational experience.

We will also be taking a deeper dive into the unhealed past as it relates to the learning of the lesson of forgiveness. Forgiveness is most certainly an instrumental part of completing our transformational experience, and until we correctly do this, we can and most likely will get pulled back into our Lower Destiny time and time again.

Block #3

The third area that can block us or hold us back from rising up to our Greater Destiny is a state of self-centeredness; the individual is too focused on the self. Often, self-centeredness is an unconscious way of being, and the person experiencing it is not even aware of just how self-centered he or she has become. One of the key ways we heal self-centeredness is to bring awareness to it.

When a person becomes aware that they've been living their life in this state, this becomes the gateway. This becomes the opening of what could turn out to be a powerful transformational healing experience. And in the months that follow, or maybe even in the next year or so, as they continue looking at this state in which they've been living and the consequences it has produced from within themselves, they become more acutely aware of this state of self-centeredness and often the unpleasant and even ugly feelings that come up.

Unconscious self-centeredness can branch off into an experience of neediness. In my seminars and within the TransCovery Process®, we refer to this as needy energy. This is where this person who's dealing with this self-centeredness can become needy for attention, validation, recognition, or for protection as a way to make sure they stay safe at all costs.

One of the ways we can spot this is that when a person is needy; even when we give them what they want, be it attention, validation, recognition, etc., it never seems to be enough. Needy energy never gets fulfilled. Unless, of course, we become aware of this and then learn how to course correct and heal it.

Block #4

The last area that can block us from rising to our Greater Destiny is entity attachments. Now, this is really tricky because as we're traveling through our life experience, we're going to attach to someone or something or someone or something is going to attach to us.

Some attachments are going to influence us by supporting us in becoming better or in having a better life. Other attachments, however, will be the complete opposite. Maybe we have an entity attachment from an old, unhealed relationship from our past that continues long after the relationship ends. We can view this as cords that still connect us to them. These cords can have a big influence over us and the choices that we continue to make, often keeping us in our Lower Destiny.

If that attachment has any kind of heaviness to it, then it's going to weigh us down. Maybe you have a friend or a sibling who was in a relationship ten years ago, and it ended. It looked like they got out of the relationship. It looks like on the surface, they're all healed. Until, of course, you mention the person's name that they were in the relationship with, and they have an immediate reaction, whether it's inward or outward, even though they are no longer with that person and haven't been for years. All you have to do is mention their name, and they begin to speak negatively about this person or you notice their physiology changes. Maybe they make a face, maybe they roll their eyes, maybe they raise a critical eyebrow.

It's really obvious that they're not completely finished with that person. Perhaps they didn't go the distance in really clearing out the attachments, the attached energetics, between them and this other person. Now if we want to be free of this block, then we've got to learn to cut these energetic cords to past relationships. Which is more than likely going to mean learning how to forgive and choosing to do so.

There's another level to consider here, and that would be the etheric level, as in non-physical entities. So, on that first level we just covered, this would be with physical human beings. In this second level, we are dealing with non-physical beings. These are non-physical entities that, for whatever reason, have not yet made a successful transition to their next evolutionary step or to their next plane of existence. Or a part of their soul fragmented and it's still here. In fact, there's a name for these types of entities. They're known as Earth-bound souls.

The point I'm making here without going too deep into this subject, at least in this book, is that an entity attachment, whether of this world or a non-physical world, becomes a heavy weight. Entity attachments weigh us down and pull us down to our Lower Destiny path because that's where they are; this is a part of their Lower Destiny. This makes it super challenging for us to rise up to our Greater Destiny.

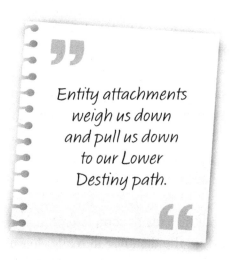

> Entity attachments weigh us down and pull us down to our Lower Destiny path.

If I have an entity attachment going on, it's like someone putting a shackle on one of my ankles. And then attached to that shackle is a chain. At the end of that chain is a steel ball weighing 50 to 100 pounds. Now I might be completely unconscious of this. On a conscious level, I don't even know that shackle has been placed on one of my ankles. But it doesn't really matter whether I'm conscious of this or not. As long as that shackle remains on one of my ankles, then wherever I go, I'm literally dragging this extra negative, heavy weight.

That in itself can hold me back. Partly because if I've been dragging this around possibly for the last three years of my life, this extra weight potentially starts to tire me out. It might even begin to drain me and deplete me.

It's like a garden hose connected at both ends. That energy is constantly going back and forth. If I have an attachment to a non-physical entity, then from the other side, it's going to wreak havoc with me by messing with my thoughts and feelings in order to get something for itself. Talk about self-centered! The entity may want something from me, or maybe it wants to use me in some way, to use my body for its expression, so it pulls on my energy and keeps me in my Lower Destiny. And next thing you know I'm addicted to something that I was never addicted to before.

If I'm conscious of this, however, then at the very least I can do something really constructive, productive, and super beneficial for myself and even for that non-physical entity or person who I am still attached to, rather than deny this attachment.

As we're going through life, there are going to be people and things we are going to get attached to. There is no way around this. We're going to be attached to our kids as we're raising them, to our husband or wife that we so appreciate, or to that career that we've come to love. Attachment is so profoundly meaningful for us when it's positive because it allows us to express ourselves in a way that's authentic or true.

Negative attachments, on the other hand, can hold us back, can pull us down, and can literally block us from moving towards the higher and greater good in our lives if we are not aware of them.

We could go on about this subject, but for the purpose of this book I'll leave you with one final thing of relevance to that of you and your transformation, and it is this: It can be easy to pick up a non-physical entity attachment when you go to heavy-energy places like bars, especially the types that are darker in nature. This is even more likely to happen when you are having several drinks in this darker establishment and are dropping into that lower state of consciousness where you have little willpower and therefore are possibly making Lower-Destiny choices.

My advice to you is that if you want to rise up out of your Lower Destiny and avoid taking on non-physical entities, avoid these types of places, and if you do spend time at places like this, drink minimally so you can stay clear and present. The more conscious you can remain, the more you will be able to continue the rise into your Greater Destiny.

REMEMBER THIS AS YOU EXPLORE KARMA

When I use this term unresolved karma, I'm really referring to negative karma, as opposed to positive karma.

This negative karma has its own weight, and it can make people more negative.

Our deepest soul's purpose naturally unfolds as our unresolved negative karma completely resolves.

If a person is carrying a lot of unresolved karma, no matter what you bring to this person—even if you bring some real sunshine into their life—they will find a way to pick it apart. Somehow, they will attempt to bring you down to their level of negativity because that's where they live.

When you're around people like this, do you feel lighter, or might you find yourself feeling heavier? Unresolved negative karma carries a weight, and negative energy is always heavy. Being around negative energy on a more regular basis can bring us into a depressed state, whereas positive energy can lift us into a cheerful state.

We're purposely going to take a much deeper dive into negative karma throughout the next two chapters and will continue to touch on this subject at different intervals throughout the rest of this book.

Let's always remember that the greater purpose of karma, whether it's positive or negative, is to help us heal, mature, and grow. Also remember that karma is there to help us transform into the greatest version of ourselves. We chose to enter this life to learn our lessons, which are often found in our karma. We chose to come here to rise up to our Greater Destiny. Ultimately, we are here to fulfill our soul's deepest purpose, and a key in how we do this is in the resolving of our karma. Our deepest soul's purpose naturally unfolds as our unresolved negative karma completely resolves.

EXERCISES

Write the answers to the following questions in your notebook:

1. What are you doing, or could you be doing, to create positive karma?

2. What are you doing, or could you be doing, to actively clear up negative karma in this lifetime?

3. Describe a time in your life that you witnessed karma return to someone or even to yourself. How did it make you feel?

   Journal how you are feeling as you answer this question.

4. As you reflect back on your childhood, what can you identify as a struggle or traumatic event that you can now see as a possible negative karmic line that you came into this lifetime to clear?

   Describe your progress thus far in clearing this negative karmic line.

   Write down the very next thing you could be doing in creating more progress for yourself on this karmic line.

5. Has there been a time in your life that you were so angry or upset with someone that you sent out hate and negative wishes for something awful to happen to them? If so, what was the outcome?

   Was there any negative karma that returned to you for this action? Or were you able to cancel out this action or resolve within yourself those negative wishes you were sending to them?

6. After learning about the blocks that keep us from rising up into our Greater Destiny, what blocks do you believe you need to be aware of and watch out for in your life?

CHAPTER 9

CLEARING OUR KARMIC AND LOWER ENERGY PATTERNS

N ow that you've learned about both positive and negative karma, let's dive into learning about karmic and lower energy patterns and hen ultimately clearing them. In order to clear them, we will need a better understanding of what they are and how they were created.

LOWER ENERGY PATTERNS

Karmic lines morph into lower energy patterns and karmic patterns. Your karmic patterns and lower energy patterns are found in the Lower Destiny. A lower energy pattern is a pattern that's created in this life.

An example of a lower energy pattern is showing up late for everything. You always leave late, show up late, and then you blame it on something like the weather or the traffic. If you just really listened to yourself, you'd hear the same excuse coming out of your mouth repeatedly.

The difference between a lower energy pattern and a karmic pattern is that a karmic pattern is five times heavier. Also, a lower energy pattern is created in this current lifetime while karmic patterns were created in previous lifetimes. Karmic patterns and lower energy patterns are both patterns of thought and behavior, but a lower energy pattern is more akin to a habit, and it doesn't have the same density.

KARMIC PATTERNS

Karmic patterns are denser and a lot tougher to dismantle than lower energy patterns. A karmic pattern comes through a karmic line. We're controlled by our karmic patterns until we resolve and dismantle them; only then do we become free of them. It's really that simple.

What's not as simple is understanding what our karmic patterns are and the work involved in dismantling them. This takes diligence and requires us to remain mindful. We're never going to know exactly how long it's going to take to completely dismantle a karmic pattern, which means we're going to have moments of frustration and impatience.

Our souls and our lives have themes that tie right into our karmic patterns. These are the heavier ones. These are the karmic lines that we were born into this life with. And, as we've now learned, our karmic lines are encoded with our karmic patterns. Around the first twelve years of life, our karmic patterns will show themselves. Now if we don't have somebody in our world who is truly conscious of this and is there to support us through the recognition of these karmic patterns, then the patterns will become buried on a deeper level in our subconscious. And even though they will be running our life in the background, like a program in a computer can do, we will have lost consciousness temporarily of them or their influence on us.

As long as you are choosing to now wake up to, or remember, the karmic lines or patterns again, you'll begin to see them—it's just a question of time. You might have one karmic pattern, or you might have five of them, depending on who you are as a soul. Because these karmic patterns are heavier, they're going to take a little longer to clear and dismantle. They are going to test your patience...count on it. They are going to test everything in your character on purpose—because on the other side of this, when these really get cleared, your character is going to become stronger. Your soul knows this. The Divine knows this. Your angels and guides know this. Everybody's on board, simply waiting for you to get this.

Our souls and our lives have themes that tie right into our karmic patterns.

One karmic pattern that I had in the beginning that was really tough to clear was the pattern of taking things personally. Early in this life, I found myself taking things very personally. My dad could say something negative about me, and I would immediately go down this rabbit hole in my own thoughts. I would become negative, judgmental, and critical. I would have depressive emotions and would be really hard on myself.

At the time, of course, I had no idea that this was a karmic pattern, meaning I brought this pattern from a previous lifetime experience into this life to ultimately clear and resolve. I was still a kid at this juncture; I had very little awareness around this and had no one to support me in remaining in recognition of this. So, whenever someone would say or do something that I felt was a criticism of me, I would immediately take it as a truth.

When I started teaching, which was at a very young age, I was presenting seminars and I was getting all kinds of positive responses from people. However, every now and then, somebody would say something negative about my teaching that day. All of a sudden, I would only be able to focus on this one person who said something negative about the material I was teaching or my ability. I would completely discard all the other positive comments that were being made from everyone else in the audience that day.

I recall a time early in my teaching career when I was giving a seminar for more than six hundred people. At the end of the seminar, we handed out an evaluation form for the audience to rate the presentation. The bottom line on this particular form was a score somewhere between one and ten—an overall rating for me as a presenter.

Later, as I was glancing over these six hundred-plus evaluation forms, I saw at least a couple hundred nearly perfect scores, as in 9's and 10's, one right after another. And then I came across the one that gave me a 3.4, and within seconds, I began to take this journey down that rabbit hole. And for the next couple of days, I found myself in this very dark place where I was being super hard on myself, over-analyzing and criticizing myself in ways that were not healthy.

What was really going on was that I was still under the influence of this karmic pattern of taking things personally. Over the next while, I did start to get an awareness around this pattern. I realized that everyone was entitled to their opinion, and the way that I was taking criticism was not really in my best interest. I wasn't able to look at feedback and say, "Okay, is there an opportunity here for me to make an adjustment? Is there something I could learn from this comment?"

I began to chip away at this karmic pattern. If I saw or heard a negative comment, I would say to myself, "Okay, am I going to go all the way into that rabbit hole this time? Or might I only go 10 or 20 percent down the rabbit hole?" With that awareness, I was more easily able to pull myself back out, and faster.

I continued to come to terms with what I was doing and was able to eventually resolve this pattern. In fact, quite frankly, I started to take advantage of criticism rather than take it personally. I started to learn, adjust, and shift to the feedback when appropriate. I began to see people's comments like gold; they were valuable tools for my improvement.

What was I to be learning from this karmic pattern? One of my lessons that was encoded within this karmic pattern was to learn how to get reacquainted with myself; to learn about who I really was. You see, back in those days I had lost touch with who I was. I was still figuring it out. I was still answering the questions: "Who am I? Who am I for real? I mean, I know I am a teacher and leader, but is that all I am?"

I began to tap into and discover who I really was, and then I was able to come to a knowing place, or a secure level of comfort, in my own skin.

As I became comfortable in my own skin, there was a direct relationship to this karmic pattern of taking things personally. I found myself not taking things personally anymore. Or if I did, it was only to a small degree, and then, over time, eventually, it was gone. I was then able to take a negative comment from somebody and I could actually handle it.

I became better at discerning, too—that was another lesson that came out of this. I could objectively ask, "Should I just be letting this go right now because it has nothing to do with me? Or, if it does have something to do with me, shouldn't I be embracing this right now?" If it was right for me to embrace, then I would fully embrace it and become enriched by it as well.

So at this point, now I am comfortable in my own skin because I've learned my lessons that were encoded into this karmic pattern. In addition to that, I'm experiencing this freedom where I really am able to capitalize on the opportunities that come with criticism—opportunities to learn more and adjust personally, professionally, and even spiritually. As a result, my life has changed for the better.

A karmic pattern is something we were born into this life with that is destined for us to clear.

Nobody knows their timeline for clearing these karmic patterns. I didn't know the timeline, and anybody I've worked with hasn't known the timeline either. Quite frankly, our Higher Self doesn't even know because we're at free will here—and that is completely unpredictable. You could take the next ten years to get done what would normally only take one year, because you might have one foot in, one foot out.

It's like a feeling. You have feelings, but you are not your feelings. It's like a thought. You have thoughts, but you are not your thoughts. It doesn't matter how ugly, how negative, or how distorted the thought is—that's not who you are. So, regardless of how heavy one of your karmic patterns might be, it's not you, unless you choose to personalize or identify with it.

When these patterns, especially the heavier ones, challenge you, you're going to have moments where you're possibly going to fall and start to think that's who you are. The process of the karmic pattern that's palying out might be very long, and as you're plowing through it, you might be 10, 20 or 30 percent of the way to clearing the karmic pattern—and then, all of a sudden, you might dip into a pocket of darkness. It's not like dark as an evil. It's just dark. There's very little light there.

This is what it means to go through the dark night of the soul. You're going through a darker pocket in one of your heavier patterns, and that's where you can really be tested—especially if it goes on for a while. It's common to have thoughts like, "I don't know if I can do this anymore. This sucks." You could even start to become down on yourself in one of these pockets of darkness that you're traversing through.

But it's important to remember that you're simply in a pocket. You're in a lower valley. There's very little light there. It might even be pitch black, but it's not bad. It's not evil. It's just been cut off from the light for some time. You're now accessing the reason why we call it "karmic." This is because it's heavy. It's got a density to it that the lower energy patterns just don't have. This is the real reason for the numbing-out strategies—because when you're here, it's downright uncomfortable, unpleasant, and could even be scary.

Again, we are not our karmic patterns, but they're our patterns—which means we get to be responsible for them. So, if we can remember this when things get tough, then we can better avoid losing sight of ourselves and our goal while we are in one of these pockets.

A karmic pattern is something we were born into this life with that is destined for us to clear. A significant part of clearing it is for us to have a conscious experience with it. And it is a part of our destiny to resolve and dismantle it, which will mean integrating the lessons contained in this karmic pattern. Eventually, we've got to take ownership of all the karmic patterns we were born with. Blaming them on Dad or Mom is completely unproductive and won't get us anywhere. In fact, it might even screw us up.

This education is critically important because without it, people don't stand a chance. They'll just keeping repeating the same choices over and over again. This is why it would be incredibly helpful to have some-body to help elevate you so that you can see it, and then you need some empowerment to start feeling the courage inside to take action and get going. We all need this, and with determination we can all do this.

Like I said before, when you're dealing with a karmic pattern, you're dealing with a pattern you might have had for multiple lifetimes. It's coming in with some weight and density. However, when you get close to the other side of dismantling one of your karmic patterns, you're going to get grace. You're going to get liberation. Something else also starts to happen, which I refer to as "karmic potential."

When talking about how to let go of what's no longer serving and growing into your full potential, that is the root. This is the higher deal, not just the real deal. This is the higher rung because there's a poten-tial inside of you that you're not even aware of yet because you're still dealing with your karmic patterns.

You might have a karmic pattern, for example, of defensiveness. Maybe you've been working on it, but there you are—somebody pushes your buttons, and you get defensive again. It's like you can't stop yourself. It might be that the karmic pattern of defensiveness was created three lifetimes ago.

You've been using the pattern as a way to defend yourself because something's going on inside of you where you have judged yourself as wrong. Maybe it's a pattern of judgment, and this pattern of judgment and/or defensiveness is karmic because five lifetimes ago, you did something before you died that you knew really hurt a lot of people, and you set in motion the pattern of self-judgment.

> *Taking ownership of our patterns is equivalent to taking ownership of our own life.*

So now, you come into the next life with this karmic carryover, but you don't recognize it. Then you do more things that create even more judgment because you're now under the rule of this karmic pattern of judgment. So then, five lifetimes later, your judgment is so freaking thick—it's so dense that almost every fourth sentence that comes out of your mouth is a judgment. It's like an addiction. You can't stop yourself. Any little thing that someone does, you take them right into judgment.

The karmic patterns that your soul—not your personality, but your soul—has chosen to clear in this life are going to come through karmic lines. Karmic lines also serve in the creation of who your parents are going to be. If you had a karmic pattern going on with judgment, you would most likely end up with a parent, or even an entire family, that has significant judgment. It's possible to be in a family where everybody ends up having similar karmic patterns or, at the very least, having similar lower energy patterns. If you are the older soul coming into that family line, you're coming in with a karmic pattern. Their patterns are probably a little lighter and may be lower energy patterns. The pattern you're coming in with is much denser and will take more work to resolve.

But resolving it is our goal here in this lifetime, and it is a worthy one. When you get discouraged, just remember those gifts that have been buried and see this as if you're digging for buried treasure. And now you've got the map that leads you to the buried treasure, of course there might be some obstacles or challenges along your path. You can pretty much count on it. At the end of that path is the buried treasure to unearth and reap the benefits and blessings from. When we look at it like this, it sounds a lot more exciting and worthwhile, doesn't it?

EASY OR HARD, IT'S UP TO YOU

Clearing our karmic and lower energy patterns is going to take some time, but you don't have to put all this pressure on yourself to go from 0 to 100 miles per hour overnight. You can, however, go from 0 to 10 miles per hour overnight. That's more realistic and doable. Get that under your belt, and then transition to 20 miles per hour. Do it in a way that's realistic, which is step by step, block by block. Because if you get in too big of a hurry to try and do all these things at once, you're going to jam up and block your progress. You can make this hard on yourself, or you can make it easy. The choice is yours.

What does it look like when things are easy? Well, easy equates to grace. Grace equates to transitioning from point A to point B while savoring things, while slowing things down, and while smoothing things out. What's the big hurry? You're going to get there—wherever *there* is. Easy is recognizing, "I'm in a real tough situation, and I recognize that I want to get out of it, so I'm ready to go into it and do what needs to be done." Then, you do it step by step.

Let's say somebody is being severely abused in a relationship. If this person is an adult, they have most likely been abused before. They might even be unconsciously addicted to abuse. I know nobody wants to hear that—I get it. I didn't want to hear it years ago either, but someone can get addicted to being abused. They can get addicted to being tormented. Once they recognize that's their situation and then choose to move beyond it, they must also recognize it's not a healthy relationship but a toxic one.

They can close the door on that relationship tomorrow morning, but they're not out of the woods yet—far from it. They've been in this relationship with someone for, let's say, five years. It is going to take some time to wind out of this relationship and heal themselves. They must be willing to allow a transition to happen.

When you're transitioning out of something, there's a point A, point B, point C, and possibly a point D. If you're going from point A to point D thinking you're just going to skip B and C, then you're missing crucial steps. This means you'll possibly have to come back to start over at some later point. That's what makes things unnecessarily hard. That's what makes life bumpy and unpredictable. You might land on your butt and hurt yourself when you show up that way.

As we learned earlier, we all have the divine birthright of grace, which means our transformation can become even more graceful—but we've got to be more attuned to doing the right thing. We must be willing to morph and transition into a better place in relation to ourselves so that we can stand up when we're called to do what's right. When we do, grace will be around the corner.

> Our transformation can become even more graceful—but we've got to be more attuned to doing the right thing.

The big challenge is in helping people see what the right thing to do is—then getting them to actually do it. Most people are addicted to their own personal agenda. They just want to do it their way. This is a self-centered approach, but they usually feel justified. They're justifying their actions, and as you know, the moment you start justifying, you're back in personal agenda land; you're back in your head; you're back in your Lower Destiny. Now, if you want to stay there, then you can choose it. That's you exercising your free will. But if you want to be conscious, then choose to stay conscious. Take it on as an exercise to see if you can stay conscious when you're operating from your personal agenda.

Eventually, as you go a couple rounds or whatever it's going to take to learn the lessons, you'll progress through it. Then, as soon as you know the right thing to do from the higher perspective in a situation, you'll just step into it. And then, shortly thereafter, it will somehow be met with grace—and you'll see it. You'll be able to recognize it and think,

"Holy cow! Look what just happened!" Exactly—all because you chose to step in and do the thing that you already knew in your bones was the right thing to do.

If that means ending a relationship, then you end the relationship because that's the right thing to do. If it's starting a new relationship, then you start the new relationship because that's the right thing to do—even though it might scare you because you may have a commitment issue. Or maybe you were traumatized in your last relationship, or maybe you were wounded in your last relationship and you haven't healed up the wound yet.

So, maybe you're not quite ready to step in. And by the way, if you're not ready to step in, then don't step in—but recognize where you are in your transition. You can morph into that place transitionally. It doesn't have to be that hard.

4 STEPS TO CLEARING KARMIC OR LOWER ENERGY PATTERNS

There's a 4-step process that I created over time to help people dismantle their lower energy patterns and karmic patterns. I've used this on myself as well as those I work with. What you're about to learn is something very powerful and yet practical. Once you step into this process, you'll be able to release and clear your patterns, little by little, slowly but surely.

STEP 1: TAKE OWNERSHIP

We live by the patterns that have become habitual. They basically run our life, similar to that of a program running our computer. That's the bottom line. We likely have more than one karmic pattern or lower energy pattern that's up for us to clear. And so, the first step is for us

245

to take complete ownership. Remember, this is our personal pattern, regardless of how we got it. This is ours and ours alone, so we are the ones that get to be 100 percent personally responsible for it. That said, we are the only ones that can really clear this. This is us stepping into the driver's seat and identifying the pattern, or eventually the patterns, that have been running our life.

It is best to do this one pattern at a time, rather than all at once. Again this is us stepping into the driver's seat and identifying a pattern that has been running our life. Now once we do this, we are going to start identifying other patterns that have also been running our life. But taking them one at a time is best so we do not overwhelm our system.

Taking ownership of our patterns is equivalent to taking ownership of our own life. This is a very significant step in the transformational journey. Earlier when we were learning about the Five Essential Keys for Personal Transformation, key number four, "Owning It," if you recall, was all about taking ownership. Taking ownership of something that belongs to only us is a very powerful way to live our life. If and when we do, we discover this is one of the master keys for rising up into our Greater Destiny.

STEP 2: IDENTIFY THE CYCLE SEQUENCE

The second step begins by identifying what I refer to as the "cycle sequence" that the pattern goes through when it's actually being played out. The cycle of a pattern is made up of three key points with a beginning, a middle, and an end. Every time one of your patterns gets turned on, again it's like a program in your computer. When the "on" button gets pushed, that pattern you've had for, let's say, 10 years begins over again.

In this first phase between beginning and middle, there's going to be something specific that occurs. It might occur with a different person each time, but once you start to dial into this, you'll see it. It's the exact same thing repeating itself. It might even blow your mind when you see how well orchestrated this is—like that precisely written computer program.

Next, it'll go into the middle phase, where it begins building its climax. This is where things usually start to get loud. Something starts to happen, and things begin to get intense—but you might not even be aware of it because you went to your favorite numbing-out strategy.

Every time one of your patterns gets turned on, again it's like a program in your computer.

Maybe you went to a candy bar and you're eating a lot of candy right now because you're coming into the middle part of the pattern sequence and things are getting intense. But you don't like to feel that way. You don't like to feel uncomfortable. You don't like to feel any of this. It feels yucky. You feel like you're spinning out of control, so you numb yourself out by going into whatever strategy you use to do that. But that doesn't really matter because once the pattern starts, like that program, it must go all the way through—unless you go in and push the delete button or the stop button. But nobody else can do this for you. You've got to go in and do this yourself.

Once the pattern goes through the middle period, it comes to its end. At the end, there'll be what looks like a completion to the cycle. But remember, it is a cycle. Which means it will repeat itself and will continue to do so until we transform, heal, and clear it.

For example, let's say someone has the pattern of defensiveness. First, somebody else comes in and pushes the program button, and the person with the pattern starts to become defensive. They might start off in a real subtle way where the other person's not even aware they're becoming defensive. Then, they move into the middle of the pattern. Intensity starts growing, and suddenly, their voice is getting louder and they're getting in the other person's face. This is where they might create some negative karma for themselves. It's going to be somewhere in this middle phase because they're potentially going to hurt someone, offend someone, shut someone down, or even push someone away.

Maybe they've done this thirty-five times with their partner before, and on the thirty-fourth time, their partner said, "If you do this one more time, I'm out of here. I can't stand this. We've talked about this before." But here they are, going on the thirty-fifth round, and all of a sudden, the consequence comes upon them. Their partner says, "That's it—we're done."

Or maybe the partner doesn't want to be conscious about being done. So, on the thirty-fifth time, they make the choice to go out and start an affair. They don't want to stand up and say, "I'm done with this relationship—this union is over. I can't stand another moment of this. This is like nails going up and down my nervous system every time you do this. I'm no longer willing to live this way."

There are some people that won't stand up. Instead, they'll cower down because they're way too afraid. They've got this frightened little girl or frightened little boy inside of them who's calling the shots—who's sitting in their captain's chair. So, they'll choose to go start an affair instead. They cannot stand this anymore but aren't willing to stand up and end the marriage. Instead, they're going to numb themselves out. They are now creating their own karma.

So, after this cycle of defensiveness goes through its final stage, everything calms back down. It feels like they've given the other person a piece of their mind, and maybe everything's fine for now, and they feel some relief from that. The pattern, like a program, then goes into hibernation and just sits there until the next trigger, when someone comes along and pushes the start button, and then the pattern begins again. It could be the exact same person or a new person who pushes the button. But that's the cycle sequence in action.

The pattern will repeat itself and will continue to do so until we transform, heal, and clear it.

What you must be able to do is slow it down and become conscious enough to recognize the sequence. Again, until you see it, how are you ever going to clear it or transform it? You've also got to understand that it's so important for you to see it, because there's something encoded in this pattern that you're to be learning. I'll emphasize that again—*you've got to learn from this.*

Some people go to healers who'll say, "Okay, now your pattern is all gone. I've taken it away from you so you don't have to worry about it anymore."

Then, 28 days later, there it is again. This person will think, "I thought this was taken away. I thought this was swept out of my field. I thought they put the vacuum cleaner in there and vacuumed it out." No—they didn't. The healer just gave them temporary relief from the pattern, but the person who has the pattern didn't do the work. They tried to go from point A straight to point D.

There's no way the pattern is just going to vanish if the pattern is encoded with a lesson for them to learn. If somebody claims to have cleared the energy for them, but they haven't learned the lesson yet, then all that means is that the pattern is coming back.

So, somebody will push the start button and...BAM! There they'll be with their pattern of defensiveness, and they'll be defending their position or defending somebody else unnecessarily. Maybe they'll be in a fight with their husband or wife over one of their kids. Now, sometimes it's appropriate to defend your child. Other times, it's completely inappropriate. The point is this person is just picking a fight—that's all they're doing. They're in a power struggle with their husband, their wife, or their partner. That's what's really going on.

And next thing you know, they become so defensive that there is no more communication. Think about someone you know who's really defensive. Now think about how their defensiveness makes you feel or react. Is there something that gets ignited within you? This is something that would be wise to explore deeper. If you're in a relationship or friendship with somebody, and they become defensive because that's one of their patterns, what happens to you when they're going through their cycle—beginning, middle, and end? Maybe you are able to remain calm, or maybe you have a pattern of attack or aggression and you come in and attack with your words as a way to protect yourself.

You might be in a friendship with somebody who has this pattern of defensiveness, and every time their pattern unleashes, it brings up one of your patterns. What happens with most people is that they are way too focused on the other person's patterns and not very focused on their own. But were you given the power to clear somebody else's pattern? No.

Now, maybe there are a few people on the planet who have the power to go in and really decode. But whoever those beings are, I can assure you, they're going to operate from a level of high authenticity. They'll make sure that you have learned your lessons before your patterns get completely decoded because they do not want your karma. If you had that ability, would you move in and strip someone of learning a valuable lesson? Not if you knew you would get a little karma for that choice.

STEP 3: IDENTIFY THE NEED AND EMOTION

Within this sequence of beginning, middle, and end, there will be a need that's influencing the sequence and an emotion that's driving the pattern. So again, if my pattern is defensiveness, then there's going to be a need driving the defensiveness. My need could be a need for control. There's also going to be a driving emotion that's literally fueling the pattern. The emotion might be anger, or it could be even fear.

But what happens if you're not quite ready to deal with your own emotions because they're uncomfortable? If that's the case, then the pattern is just going to continue. It just becomes a question of time until somebody comes in and pushes that start button, and the pattern starts the cycle sequence all over again.

STEP 4: LEARN THE LESSONS

Finally, to successfully break down the pattern and advance the resolution of our karma, we must learn the lesson or lessons encoded in the pattern itself. That's why if somebody comes in and erases the pattern, assuming they have the ability to do so, they've potentially robbed you of learning the lesson. And the bottom line is, you'll have to come back and repeat the lesson all over again because you haven't learned it—similar to being in school. If we don't learn what we are supposed to learn in whatever grade we are in, we simply get to repeat that grade all over again. Remember, Earth is very much like a school—a school where we are to be learning the lessons that are unique to us.

The design of every karmic or lower pattern that we have at its deepest core is for us to learn a lesson. Every single pattern is encoded with at least one very specific lesson that comes directly out of our Higher Self—our soul self.

The reason many of us are still struggling with our lower energy patterns or karmic patterns is because we ultimately haven't learned the lessons yet. We must master the lessons that are encoded in the patterns. This is the key here. Once you master a lesson, you'll know it because if there's any of that pattern left, it crumbles quickly. You might even feel it in your bones because there's a real breaking down of whatever the last steps are to completely dismantle this karmic or lower energy pattern. And then, you'll be completely free of it. You'll know this because somebody will come into your life and attempt to push the button, and there will be no button left to push. How bout that?! You'll remain completely calm. And then, at some point, you'll say, "Holy cow! Look at that! It's really gone! There's not a part of me left that was tempted. This is really freeing!" There's that first divine birthright—freedom.

EXAMPLES OF PATTERNS

Let's take a look at some examples of patterns, but keep in mind that there are many more patterns than this. These are just a handful of examples that will get the wheel spinning in being able to better identify some of your own patterns.

The Pattern of Holding On

Here's an example of a pattern with an encoded lesson. Let's say you have a pattern of holding on, or maybe you know someone who has a pattern of holding on. This is the person who refuses to let go of what they're truly supposed to be letting go of. They won't let go of something that's no longer working in their life.

Most people are way too focused on the other person's patterns and not very focused on their own.

Depending on the strength of this pattern, it would be like they literally get a vice grip and squeeze onto whatever this thing is or whoever this person is that they're so desperately holding onto. This could also be the pack rat who's always collecting stuff that they're never going to use. They've got this pattern of holding on, and they're literally being ruled by it. This is a biggie. This could also be a pattern of holding onto your fear, your insecurities, your jealousy, your possessiveness, and/ or holding onto the past. Remember, this lower energy pattern will always have us holding onto something that is no longer serving us and possibly hasn't been working for some time.

Next comes the lesson. This could be a lesson in trust, a lesson in letting go, or both. You have to trust when you're letting go. This could also be a fear that you might not have enough or be good enough. So, it could be a lesson in knowing your true worth or value. Or this could be a safety issue tied in with the fear of change. Someone might be holding onto memories and things, and those things start to define them. And if they don't have those things anymore, then who are they without them?

The lesson here might be around developing the courage to step into the unknown. This could be the pattern of holding onto a story. This person might feel that hanging onto the story is somehow keeping them safe. The lesson might be how to become safe within themselves and trust that they're already safe. That's their lesson because they bought into the illusion that they're not safe. That's their story they've been holding onto for who knows how long.

The Pattern of Being Attached to Outcomes

Another common pattern is the attachment to outcomes. This person immediately goes to whatever outcome they're attempting to accomplish with a person or project, and then they get overly attached to it. Once that attachment happens, the outcome starts to control them. It begins to consume them, and they potentially lose themselves in the process of it now controlling them.

In the process of learning how to detach yourself from outcomes, you still want to be connected to people—the people that are right for you to be connected with. You want to honor that and cherish that. You want to be connected to your business. You want to be connected to your projects. You want to be connected to your clients. At the same time, you want to learn how to detach yourself from outcomes with these people so that you become free to express, flow, and be in alignment with each other. Then, you're allowing something powerful to be revealed in that dynamic.

This lesson requires you to become connected to your Greater Destiny. In other words, if you're living 90 percent or more of your time in your Lower Destiny, it's going to be an incredible struggle for you to trust in the invisible because if you're waiting until you can see it, you could be waiting for a very long time. Learning to detach from outcomes is a lesson of trusting in the unknown, trusting in the invisible, trusting in the energy of your guides, trusting in your Higher Self, and trusting in a higher and greater process that's at play.

The Pattern of Exaggeration

Another example is the pattern of exaggeration. The person with this pattern takes something small and blows it out of proportion. They take a little story and turn it into a big story. The lesson could be to see the simplicity. This could also be a lesson in being truthful. How about something as simple as being honest instead of turning a molehill into a mountain? Is this person being honest? Are they being truthful? No— they're not being real. They're not being authentic. Are they in their real power? The lesson here is to learn how to be honest with themselves, and then, of course, with others.

Maybe this is a carryover from a previous time. Perhaps in the last three lifetimes, they've lived in such a way where they were always dishonest. So now, it's created a pattern of exaggeration.

Some people exaggerate their fears. As they become aware of a fear, over the next hour, they blow it out of proportion. As a coach, there have been many times that I've literally had to pull people back into reality. And sometimes it's like pulling a bad tooth. They will fight because they're convinced that what they're telling the world is absolutely the truth. In reality, what they're saying is at least 90 percent off, but they're convinced that they're 100 percent on, and they're willing to fight for it. They're willing to get mad at me. They're thinking about hanging up the telephone on me.

To advance the resolution of our karma, we must learn the lesson or lessons encoded in the pattern itself.

This is another pattern that has a beginning, a middle, and an end. There's a possibility that when this cycle of exaggeration is going through its sequence, that person might actually create more karma for themselves. So, their lesson at soul level could be as simple as learning how to become brutally honest. They might also have another lesson here of discipline.

When somebody has the pattern of exaggeration, what that really means is they often literally spin out of control with themselves. They spin out of control with their minds. They spin out of control with their emotions. And they could be here at soul level to learn how to discipline themselves—how to pull back the reins and recognize, in which they might say, "I've got a lot of emotions coming in right now. I've got all these thoughts that are literally overtaking my mind. I'm going to hone in on them one by one, and I'm going to pull them back." This is an act of self-discipline.

The Pattern of Moving Too Fast

Another pattern is moving too fast. We've all heard the phrase, "Slow and steady wins the race." This one is about having patience and persistence. When we're under the influence of the pattern of moving too fast, we're literally covering up our intuition. We're not even hearing it. So, might there be a lesson in this pattern that shows we're to be learning how to really honor and trust our intuition?

Everybody has some kind of an intuition. Everybody has some kind of an inner GPS. The question is, do you trust yours? Or maybe the bigger question is, have you learned how to trust yours? Have you learned how to follow through on yours without hesitation? Do you really know what that feels like? Do you know what it sounds like?

When somebody has a pattern of moving too quickly, there's no way they're even listening to their intuition. This is the person who might say, "I want what I want, I want it right now, and I'm going for it—and that's it! I don't care what anybody says."

Meanwhile, their intuition is saying something completely different. But they are hell-bent that this temptation is exactly what they think it is, and nobody, including their own intuition, can convince them otherwise. Obviously, this would produce a pattern of moving too quickly. It's all about how fast they can get in there and sew up the deal so that they can secure this thing.

So, there is going to be an emotion associated with this pattern of moving too quickly. What might the emotion be that drives this pattern? Anxiety is a branch to the rooted emotion, and the rooted emotion to anxiety is fear. The reason why we move so quickly is because emotionally we're really frightened. It's 100 percent fear. We are afraid of something, whatever that is. So, of course, we're not going to listen to our intuition because our intuition would tell us to slow down. Our intuition might say, "This is not who or what you think it is. Go in another direction. Let this go." However, we don't want to listen because we're really afraid of losing something.

Another example of moving too quickly can be seen in relationships. Do you have a pattern of moving into a new relationship before resolving your current one? Do you have a pattern of jumping from one person to another because you are terrified of experiencing the gap? Do you have a difficult time being alone for a sustained period of time? Is that tough on you? If it is, then that ought to be a message here for you. That's your Higher Self attempting to get through to you, letting you know that you've got an issue with being alone. You've got an issue with experiencing the gap or the void.

So, therefore, you need a new relationship to cover that up because it's too scary for you to traverse through. If that's where you're coming from when stepping into a new relationship, you're coming from a weakened place.

For some people, it's only five minutes, perhaps five months, or even five years all by themselves—and they can't bear the thought. "I'm terrified of being alone," they might say. "I'm terrified of experiencing the gap. It's way too scary to be all alone, to learn about myself, to develop a relationship with myself, to strengthen the relationship with myself. Oh my gosh! I've got to have somebody here right now—somebody to remind me how beautiful I am or how handsome I am. I've got to have somebody to have sex with—like right now. I might actually have a sex addiction, and I don't even know it. Maybe that's what's been driving my relationships. I need to fill up my sex addiction. So, I need the next person. Who's available? He looks really good—he's got big arms. She looks really hot. That's my next one. Are they willing to go there with me?" Next thing you know, that person is in a new relationship, but they haven't taken care of what's happened in the past, so that unresolved stuff they're walking around with is going to affect the new relationship.

> Everybody has some
> kind of an intuition,
> an inner GPS.
> The question is, do
> you trust yours?

If this sounds familiar to you, the first step is to recognize it. You might say, "You know what? I'm not going to go into any deep relationships right now." Maybe you go through a period where you just date—no commitment. You've got to decide that for yourself. And, if you're not at the place yet of being able to wait, then maybe you need more pain. Maybe you need to go back into a relationship again to realize you really do have a lot of unresolved stuff from the past you haven't cleaned up yet.

That unresolved stuff is eventually going to seep into that new relationship. It's going to cause a whole other problem—a whole other piece of karma for you one more time. Maybe that'll be the last time for you.

Maybe that'll be the time that makes you say, "You know what? That's it—I'm done with this. Now I'm really ready to get my sleeves rolled up higher. Not that I'll never date again, but maybe I'll just keep it to a date. No more commitments until I clear this stuff up because this stuff is too difficult to deal with when I'm attempting to start a new relationship. And especially if what's really going on is I'm attempting to start something new as a way to cover up something else that I don't want to deal with—to cover up something I don't want to experience because I'm afraid of it."

The Pattern of Having No Boundaries

Another pattern example is having no boundaries—or not staying true to your boundaries in order to make someone else feel better. A need possibly influencing this pattern is a need to play it safe or a need to protect ourselves from something we don't want to feel or experience. The emotion that's driving this pattern could be fear, as in possibly the fear of rejection. If you have a very specific fear of rejection, of course, you're going to abandon your own boundaries; you're going to abandon your own rules and your own truth because the whole focus is on making sure that you never have to feel the fear of being rejected by whoever this person is.

If this is the underlying emotion, now somebody can enter your world and basically walk all over you. That somebody might always be asking you to do things for them without doing anything for you in return. Or it could be that you're always reaching out to this person out of care for their wellbeing, but they never reach out to you. Whatever it is, it's going to show itself. These types of imbalances will get played out in our relationships, friendships, or partnerships.

At some point, you might even find yourself feeling resentful and angry—like you're the one always doing the sacrificing and giving. Maybe you feel like you just want to give up and not spend this much effort on this person anymore.

If you're unaware of this pattern, you might blame this person for showing up the way they're showing up and therefore remain in denial that you have this pattern of sloppy boundaries.

Any of these lower energy patterns bring us down into our Lower Destiny and can keep us there for quite some time.

Let's say you came from a childhood where nobody around you exercised healthy boundaries. It could be extremely difficult for you to set them later in life if you didn't have a good role model, and you might find yourself getting walked on all the time. This is a common way in which this pattern manifests.

Then, later on in life, you find yourself with this pattern of being unable to set boundaries and find yourself in these situations with different people where your lines are being crossed constantly because no lines have been drawn. Like I said, you might feel resentful and angry because your genuine needs in a relationship or friendship are not being fulfilled. Should you live your life this way, it can cause a deep level of pain, keeping you in your Lower Destiny.

I think at this point, one of the things that's important to remember is the greater purpose for a relationship or a friendship with someone. This has to do with our genuine needs being fulfilled on both sides of the relationship. In other words, it's not healthy to have a relationship or a partnership with someone where just one person appears to be getting their needs met. This causes a deeper problem long term because we're in denial of this deeper, greater purpose of the relationship experience, which is that genuine connection and a fulfillment of both parties' needs.

The lesson here could very well be on how to actually set, establish, and enforce healthy boundaries. Would this be a wise thing for you to learn how to do, starting right now? If this is resonating and it's something you haven't previously been very good at, then a strategy might be to begin setting one or two boundaries with someone in your life where you can practice, giving you the chance to eventually get better at this. This would be you establishing a higher energy pattern of creating healthy boundaries.

The Pattern of Judgment

This pattern is a common one. We've all experienced a friend, family member, or even a complete stranger judging us for something we did or even said. They may have not even verbalized their judgment, but we could feel the energy of judgment being directed at us.

Judgment in itself does have a positive place with us. Being a good judge of character or being able to make a good judgment call are great qualities. However, living with a lower energy pattern of judgment is very different. This pattern has to do with locking something into place. You might recall from earlier in the book when we discussed the ego and that it's always looking to maintain the status quo because it senses that moving forward would be detrimental to its existence and possibly to yours as well. The ego believes that it needs to keep us safe and needs to keep itself safe. Because of that it can most certainly influence this pattern of judgment as a way to maintain the status quo in our lives, by holding someone or something in judgment.

If we're experiencing this pattern directly, we are holding someone or something in judgment and, in turn, holding some part of ourselves or something we've done that we disapprove of in judgment.

If I'm judging someone or something else, it's only question of time before I start holding myself in judgment.

When we lock this pattern of judgment into place, we are going to get more of whatever it is we are judging in our lives. For example, if I'm judging you for always being negative, then there's a real likelihood I'm going to get even more negativity from you or in my life in general. You see, this energy I'm locking into place will begin to grow and strengthen, which means it can and will attract more of the same.

Say I have one negative person in my life that I've been holding in judgment for being too negative. Then, I have a second person in my life that I find myself having a similar experience with. It's because I'm the one who has been holding negative energy as a judgment inside of myself. I'm not releasing it, so it is accumulating more of its like. That's ultimately what judgment that's held over a period of time does. Even though I'm projecting it outward onto my mother, my father, my best friend, or my next-door neighbor for something they did that I dislike, it all comes back to me.

This pattern is such that if I'm judging someone else or something else, it only becomes a question of time before I start holding myself or some part of myself in judgment. Eventually, if not cleared, we can become so hard on ourselves that we start believing we can't do anything right anymore. Nothing is good enough for us anymore. This is where we, over time, start to lose our own freedom. Energetically, we're living in a self-imposed prison cell.

If you have this pattern of judgment and you dig deep into this feeling, you'll likely find it's been you holding you back over time. That's ultimately what judgment does.

Do you know of anybody who has the pattern of judgment? What might the lesson be when somebody has a pattern of judgment? The lesson here could be acceptance. It could also be a lesson of forgiveness. Another lesson could be compassion and understanding.

Other pattern examples are:

Control, perfection, holding a grudge, procrastination, self-doubt, laziness, making others wrong, shutting down, overthinking, pushing, avoidance, worry, negativity, frustration, fantasizing, or always having to be right.

Any one of these lower energy patterns bring us down into our Lower Destiny and, quite frankly, can keep us in our Lower Destiny for quite some time. The key here is, once again, to become aware of what the pattern is. It's that awareness, that acute state of awareness over time, around this lower energy pattern, that's the first step. Then, we are able to do the work to clear the pattern and eventually release it.

EXAMPLES OF LESSONS TO LEARN FROM PATTERNS

- Learning how to trust
- Learning how to let go
- Learning how to have faith
- Accepting what is
- Learning self-love and self-care
- Learning to trust yourself
- Learning how to manage your emotional energy
- Learning how to correctly utilize your power
- Learning self-discipline
- Learning how to effectively work with failure
- Learning how to respect the process of taking small steps
- Learning how to let go of control
- Learning how to take ownership for your career
- Learning how to trust in the Divine
- Learning how to make healthier, wiser choices
- Learning how to believe in yourself
- Learning about commitment
- Learning how to heal yourself

TRANSFORMING YOUR PATTERNS

Your patterns run your life. These lower energy patterns cause you to make choices that create more consequences for you. This is up for you to uncover and get to the core of. You've got to discover what's driving this way of making choices that cause negative consequences to show up in your life. When you start to uncover and dismantle these patterns, you'll receive more blessings and more positive consequences, partly because you will begin to recognize the value of the higher energy pattern such as the pattern of worthiness, receptivity, progress, consistency, or forgiveness to name a few. When this happens, it can completely change your trajectory. Choosing not to do this, however, will simply result in a repeat of what you've already been doing and getting.

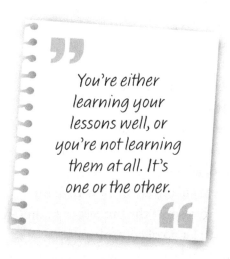

> You're either learning your lessons well, or you're not learning them at all. It's one or the other.

It's important to understand that your patterns can also merge. You could literally have one cycle sequence involving three or four patterns, especially the longer you let this stuff grow. These patterns are like weeds in your garden. When you get enough weeds, they start to entangle with each other. When you get enough of these lower energy patterns going on, at some point, they're going to cross over—and that in itself makes them heavier and more complex to unravel.

Uncovering some of these patterns may shock and disgust you. You might wonder, "How did I not see this before?" But with this newfound awareness, the next time a pattern cycles, you're going to see it in a whole new light. You're going to get more details, and then you're going to be simultaneously moving towards clearing it. Then, at some point, it's just going to loosen up and lighten everything up for you. You're going to start having new experiences or experiences that perhaps you haven't had for some time as the pattern starts to release.

Somewhere along the way in life, many people develop the habit and/or idea that it's safer to focus on their outer world than to focus on their inner world.

Many people are downright terrified to go inward; subconsciously, they feel it isn't safe. Perhaps something traumatic happened in their past when they went inward, and then, out of that, the conclusion was made that it's not safe to go there anymore. In order to survive, they shift focus from the internal to the external. They just start focusing on everybody else and take the focus off themselves.

It's possible that they could actually completely forget about themselves. This can get very extreme for some people. They might never understand it in this life, which means they're coming back in another lifetime to learn this lesson since they couldn't resolve it in this one. And whenever they come back, they're going to come back to where they left off. They're going to come back into a reality with a group of people where the focus is on the external. And somehow, they're going to have to navigate through that and start to realize that they really need to focus on the internal—on what's going on inside themselves.

If someone has a big issue with going inward that's rooted in fear (because of some previous experience they haven't resolved yet), then it's going to ignite these patterns where the focus is always on other people. This could be so extreme that it might even confuse them. They might wonder, "Why can I do this for everybody else, but I can't do it for myself?"

I see this all the time with entrepreneurs and with outwardly successful people. On the inside, they're not successful. They're shallow, unable to go deep—and they're really scared. When they get to a vulnerable place where they're willing to be brutally honest, they'll loosen up and start sharing what's really going on inside of themselves with me. That's why they're always so busy on the outside—doing this, doing that, taking care of this, taking care of that. They are always living outside themselves, busy and distracted, as a way to keep them separate and safe from whatever it is that's going on within. They don't want to go inside because they're afraid to confront and ultimately deal with what needs to be seen, felt, and healed. Speaking of feelings, they are often afraid of their own feelings and most likely don't even know it yet.

> Your biggest purpose, should you choose to accept it, is to identify your unique lessons and then choose to learn them well.

When we get serious about rising up into our Greater Destiny, it's only a question of time; we're going to have to go face to face with our fear. And we're not going to clear it overnight. We're not going to clear it over a weekend. There are a handful of core fears that we all share, but once we transform them and literally clear them out, we're completely free to now be the most authentic version of ourselves.

Get excited, knowing that you can get in and start clearing this stuff! This is going to change your life in the biggest, best, and brightest of ways.

CLEARING PATTERNS AND LEARNING LESSONS

While you're clearing your patterns and learning the lessons, you could discover additional lessons along the way. And they'll keep on coming. Just focus on the lessons that are in front of you right now. They are at the core of everything. You're either learning your lessons well, or you're not learning them at all. It's one or the other.

So, my message to you is to identify these lessons and then go to work on them with a very specific intent to master them. If it takes you a year, then take a year. If it takes you five years, then take five years—but get it done. Your soul will be thrilled with you. The Divine will be thrilled with you. The Universe will be thrilled with you. Your guides and angels will be thrilled with you. Those people in your life who really get you will be equally thrilled with you, and they'll want to celebrate you because they recognize that what you just pulled off is huge.

Setting this intent means that now you're going to recognize rather quickly when you're not clearing these patterns. You'll think, "Here I go again, jumping ship. I promised myself and I promised those close to me I was going to do this. In the moment, I convinced everybody. They really believe that I'm going to do this." If you can recognize this, you can get back on track.

Let's say you have a lesson to learn around acceptance. Then you're going to have somebody or something come into your life that's going to bring up the part of you that's having a difficult time accepting. It's going to feel uncomfortable. It's going to challenge you, upset you, and activate you. As I wrote in book number one of the Transformation Trilogy, "What challenges you is designed at soul level to change you." The difference now is that you are aware that this is your lesson—to learn how to accept things as they are and to learn how to accept yourself as you are. What empowers you is the pure and complete

269

acceptance of where you're at in current time, or where something in your life is at in current time. That's what opens up a doorway to allow you to see something else.

> *What challenges you is designed at soul level to change you.*

But, if you're fighting learning your lesson of acceptance—which means you're not going to accept this person or what they've just done, or you're not going to accept what you're doing—then that means you've got your foot back on the brake pedal again. You're literally holding yourself back from your own higher and greater good that awaits you. You're hurting yourself when you do this. You're disempowering yourself and weakening your system.

Your lessons have been encoded in your soul and your field of consciousness. Your soul agreed to set this up in advance. Whether you have a total of half a dozen lessons, a dozen lessons, or fifteen lessons—whatever that number is—it's already encoded. It's waiting for you to discover.

The soul takes on a lesson for the purpose of the growth it's going to gain from learning and ultimately mastering the lesson. There's something wonderful that happens for the soul when each lesson becomes mastered. This is the soul advancing and expanding in its own evolutionary process of becoming wiser, healthier, and happier.

You're here on purpose—and your biggest purpose, should you choose to accept it, is to identify your unique lessons and then choose to learn them well. Choose to take them all the way through to mastery, to where you'll never, as a soul, have to learn those lessons again.

CONFRONTING ONE OF MY DARKEST FEARS – PART 2

Speaking of learning lessons, back in Chapter Two, where I began the story of Confronting One of My Darkest Fears, you may recall that I had died in the middle of the night. At that point, my inner eye, or my inner vision, was now fully open. I could both see and feel these hands of light on my chest, just like someone would if they had a heart attack and the medics were trying to revive them. The hands were pulsating, and as soon as I saw this being of light, I opened my eyes, and I realized my body was ice cold. It felt like I had been laying in a tub of ice for some time. I had never, ever experienced that level of coldness before.

My body was just frozen, and I could see my skin was not even purple. It was this other strange color.

At that point, I got a little scared and thought, "Where am I? What just happened?" My physical eyes were now open, but the room was pitch black. I tried to get off the bed, and I couldn't move, so I rolled over. My body was paralyzed and lifeless. Somehow, I was able to will myself to roll to the left, and I rolled over and landed on the floor, falling off the bed.

I didn't have any bodily function. My body was just frozen, and I could see my skin was not even purple. It was this other strange color. I was fully aware that my body was completely lifeless, but I wanted to get to the phone and call Dr. Greenawalt and just have him check me. This is something he had done for me a number of times prior to this moment. I just knew that I had died and had been dead for what seemed like a long time, but I'm really not sure exactly how long it was.

It took me the better part of a half hour, as I could only crawl to where the phone was in the other room in the kitchen nook. The phone was up on the table. I had to climb and get up onto a chair. Then I grabbed the phone, found the number and dialed. At that point I could hardly move. It took all my willpower to get to the chair and turn on the light. I was trembling with cold, as I was still in the process of coming back into my body.

Dr. Greenawalt answered the phone and right away started testing. He said, "Wow, I've never seen this before. Wow. Wow." It felt like I was resurrecting from the dead. In that moment, I acknowledged and fully realized that this was me finally confronting death. Which is something that I had been moving towards for a part of my life. From that point on until now, I've never been afraid of death.

I feel like I'm not going to go anytime soon, but I could go right now. I am so at peace and so welcoming of death on all levels. I've noticed how honoring I've become of death. In fact, I've become equally honoring to the many transformational deaths that I've experienced since this year-long cleanse. This life-altering experience literally opened everything up inside of me and allowed me to really confront the fear of death.

Among my other near death experiences, this one was like nothing I'd ever experienced before in this life. But it was the time along my journey to confront my own death and then come back to life.

> It was the time along my journey to confront my own death and then to come back to life.

The lesson for me here was in learning how to fully embrace and welcome death—that death is just as important to me now as life is—and to appreciate it. They are the opposite side of the same coin, meaning that as we are going through life, there is some part of our life that is to be dying off so that it can be replaced with something new. In order to have the birthing of a new season come upon us, it is only possible as a result of the death of the old season that we equally honored and let go of. As in the death of winter being followed by the birthing of spring.

Something must die for something else to be born, and this became clear to me in this death experience that I now see as one of the most powerful experiences of my life. Since the time that happened, not only did a part of me die, but my mystical abilities came online and were reborn from that of a previous lifetime.

As we continue to go through this book, *Transform Your Destiny*, I want you to have the insight that there are different areas throughout the teachings found within the entirety of these pages where I am accessing from that mystical side that came online during this lifechanging experience.

THE ELEVATOR APPROACH

As always, when you're taking something on, it's always better to recognize this and do it in steps. Like the ascension ladder, make the decision to go one step at a time. Decide that you're no longer going to let your ego hoodwink you into thinking you have to take the elevator and not the stairs. With the elevator approach, it's just a question of time, you're going to hurt yourself, which means you're going to create more karma and have to go back and repeat the steps you tried to skip.

I have many students that come to my seminars that comment on the practicality of my teachings and how they take the student ascending upward one step at a time in a practical yet powerful way. A part of the reason why it's so powerful is that it works for everyone that practices it by taking it step by step in a progressive manner, rather than looking for the fastest way to get there.

The key here is to recognize what step you're currently on, and then what step is next. The other part of that key is to recognize where you're at in your completion of that step because this is where your ego will try to trick you yet again—you'll think you're ready for the next step, but you haven't completed the step you're currently on. If you jump too quickly to that next step, there is a chance you're going to hurt yourself.

That's like a sensei saying, "You know, I'm just going to give you a black belt, even though you're still only a green belt." That's not okay because you're not quite ready. It might appear like it's going to take a long time. Okay—then let it take a long time if that's what ensures that you get this right to where you can completely own this step, as in "You've now got this now!"

Again, it appears practical but it is equally powerful, as you're now on the path of ascension, progressing upward one step at a time.

EXERCISES

Reflect upon the following questions and as you do write out your responses in your notebook.

1. Are you able to recognize a pattern with a cycle sequence that's been playing out in your life?

   If so, describe the beginning, middle, and ending of it.

   What is the need that's influencing the sequence (as in the need to control, the need to be right, the need to play it safe, or the need for something else)?

   What is the emotion that's driving the pattern (as in anger, jealousy, sadness, fear, or something else)?

2. What happens when you're around somebody who's really defensive?

   What kind of a pattern or feeling does that ignite within you, if any?

3. Do you know of anybody who currently has a pattern of holding on? If so, describe this pattern of theirs. What do you notice?

What happens to your thoughts towards them? How do you show up with this person?

Check and see if you might have this pattern and if so, what do you see? Explain.

4. Do you have a karmic pattern that you are aware of to clear in this lifetime that has been reflecting back to you in some area of your life? If so, describe it and why you think it is a karmic pattern.

5. On a scale of 1-10, 1 being very little, and 10 being a lot, how much do you blame others? Whatever your number, why did you give yourself that number?

   Describe a time when you blamed someone else. What feelings are coming up for you as you are reflecting on this experience of having blamed someone?

   Now describe a time when you took ownership. What feelings are coming up for you as you are reflecting on this time of taking ownership?

6. When it comes to relationships, partnerships, or friendships, how quickly do you move to the next one? Or do you give yourself some time in between each one to fully complete and move on?

   Do you recognize any patterns you might have in this area? If so, describe what you see.

7. As previously mentioned, one of our greatest reasons for being here in Earth School is for us to be learning lessons. So if there was a lesson you were to be learning right now, what would it be? (See examples of lessons earlier in this chapter.)

   And if you were to actually learn this lesson really well, what would this do for you? How would it change your life?

CHAPTER 10

THE WHEEL OF KARMA

In Chapter 8, you learned about the Law of Karmic Return. But this law has a secondary law, which is the Law of Reincarnation. There's a direct relationship between karma and reincarnation. Once we enter this third-dimensional reality, at soul level, we all know there's a chance we're going to create karma. We also know that once we create negative karma, that karma has to be resolved. There's no escape from it.

So, when you, as a soul, consciously choose to come here, the risk would be once you created the karma, would you resolve it? And would you resolve it rather quickly? Or would you put it on hold for a while? Now if you put it on hold, then you enter into the wheel of karma. Sometimes, depending on the intensity of the karma, souls are literally forced back into their next life right away. In most cases, however, they get a reprieve to reorganize themselves before they make their way back.

When I was a young guy, I didn't know all of this. I knew that I had karma, but I was like most people on the planet and thought (at least on an unconscious level) I could somehow escape it. Well, it turned out that not only could I not escape it, but I started creating more karma on top of the karma that I came in with. I went down that rabbit hole for a while, and once I realized what I was doing, I thought, "Oh my gosh! I'm going to be here forever." That's when I made the decision to resolve my karma.

Over the years, I've heard all kinds of spiritual people say that this is their last lifetime, but I know it's not their last lifetime if they're not truly resolving their karma. They might be hoping, or even be desperate for it to be their last life because they don't like it here and they want to get away. But once again, what I've come to appreciate under this law is that nobody escapes the resolution of their own karma.

Sometimes, depending on the intensity of the karma, souls are literally forced back into their next life right away.

An authentic ascended master wouldn't take your karma away from you because that would mean they would have to put it on their shoulders. They would be in violation of the Law of Cause and Effect, which means because of the choice (at causal level), this would now produce the effect of more personal karma. And when they do that, that means they have to get back on the wheel.

This wheel is a very important component of destiny for us to understand. It's a deep subject, and that's why a lot of people stay away from it. They don't want to go there because of what it implies. It demands a much higher level of responsibility than we are used to. If you're not ready to take on this responsibility, then you're simply not ready—and this might be something you'll merely want to only have an intellectual understanding of but not work on, at least just yet.

You might say, "Oh, that's good. I'll come back and revisit that 10 years from now and see if any of its true, but right now, I don't want to do anything because it implies that my only way out is to resolve my karma. And, if I don't clear it all up in this life, no worries." From a Universal-Law perspective, it is not an issue because if we don't resolve it, we'll simply get another chance. Which could very well mean to reincarnate again, but perhaps not right away, as we might not reincarnate for another fifty years.

Until you strike your last lifetime for real, you're on that wheel. It's like a hamster wheel. You can't get off until you completely resolve your karma and ultimately fulfil your deepest soul purpose. Once you clean it all up and fully complete this, you can get off anytime you wish. Which means you're no longer required to come back ever again, should that be the choice you make as a soul.

REINCARNATION

The subject of reincarnation gets really interesting here in the Western world, as some people and some religions don't believe in it. This very well could be because it's been plucked out of the original texts. In other words, it was there all along from the original ascended masters.

Some religions were created from whatever the master was teaching, hundreds of years after he or she left the planet. And then, over time, there's the possibility that it didn't stay in its original form. Most of our religious texts have been translated many times, and now, thousands of years later, many in the Western world have a difficult time with the idea of reincarnation. But that has been changing in more recent years.

About thirty or forty years ago, there were studies done on people who believed in past lives. Back then, a smaller percentage of Americans believed in reincarnation and the larger majority didn't.

These beliefs are shifting as people are awakening and more are believing in reincarnation, though the majority of those people have never had any kind of a recall that they're aware of.

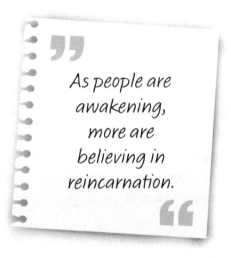

As people are awakening, more are believing in reincarnation.

I was talking to a friend, and we got talking about reincarnation. This friend had a dream that suggested they had a past life. It was so detailed and real for them that it made them a believer.

Now there are some that no matter what you do, there's a chance they will never believe that reincarnation is possible. In this case, hopefully this doesn't offend them since this is a generalization about beliefs shifting in the mass populous.

When someone has a past life recall, this would be some kind of a memory within their subconscious that pops up from a previous time. It might show up in their dream space. Or it could show up in their meditations. Perhaps they go into regression therapy or a similar modality. In other words, something happens inside of them, and they tap into their inner knowing.

Of all the planets in our galaxy and all the galaxies in our Universe, does it really make sense that there's only one life on one planet? There are almost four billion other planets in the Universe, and many are declaring that this is the only life there is in this vast, infinite place we call the Universe. Where's this coming from? Do we even know who started this teaching that says reincarnation doesn't exist? When we sit back and objectively listen to the narrative that there's only one life, and that life can only exist on this planet in this vast Universe, does that make sense? Or does it make you question this and make you want to know more about your own past lives?

Hopefully this has made you curious and this prompt will awaken something within you where you will begin to earn more, if that hasn't already happened for you.

PAST-LIFE DREAMS

Some of the parents I've coached have kids who started having dreams of past lives. Because I'm very skilled at translating dreams, it was obvious to me that these were past-life memories showing up in these dreams, but the parents didn't usually believe it at first. The good news is, in this context, Mom and Dad had somebody like me in their corner. So, they were at least open enough to run it by me, and then I was able to help them understand what was happening with their young child.

When this happens, the child is having a recall in their dream space. The parents would sometimes say, "I don't know about this, Dale. I think this is kind of weird. Are you sure they're not making it up?"

I'd respond, "Well, let's find out. Let's go ahead and turn it over to their Higher Self. Let's put it out there and ask that if there's any truth that your son or daughter has had a past life prior to this life, then let's ask your child's Higher Self to let us know by producing another dream of its like."

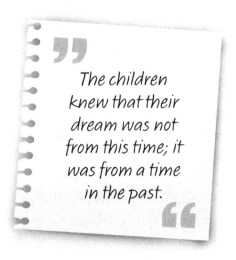

The children knew that their dream was not from this time; it was from a time in the past.

Two weeks later, my phone would ring, and the parents would say, "You aren't going to believe what happened. They had another dream, and it's a continuation of the dream they had two weeks ago."

At least then the parents started to open up to the possibility behind their child's experience. What's interesting is that the children knew that their dream was not from this time; it was from a time in the past.

Children are usually far more receptive because they don't have as many limiting beliefs inhibiting their experience. So for them, this often just makes sense.

Understanding reincarnation is similar to understanding death. Humanity as a whole doesn't really understand death, which is why most people are terrified of it. And, quite frankly, a lot of people are terrified around the idea that they've had one hundred lifetimes before this one—or even ten lifetimes before this one. In the Eastern world, it's very different. They've used reincarnation as a tool and sometimes as an escape route. Towards the end of their life, they'll literally say, "Oh, no worries. I'll take care of it next time."

This is because they already know there's going to be a next time. They understand it. They know it to be true, and we're not going to change their mind.

PERSONAL KARMA

Personal karma is the karma you came into this life with. Remember those karmic lines we covered in the previous chapter? When you came here, you came in with a pocket of personal karma that you ultimately cannot avoid because it's already been destined; those are your karmic lines. Now, will you resolve this in this life? That's where your choice, awareness, and understanding comes into play. You might resolve 70 percent of it. You might resolve only 30 percent of it. Quite frankly, you might not resolve any of it and you may actually create a whole lot more of it, which will make your next lifetime heavier.

For some people, this is one of the reasons this lifetime has been so heavy. They've gone through the last three or four lifetimes, didn't resolve diddly squat, and literally created more karma. Every time we do this, it sets the next life up to be even heavier.

Again, in the Eastern world, they understand this—so they consciously work with it. And, in the context of life, they will successfully move through some of that karma—at least, they usually do. Now, will they resolve it all? That's all choice and awareness. They might or might not. But, clearly, in the Eastern world, they're going to get to a chunk of it. They're going to clear out a portion of their personal karma that they were born with from whatever previous time it dates back to.

INTERFERING WITH OTHERS' KARMA

We are accountable for what we do—period. We are not accountable for our next-door neighbor. We are not accountable for our boss. We are not accountable for our child, not when it comes to their karma at soul level. When we take something out of balance, it immediately causes the creation of karma.

Keep in mind that interfering with someone else's karma is far different from having energy spun back around on you—when that happens, it is a message, a boomerang of your own energy, sent by the other person; it is a gift. It comes from the Divine as a highly conscious act, an act designed to help you possibly finally get it. Whatever it is that you've been sending out is now coming back to you so that you can see what it is that you were sending out and if necessary, correct it.

So, let's look at an example of interfering with someone else's karma. Let's say I have a friend who is an alcoholic, and he's out driving his car drunk, and dangerously, which means he's putting other lives at risk. He gets pulled over, arrested, and is facing DUI charges. He calls me for help, knowing I have connections with the courts, and is now pleading with me, saying he could lose shared custody of his kids and possibly his job. It's a choice for me to interfere with his consequence. And I may come up with all the reasons I should save him—like he's my best friend, I love him, I can't bear the thought of seeing him lose all that, it would devastate him, etc.

But it doesn't matter what my reasoning is. Once I make a choice to go in and interfere and save that person from their own consequence, I've now just created karma for myself because I'm the one who's out of alignment. His Higher Self and the Universe were working together and beginning to intersect on his behalf so he could get whatever consequence he had coming, so that he didn't have to put any other lives or his own at risk.

Perhaps this is exactly what he needed. He needed to be pulled over by the police. He needed to be charged with a DUI. He needed to go to jail for the night. Maybe this is the very thing that would cause him to change what was up for him to change about himself.

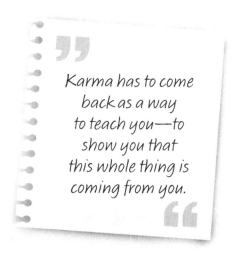

> Karma has to come back as a way to teach you—to show you that this whole thing is coming from you.

If I got him off easily, with no consequence, what if it resulted in him doing it again, but next time, he got into an accident and killed the family in the other car? What kind of karma would I potentially take on then? This could be a karma string that keeps on coming due to that one choice I made to interfere with someone else's consequence. This person was coming into some karma, and if they continued on living this way, it would get worse. But I interfered.

Maybe had he gotten the DUI he would have turned his life around, stopped drinking, and been a better father. That could have been the very thing that caused my dear friend to make the change in his life that would be a benefit to him and his family. Can you see what's happening here when we interfere and take on someone else's karma?

Once I make that choice and lock it into place, meaning I now act on it, I get to be accountable for my actions. There are all kinds of applications for this in your own life, and I challenge you to reflect on your life and see where you've interfered with someone else's karma—and therefore, taken on their karma. My hope is that understanding this law changes you for the better to start making the right choices in the intensity of the moment. Part of making the right choice is understanding that it is a personal choice to take on someone else's karma.

You might be completely unaware or unconscious to what you've done, but the Law of Choice says, "I don't care," because the law is completely impersonal and precise. It challenges you for the better to start making the right choices, where it can matter the most in the heat of the moment.

THE SPIRIT OF MALICIOUS INTENT

When creating karma on a personal level, it's the spirit in which we do things that also causes negative or positive karma. So, if I go into something with malicious intent because I'm so bitter about my ex to the point where I hate them and I want them to pay, that will create negative karma for me. Even though nothing might happen to them, at least in the next little while, that spirit could potentially destroy me. So, when I'm holding the spirit of malicious intent, even though I'm not acting on it, I'm still broadcasting. It's going out into the Universe.

Remember, the Karmic Law of Return which says whatever we send out has got to come back. If you want to see somebody hurt, or pay, or be punished, then you're still sending. And, if that energy is intense and focused enough, all that upset energy inside of you is now being sent. Even though you haven't said a word, it can still create negative karma for you.

When you perceive that someone has wronged you, you might visualize or fantasize, thinking: "This person sucks! I'll let them have it in my mind. I'm going to think about all the different ways I can make them pay."

When we take something out of balance, it immediately causes the creation of karma.

That's holding negative energy in place, and even though you think it is secret and therefore safe, you are governed by this law which clearly says that whatever you put out into the Universe, whether you're con-scious or unconscious, must return back to you. Now it might not be right away, but it's got to come back because clearly, you're not learning. So, it has to come back as a way to teach you—to show you that this whole thing is coming from you.

Very seldom does this come back to the sender in the same form, but it'll come back with double the intensity. When it's time for it to boomerang back, it's going to be difficult for them to actually see it coming because they're not going to recognize it until it strikes. Whether the sender was conscious or unconscious, it doesn't matter. They're sending, even though they haven't said a word—even though they haven't picked up the telephone. That's the piece that people often don't understand.

Then they wonder why, all of a sudden, they get struck with something out of the blue. They're not able to pinpoint it or trace it back. But, for the last, let's say, 128 days, they have been sending out negative energy because of their bitterness, resentment, and hatred—feeling like this person wronged them somehow, which was being used as a way to justify what they're sending out. And that's where this consequence comes from.

When we live that way, we are asleep and ignorant of the consequences of our actions because what we don't realize, when we're so busy inwardly cursing another person, is that we're the ones who end up paying. Our dear friend, the great Wayne Dyer said it best in this quote, *"How people treat you is their karma; how you react is yours."*

We've already paid once in the experience we had with this person, and now we're just setting it up to continue. This is one of the ways in which we create personal karma.

IMPERSONAL KARMA

Another type of karma that is really misunderstood is what's known as impersonal karma. Impersonal karma is very different than personal karma. Carl Jung was one of the first people in the last hundred years who wrote about this, and back then, people criticized him because nobody understood it. When people don't understand something, they get really afraid and then attack to protect themselves. That's why educating ourselves is so important—especially in today's time. We as a race are more ready than ever before for higher education, and we need to immerse ourselves in it on purpose on a regular basis.

Carl Jung proposed that karma impersonally recreates itself by the impersonal actions of an impersonal Universe. What he meant by "impersonal actions of an impersonal Universe" were the acts of God. This would include hurricanes, tornadoes, and earthquakes. This also extends to cultural and economic factors, such as how the economy is doing and its effect on you. You didn't do anything to create it, but you're now impacted by the impersonal effect of the economy going through its next cleanse.

It's the spirit in which we do things that also causes negative or positive karma.

You can receive messages from those who have the ability to pick up information on the future, and if you take it seriously, then what's coming doesn't have to affect you at all. Or you might get a dream one night that warns you something is coming. It's your soul, your Higher Self, coming through and giving you a warning. You might completely discard it, or you might start preparing so you don't have to be affected by the impersonal karma.

After the crash of 2008, there were millionaires and billionaires who committed suicide. Would you do something like that if you had a billion dollars, and you happened to lose $250 million of it? Say you've now got $750 million—would you end your life? That's impersonal karma. In other words, the crash was being caused by something outside of them and had nothing to do with them, but the impersonal karma came in, and they took it personally. And then, they potentially created more karma for themselves by committing suicide. That was their personal choice. They reacted to something that somebody else was causing and then personalized it. That's another way impersonal karma shows up.

IMPERSONAL KARMA THROUGH THE NEEDY SELF

The most common way, and probably the most destructive way, that impersonal karma shows up is through your needy self. Let's say you have a strong need for attention, and you just can't get enough. Your husband or wife can't give you enough, or maybe they're not giving you any attention at all. You're just not getting it from anywhere. So, then you go out and flirt with somebody else because you're now desperate for attention.

Or let's say maybe you get really sick. Some people can literally make themselves physically ill because they know that when they do, suddenly, their family comes over or writes get well cards and sends flowers. So, they get the message—just get sick, and you'll get all kinds of attention.

If you have a strong need for attention, you'll take that need and hook it into someone else's psyche. Now you'll likely do this more unconsciously than consciously, until, of course, you become fully conscious of what you are doing. Whether at a conscious or an unconscious level, you are creating impersonal karma by doing this because the moment you do it, you're going to be affected by someone else's karma.

Now consider for a moment that you have this strong need for attention and there's nobody who can give you the amount of attention you so desperately need. So, now you take that need—and, once again, you might be unconscious while you're doing this—and you plug it into your next date or the person you're flirting with. Once it gets plugged in, from that point on, you start to take on their karma, which you become affected by. When that happens, the ego now gets what it wants; which is for this to be a big distraction—and more specifically, a distraction from the healing and resolving of your own personal karma.

You could hook this needy energy into whomever. It could be one of your kids, your parents, your next-door neighbor, one of your coworkers, or one of your clients. And, from that point on from the hooking in, you're now at the effect of an aspect of their karma. You've literally plugged into their psyche.

If they're creating more of their own karma, the act of them creating it is going to affect you. You're not going to take on all of their karma, but it will have an effect on the choices you make and how you show up in life. It could affect how you are with your body, with your finances, with your business, or with your career. The longer you stay hooked in, the deeper, greater, and more intense the effect is going to be.

Once again, while this is all going on, from the ego's perspective, it's one big distraction. This keeps you from connecting with your own personal karma and resolving it. And in this process, once it starts affecting you, playing with your head, and creating havoc with your energy field—next thing you know, you're doing things that you wouldn't normally do at all. You're literally out of whack due to the person you've plugged into and possibly one of their karmic lines.

In this case, you want to put an end to this because this is the part that's not serving you. It's actually keeping things messy, heavy, and extra dense because ultimately, this is not your karma. This impersonal karma stops us from stepping into resolving our own karma.

We need to recognize that this type of situation is detrimental because it's affecting us to the point where we can't be who we truly are. We can't step into our own power. It weakens us and keeps us from our own truth. It can literally make us become somebody that we're not even intended to become. That can be one of the effects of impersonal karma.

Your karma has your name written all over it. And the only one that can ultimately delete your name from it is you.

Many people in the Western part of the world do this every single day. They're hooking into others, and their needy energy is running the show. They often hook into people who don't even know they have personal karma, or, if they do know, they're resisting it like the plague when it comes to resolving it.

Some hook into other people who are in their process of creating even more karma on top of the karma they were born with. So that means when we hook into someone like this, the effect is going to become even greater. This weakens us, lowers our self-esteem, and causes us to have all kinds of negative thoughts that aren't even our own.

This is a real tricky situation, partly because we haven't been educated about it yet. In order to reroute this dynamic of hooking into others, you've got to get into the captain's chair of your own ship and learn to recognize where you're hooked in.

Let's go back to the example that I gave with the economy. When there's an economic crash, the wealth transfers by billions of dollars in a matter of probably twelve to eighteen months. Most people are so hooked into the economy that it's scary. And when the economy falls, you see how it affects them. Those who are hooked in, which is the majority of people, might get wiped out. Some will even commit suicide. On the other hand, the people who are not hooked into the economy with their needy energy are simply not as affected by it when it's in the process of going through its own economic cleanse. So, you've got to recognize what it is that you're hooked into.

When people are hooked into needy energy, they can take on the impersonal karma of geological events like the weather. When rough weather happens, they can't even listen to their Higher Self. Their Higher Self sends them a message, "You need to get out of town this weekend." Their Higher Self already knows a fire's coming. When the fire shows up, their Higher Self is not shocked by it at all. Their angels are not surprised. Their guides are not caught off guard because they already knew at least two or three days before when it's going to strike in linear time. So, you can be assured that their Higher Self is prompting them to do something to get out of harm's way. But they can't hear it.

Maybe they're so busy numbing themselves out that they're not paying attention. If they were paying attention and were not hooked into some needy dynamic—if danger was coming into their community—then they might say something like, "You know what? Why don't we go to Grandma's this weekend?" They'd just get a sense, and they'd follow it. Then, suddenly, they'd be out of harm's way, but without all the stress and anxiety. They didn't wait until the very last minute, when everybody else started to panic. When people get scared, that's when they can step on and hurt other people.

> If your ego's got you tricked, then it's creating a distraction from you clearing up your own personal karma.

Another example of impersonal karma in the world is politics. Let's say our politics are now dividing us as a people. The byproduct of this type of division is that people are willing to physically hurt other people or even kill them. Now when this sort of thing is happening, at some point, it usually gets much louder because the people themselves are so hooked into one side or the other. And, as always, when you're hooked into one side, that means the other side is wrong—and now you're in for the ride of your life. It might literally wipe you out. You might find yourself in a situation where something terrible happens because you're in this dynamic. Whether we like it or not, when this division is occurring, we as a people are going to play this thing out—and while we're playing it out, we might create more karma. The question here is—will it be negative or positive karma?

That's what happens when we do the division thing, where only one side has all the answers, and they believe the other side is really stupid. It's like in religion when people say, "My religion has all the answers. I'm the one who's got the ticket to paradise. You don't." And so, for those of you who have a political interest, you want to be very mindful of whether or not you're hooked in. If you are hooked in, then you're going to be a part of that dynamic, which means you're going to be at the effect of that impersonal karma. And that might be the perfect thing for your ego because if your ego's got you tricked, then it's creating a distraction from you clearing up your own personal karma.

To become less affected by impersonal karma, first you've got to identify where you're hooked in, and then you've got to learn how to pull back the hooks and place them where they belong. Second, once you get on the path to dismantling your own personal karma, then, at some point, you're going to have to pull all these lines back in—all this needy energy that you have hooked into your ex-husband, your ex-wife, your kids, your mom, your dad, your brother, your sister, or whoever it might be.

As you become the real deal along your own pathway of resolving and healing the personal karma that you were born with, impersonal karma is no longer a big deal because now you're focusing on what you're really to be focused on. And, what happens when you do the right thing? You are graced by the Divine and even less impacted by impersonal karmic situations.

PEOPLE GETTING LOST IN IMPERSONAL KARMA

People often get lost and swallowed up in impersonal karma. They can become incredibly confused because they're living at the effect of something else outside of themselves. The most difficult part to understand, or to really connect with, is the part of them that's hooked into it. That's all underground stuff. It's all unconscious stuff driving the choice to hook into this or that.

Of course, once someone is hooked in from that needy perspective, it's going to have an effect on their psyche. Although they're not directly taking on the karma, it affects them now in terms of who they become, what they become, and the choices they make. It can directly affect the thoughts that show up on the screen of their mind and the behaviors they take on.

Sometimes people are addicted to certain things, and it's not even their own addiction. But they can't get rid of it because they're not identifying it properly. They think it's theirs, but it's really the effect of someone or something they've hooked into because they were so needy for something. Maybe their need for love was so great, or their need for approval was so strong.

It's like when someone goes and makes a deal with the devil—or the mafia or the illuminati. They've got to have a weakness to do that. If they're super strong, they're not making a deal like that. They've got to have something going on inside of them that they haven't dealt with yet. They've got to be disconnected from themselves in order to go make those kinds of deals.

That's why those groups attempt to get to us before we get to the clearing of all our karma. If you clear out all your karma, you're back in your strength and in your centered self, which means you're no longer going to be tempted.

When you get to this place of centeredness, you're in a very fortunate place. You're now literally living your life of your own volition, no longer at the effect of anyone or anything outside of yourself. That's you now being a true sovereign being, living the life that you truly are meant to live—but you've got to reclaim that. You've got to learn how to bring it to you.

A significant piece of this is getting in touch with your needy energy—and more specifically, the needy energy you've got hooked into whoever or whatever. So, you're going to need to be motivated, diligent, and mindful of your own needy energy—and more specifically, who or what you have your needy energy hooked into.

> Sometimes people are addicted to certain things, and it's not even their own addiction.

Here's another example. It would do people good to think twice about having sex with someone they've just met. They might try and justify it by saying, "I haven't done this for a long time, and I've been working so hard for the last year. I just need to have some fun. It's going to feel amazing." But it would be good for them if they asked themselves, "Might this be a way to get hooked into that impersonal karma business? Hmm. Do I want to risk it?" I'm not saying you shouldn't have sex, but whether you want to have sex on the first meeting or on the fourteenth meeting, that's a personal choice, and all actions have positive and negative consequences. As such, behave responsibly and mindfully when it comes to relationships with potential karmic consequences.

IMPERSONAL KARMA WITH PARENTS AND CHILDREN

Let's say someone were to dial into a radio station, and whatever was playing on that radio station gets broadcast to another person's radio. If you think about the song and the broadcast as a person's thoughts, this is how impersonal karma can influence that particular individual.

This can happen when children receive broadcasts from their parents. The parents' issues can be part of one of their own karmic lines. When you're the child of this person, and this broadcast exchange makes a strong impression upon your psyche, this is often because your need for their approval is great, or you have some other kind of need hooked into them.

Because the person affected was a child at the time, they were influenced by what was going on with their parent. So, the thoughts that the parent was having became the child's thoughts—even though they never were the child's thoughts in the first place.

Again, it all comes back to that deep-seated need for a parent's approval. That keeps the underground cable, if you will, alive and well. What that means is whenever we desperately need approval from someone, we become hooked into them—and now we're affected by whatever they have going on. The parent most likely didn't even know what their personal karma was, so they ended up on a mission to create even more karma. The child couldn't get their parent's approval, so their need for approval became stronger. This caused more of a transference. The child had an open inner channel that was literally being flooded with somebody else's thoughts. And, later on, they become bombarded with negativity, but only 60 percent of it actually belongs to them. The other 40 percent was never theirs in the first place.

ANCESTRAL KARMA

Another type of karma is ancestral karma. An example of this would be the Kennedys. They're literally part of a soul group, and they haven't yet gotten to the point where they've freed themselves from that group. What we are aware of publicly is that the head patriarch of the family, Joseph P. Kennedy, Sr., the father of John F., Ted, and Robert Kennedy, made his fortune playing fast and loose with the pre-1929 stock market crash by teetering the line of various legal and illegal trades and by being the first of the Kennedys to hold public office. He was a powerful influence behind the scenes in a turbulent time in history.

So, when you consider the negative effect many events of that time had on so many people—as in those who became alcoholics or committed some act of murder under the influence, or took their life during the stock market crash—on one level, it looks like the Kennedys became a wealthy family. But at some point, we must take a look at the effect the patriarch's actions had on people's lives.

The karma runs so deep that it has affected each of the family members—to the point that one family member stated it was like they were cursed. Just take a look at all of the deaths and how many of the Kennedys died. Some would say that the great, great grandfather in the lineage affected the entire family line to the point that they're still having consequences from it to this day.

The Law of Karmic Return says it's going to bounce back. So if we're building a business that's going to affect the many, and if the way in which we are affecting the many has a greater positive effect, making a more significant lasting, difference in the lives of the many. Then it will come back to us at some point along our timeline in some form of a blessing, as in a positive consequence or positive karma. If, on the other hand, we've been building a business in an industry or in a profession where a lot of people are getting hurt or this is causing harm, then at some point that will return to us in the form of negative karma.

One of the key ways to free yourself from ancestral karma is to become responsible for your own personal karma and get it resolved. That's where your freedom lies. That's your liberation. That's where you discover what the right thing is for you to be doing—the right path that you're to be walking on.

PARENTS THAT TAKE ON THEIR CHILDREN'S KARMA

Here is another scenario that can play out between parent and child in relation to karma. Parents can get caught up in trying to take on their children's karma without being consciously aware that this is what they are doing.

An example of this is when a parent has a deep-seated need to win their child's approval. Talk about creating a life of complexity—getting hooked into their kid's karma and attempting to take it on. They think they're the hero. They think they can shield their kid from anything. Look at the mother of the fourteen-year-old daughter on the *Dr. Phil* show. She was almost too weak to let Dr. Phil go through with the plan; you could see that she was about to cave. She managed to go through with it, though her daughter was doing her best to manipulate the situation. Had the mother intervened to stop Dr. Phil from helping her daughter, that could have created even more karma for her, the mother. Are you able to see this?

A parent in this situation hasn't dealt with their own karma yet, but confidence sometimes comes with ignorance. They're unconscious to what they're really doing. And so, they might need more pain before they're willing to become conscious. Their kids might need more pain, too, but the parent is literally getting in between their kids and their own pain. Can a parent even process their children's pain? Can they resolve their pain? Can they really resolve their children's karma for them? No—they cannot.

But they'll try to take it on because they're possibly so needy for their children's approval, attention, or love. They're scared that they're going to lose something that their children are "giving" them. And that's what they're having a difficult time dealing with. So now, they'll do an exchange.

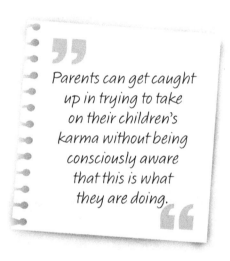

> Parents can get caught up in trying to take on their children's karma without being consciously aware that this is what they are doing.

They'll do the big negotiation at the level of unconscious, which might sound like, "All right—here's the deal, son or daughter—just keep on approving of me, keep on giving me attention, keep on loving me. Make sure you make me feel really secure in this role that I have with you, and in exchange, I'll take on all of your stuff. Now, if I'm really to be honest, I must tell you that I don't even have the power to clear up your stuff, but I'll take it on anyway. I'll shield you from it. I might even literally hurt myself in the process. I'll weigh myself down to where I might literally drown, but I'll take it on as long as you assure me that you'll always love and approve of me."

If this parent had any idea what was actually going on inside their child, they would support their child in working through their own consequences, without trying to take those consequences on for them. The child needs to embrace and process through their own consequences. They need to resolve their own karma at some point along their life's journey. By letting and encouraging our children to work through their own consequences, we as parents are dramatically increasing the odds that they will go on to ultimately resolve all of their karma that they at soul level took on for this lifetime experience.

But often, as parents, we get in the middle of it and try to protect them from that—not because that's the right thing to do but because the parent has one of their own needs hooked into the psyche of their child. Imagine that.

And, if the parents continue choosing to do this, they're the ones who are going to pay the piper. They're interfering with the process of the child as a soul. The child at soul level came here to accomplish certain things, and the parent is elongating that process for them. There will be karma for that parent because they're trying desperately to be the General Manager of the Universe.

Our role as parents is to be our children's care provider. And, when it's time for them to learn their lessons, one of our roles is to let them learn those lessons. Remember, they, too, have a soul—they are a soul. And quite frankly, their soul might be wiser than ours. How about that?

But, of course, many of us, at least in the past, couldn't see it that way. We were seeing it through the eyes of the ego. We were seeing it through the eyes of the smaller perspective. And, for those who don't have offspring, you might have a girlfriend, boyfriend, husband, wife, or a best friend that you've been doing the exact same thing with. Or maybe you have a career where you have clients, or you're working with co-workers, and perhaps you've been playing this out with them as well.

Where are you at with creating more karma? Are you done yet? Or do you need another month or another year to figure this thing out? Are you willing and ready to make the choice to get off the wheel of karma? Or is it right for you to go out and create more karma for yourself?

I'm not here to make you do anything, mind you. I'm just here to bring this to your awareness so you can choose what's right for you. Perhaps it is right for you to buckle down and get focused with a clear intent to clean up your personal karma. That's the big decision we all eventually choose to make, for that choice is a part of our Greater Destiny.

TRAUMA AND SHAME

When it comes to trauma, whether in this life or a previous life, if someone hasn't cleared it yet, that means they're likely going to be dealing with shame. This is especially true for someone that has been sexually traumatized, whether in this lifetime or a previous one—or both. When they enter this life, if it's a carryover coming in through a karmic line, they're going to more than likely end up with some sexual trauma or extreme emotional trauma early in this life, most likely by the age of twelve.

Those who are dealing with shame can be pretty much assured that somewhere in their past timeline is some sexual or emotional trauma, whether they're able to remember it yet or not. It doesn't necessarily mean that they were molested on a physical level. There are various ways in which a person can be molested or violated, including mental and emotional torture. But these acts always produce an emotion of shame. So, as a karmic tone or a karmic line, when this person comes into this life, there's going to be something that goes on in their upbringing where shame is involved. Perhaps a parent is always feeling ashamed of them, or the child is constantly feeling ashamed of something that is going on within the family, or possibly even feeling ashamed of the family.

Shame as an emotion carries a very low vibrational frequency. It's designed to literally pull or push you down to the depths, like being sunk to the bottom of the ocean floor, or being pulled into the depths of quicksand, slowly, like something that's moving through molasses. It moves so slowly that you can't even see it moving. It's a heavy, dense emotion, and sometimes it will manifest in your physical body, such as getting a sexual disease.

It'll show itself somehow because at soul level you are destined to come in contact with this karmic line, which means you are bound to experience it at some point in your life's journey. Carl Jung said, "Until you make the unconscious conscious, it will direct your life and you will call it fate." Now here's how it might look when the unconscious is directing your life and you're calling it fate: You'll blame it on destiny. You'll blame it on somebody or something else. And it won't even dawn on you that this whole thing is coming from inside of you. In other words, you'll potentially miss the mark and therefore, you'll create more karma. And you could even set up the next energetic tone for the next lifetime. Or you'll start to consciously connect with it, no matter how uncomfortable it is, with the intent being to ultimately learn how to clear this—and how to resolve it at soul level.

What might it be like for you to come to a place and time along your life's journey where you are totally resolved of all karma from your past actions in this life as well as in previous lives? What might happen next for you? No really, imagine right now what might happen next. How might the resolving of all your karma impact the way you live your life?

Your light would most certainly become stronger, bigger, and brighter as you become more of who you truly are. And, after all, isn't that what this is really all about?

KARMIC LESSONS

The next karmic piece is karmic lessons. They're encoded by the soul, which means the soul has chosen this in advance of your first breath. It also means this could be a carryover from literally eight lifetimes ago.

Karmic lessons are going to be the long-standing ones that go on and on.

Say this is the case and you have a lesson from eight lifetimes ago. For the last seven lifetimes, you haven't been completing this lesson, so the soul pulls it back out of the archive and says, "Okay—this is the lesson that we didn't take seriously seven lifetimes ago. This lifetime we're now going to get it." This lesson has been around for a while. You've struggled with this one before. This is not your first rodeo, even though you might think it is because you might still believe this is your only life.

Karmic lessons are going to be the long-standing ones that go on and on. Sometimes, you'll feel like you're in Groundhog Day. Remember, your character, resolve, commitment, faith, and integrity are being tested when your soul has signed up for a karmic lesson.

Once again, there's no timeline on karmic lessons. Let's say you came in with four karmic lessons. You could literally be mastering one of them in a year or you could find yourself struggling with one lesson for your entire life. If you have not mastered a karmic lesson, it's going to somehow find its way right back to you where you'll be forced to look at it. Then, you might get frustrated and choose to go and pull up one of your old addictive behaviors and numb out for a couple of months. You might say, "I just can't stand working on this thing. This is ridiculous. I've been at this for three and a half years now." That's the karmic lesson. You're always at choice when it comes to resolving it and as to whether you're going to do so in this lifetime.

As I've often said when I'm teaching about karma in one of my classes, "Your karma has your name written all over it. And the only one that can ultimately delete your name from it is you."

THE KARMIC WALL OF RESISTANCE

You usually have to be in the older soul category in order to have a karmic wall. These are really tough. A karmic wall energetically is like a fortress that you've got to climb over. It might be equivalent to climbing Mount Everest. It goes on and on. It has the heaviness of more than one karmic lesson or karmic pattern.

A person who has a karmic wall is usually somebody who has a handful of karmic lessons that they've resisted for lifetimes. In that, they've got at least two or three karmic patterns, meaning two or three karmic lines, that they've also resisted for lifetimes—and now the soul has said, "That's it." So what happens then is all of that becomes the wall.

In my book *Being Called to Change*, I refer to this as the "stripping." This is where the individual might choose to cower down and say, "I'm not doing this anymore," and check out of this lifetime.

The karmic wall is not destined for everybody, but it is destined for those who need it the most. This also depends on the age of the soul. If you've been around for a while—and more specifically, you have been resisting a lot, not just in this life but for a number of lifetimes—then your karmic lessons and karmic patterns that you've been resisting for let's say, the last four lifetimes, come together and create a cluster.

The karmic wall is not destined for everybody, but it is destined for those who need it the most.

So now, the karmic lessons and patterns are no longer individuated. They combine and produce a wall. This wall can give you the feeling you're never going to be able to do this. It's the consequential effect of the amount of resistance you as a soul have been in for the last four lifetimes.

You're going to have to break this wall down in order to ultimately clear it. And if you're feeling heavy and discouraged thinking that you have a karmic wall that is going to be too much to face, then stop now and take a breath.

Know this—you can break through a karmic wall. The first and most significant piece would be to fully relax and surrender to it. The idea or strategy here would be to let go of all that built-up resistance, little by little, slowly but surely, regardless of how long it will take. Use your transformational modality or the TransCovery Process® to aid you in this work.

A mantra that most of my students adopt over time is, "I relax. I surrender. And I let go." This would be a good mantra to adopt for anyone reading this, whether you have a karmic wall or not. Surrendering is the key to making ultimate progress in this work.

Remember, whatever we choose consciously or unconsciously will be followed by an effect. When someone chooses to resist and then makes another choice to dig their heels in and resist again and again, what kind of effect is that going to produce on their energy level? It's going to zap it. They're going to get exhausted.

One of the reasons people struggle with staying awake is because they've been in so much resistance that their body is exhausted. And they're exhausted because when they're in resistance, they cannot accomplish anything. They can't move the needle forward.

Resistance is also a choice that we all get to be responsible for. Resistance is like an onion—it's layered. Some people have been resisting for so long that they've created two or three onions in their subconscious. You've got to let go and peel away all of the layers of resistance that you've created inside your field.

It just doesn't dissolve because, "Hey! I had an epiphany when I read this Dale Halaway book! I'm so glad I read it. I learned that I've been resisting all my life. That's it! As of this day, I'm going to have a drink to salute that there's no more resistance. I'm now free." Wouldn't that be great if we could do this bypass? But no, that's not the way this works—you're not free. Not yet anyway. But you could be.

If you have now decided that you're not going to resist anymore, be aware that you're still going to be challenged because your whole way of living has been to resist for so long. This is going to be a process to change, but a worthy one.

Anything that frightens you—anything that activates you or triggers you—puts you in resistance right away. You go into tight or tense energy. It's not an easy fix because you've been resisting for however long you've been doing it for, and it's built up its own energy and created its own karmic wall.

The karmic wall causes you to avoid the mastering of your karmic lessons, the dismantling of your karmic patterns, and the resolving of your personal karma. Choosing to resist over a long period of time creates its own consequential effect. In this case, the consequential effect is the karmic wall. If you have one of these to deal with, that means you have become a master in the most negative of ways. You've gotten so good at resisting that you don't even know when you're resisting anymore. Heck, you could be resisting your own resistance!

One of the symptoms of somebody dealing with a karmic wall is that they normally find their life being really hard. You might hear them say, "Why does life have to be this hard? What did I do that was so awful to deserve such a hard life?"

Another symptom or gauge of someone who has a karmic wall is there's a heaviness in their life that doesn't seem to go away no matter what they do. The heaviness could be depression—the person lives in some kind of a depressed state for a good amount of time. Maybe this person goes and seeks help. They get counseling, coaching, or psychotherapy.

Perhaps they've even gone to a psychiatrist and are on some kind of an antidepressant and yet they find themselves still dealing with this heaviness. Like this heaviness doesn't seem to go away.

If you've got a heavy karmic load, declare it out loud. Surrender it to the Universe. Part of clearing this is to choose to remain conscious when actually experiencing the heaviness because it's only in the conscious experience of this heaviness that a person will learn what it is they need to be learning.

> I relax.
> I surrender.
> And I let go.

If I was the bully at school, for example, and I bullied X number of kids, and I never learned anything about the bullying that I was engaged in, then later on in life, I will likely find myself being bullied. Maybe not physically; maybe I'm now being bullied financially or legally. Maybe I'm being bullied at work by something that's going on in my organization.

One of the ways that helps us a lot in resolving this type of heavy karma is when we find ourselves on the receiving end of what we initially put out into the world that caused the karma in the first place.

If I end up bullying a lot of people, and if I'm not able to learn whatever the lesson might be around me hurting someone else, that's what turns into heavy karma. Which means now pretty much the only way I'm going to learn from this experience is to be put into the receiver's position. In other words, someone who has this heavy karma is now being forced (on purpose) to endure what they've done to others. They're now having an experience from a completely different perspective. The idea here would be that we might actually learn our lessons and learn them well as a result of experiencing what it would be like to be on the receiving end.

Remember that which we send out comes back to us. A karmic wall gets created because we have not been learning—and we have not been learning for a while. And while we've been in this place of not learning, we've likely been putting out a certain kind of harmful energy that we're not even aware of, and in doing so, we've been hurting other people and ourselves. Because as always, if I'm hurting other people on some level, I'm hurting myself as well. I'm simply unaware while I'm doing it. But the longer I do it, the more likely it is that I'll create a karmic wall. Then, it becomes a question of how long I will do it for, which then determines how thick the karmic wall is going to be.

"Karma is a bitch." We've all heard or seen this saying before, right? But what you might not know, at least just yet, is that, to the contrary, karma is not the bitch, but rather it's the teacher. It only becomes the bitch when we're in resistance or avoidance of it. In other words, karma is not here to curse or punish us. Its essence is also to keep us from our deeper soul's purpose until we learn the lessons that we really are to be learning. You see, in truth, its essence is to help us heal, grow, and evolve.

When you're dealing with karma and/or a consequence from a previous choice or choices, the question becomes: Can I give myself permission to get better at embracing this consequential effect or karma that I'm

311

now encountering? Can I get better at embracing this struggle that I'm currently going through? Can I get better at embracing this depression that I'm feeling versus always fighting the depression?

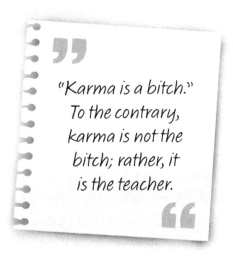

"Karma is a bitch." To the contrary, karma is not the bitch; rather, it is the teacher.

If this is you, and if you can get better at embracing, this is where you'll dramatically increase the odds that those lessons you really are to be learning will become more clear to you.

KARMA RELATED TO ENVIRONMENTAL IMPACT

A student asked me once about environmental impact as it relates to impersonal karma. They asked, "We use a lot of fossil fuels and build a lot of roads in order to get to the places that we go. I'm benefitting from the use of those things, and yet, they have a huge impact on animals and the environment. Now that I'm seeing and understanding those impacts, am I encountering karma from that?"

The answer is "yes and no" because it really comes down to a personal choice. It is impersonal karma, meaning it is beyond our control; it's something going on that you have nothing to do with.

Impersonal karma can still affect us, but you always have a choice. You can choose to let that impersonal karma affect you, or you can choose to not let it affect you. If you choose to let it affect you, you might be dropping some of that unconsciousness; maybe there really is something that you could be doing to help. Or you could choose to not let it affect you but to remain aware of it. You could say, "This is my little piece of the puzzle, and I'm going to start doing something that contributes to that larger overall movement." You could start recycling or stop buying plastics—choose to be responsible in that way.

When you are aware of them, even those little things are now contributing to a larger movement in helping to move the world in a healthier direction. Our economy and the powers-that-be literally prey on supply and demand. What we've forgotten as a people is that we do have power—power in numbers. When enough of us get together in a unified field of consciousness and create a movement from this place of unity, it can impact the powers-that-be more than anything else because it changes the flow of supply and demand.

We've all heard it said that united we stand, divided we fall. And even though we've heard that, we might not yet know how powerful this really is for us to come together in a unified way. And perhaps this might be one of our key lessons as a people that we are to be learning.

What is happening right now, on an unconscious level, is that everybody is looking at themselves and making those little minor choices that will help to force a new flow of supply and demand. More than ever before, people are looking to make those little choices, like using recyclable products or cutting down on their paper usage or on the unnecessary wasting of water. It's a great illustration of the fact that there are two levels of choice making. There's the conscious choice that you're knowingly making, and then there's the unconscious choice, where you might not even be aware of what you're doing—like wasting water.

Or another example would be smoking cigarettes. When lit, cigarettes produce dangerous, poisonous gasses, and if we're not aware of that fact, then that means those poisons are going into our system. But as soon as we become acutely aware of that fact, we start to make different choices. We say, "You know what? I don't want to contribute to smoking anymore. First of all, for myself and the state of my own health and well-being. But secondly, because I don't want the possible karma." Once we realize that we're blowing out all this secondhand smoke, and that our kids or our friends or our loved ones are breathing it in, it hits us: we're contributing. We're letting all that stuff flow through our system, and we're responsible for it. We're creating negative karma for ourselves. We may not have realized it consciously, but unconsciously, those cigarettes we've been smoking may have been contributing to someone else's demise.

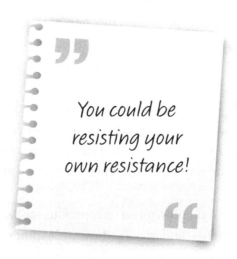

You could be
resisting your
own resistance!

Of course, once we become conscious of this, we can recognize that our decision doesn't feel right, so now we become more willing to change it. We step in and do what we need to do to let that habit go. Once we recognize the karma that we've been creating for ourselves, we start becoming more responsible in that way. As more of us on this planet continue to make these kinds of choices, we're going to create a strong and powerful movement.

In order for anything to collapse, it's going to require more people to really wake up. Quite frankly, more people are going to need to wake up and step up so that they can become more acutely aware of their own choices. When freedom of choice was originally spoken about, it was with the intention of empowering the people. It was to let the people know the truth: that if you don't get things right in this life, you are going to get a second chance. At some point, you're going to get it right so that you can become a truly empowered being on this planet—and then you would do your *real* work. You would move into complete alignment with your deeper soul's purpose and Greater Destiny.

How do we get back to that? How do we get back to this concept of freedom of choice as it was originally spoken about? We change this by getting more people involved in their own transformations. More specifically, we change this by getting more people involved who are willing to rise up into their Greater Destiny and develop an acute awareness of their choices.

As far as environmental impact goes, reducing our carbon footprint is something we certainly can do that will help Mother Earth. Maybe this conscious awareness as it relates to karma has got you thinking about what you could do differently to help the planet in this way. It certainly is good food for thought. And if you find yourself thinking about this after setting this book down, then maybe you will want to make some different choices and personally up-level this area in your own life. Or share this with others to get that movement going that can create bigger changes on a community or global level. And in the process, you'd be contributing to your positive karma and adding to your cosmic bank account.

POSITIVE KARMA AND YOUR COSMIC BANK ACCOUNT

We each have a cosmic bank account or a spiritual trust account—also known as a divine trust account. And this trust account was set up prior to us taking our first breath in this life. It is similar to a trust account that is set up by a parent for their child.

Parents, especially wealthier parents, will take a portion of their money and assets and put them into a trust. And that trust account belongs to one or a couple of their children, but the kids have no access to that account until a certain point in time or age.

Once they reach that time or age, they get access, maybe only for college or for university tuition. And then again, at a later age, they get another lot of money to support them along their journey. They might even get allotments periodically thereafter. In that trust account, there is something of a reward. There's a form of support that has been created specifically for that person.

Well, the same thing happens here, spiritually speaking.

But just like a trust account here in the physical, that spiritual trust account also has guidelines that have been set up. And these are the types of guidelines that cannot be violated, banned, manipulated, or changed. Just like the executor of a physical trust account is the one who calls the shots, your spirit in partnership with the Divine is in full control of your cosmic trust account.

Instead of money being released, in a spiritual trust, our positive karma that has already been created is released. It's sitting there in this metaphoric bank account as a positive balance, and once we come to a point in time along our journey, when we've risen up to a certain place, which will be unique to each of us, then part of that trust account gets released.

The part that gets released now becomes a reward, an extra support, or extra grace. It can be such a beautiful thing because when that reward, grace, or support is released, you'll know it—because it comes up and lands on your doorstep naturally and organically.

Sometimes we look at people who seem to have it easier than we have in certain parts of their journey, and we say things like, "Well, you know, he's lucky, she's lucky. I guess they were in the right place at the right time doing the right thing." Well, some of that is true. The other part is that the luck that we perceive them experiencing could very well be a part of their divine trust account that has been opened up for them to access.

Maybe they just learned they won the lottery or that some inheritance came to them from someone way back long ago in their past. Maybe it was a family member or simply a friend of the family. In other words, they did not see it coming. Maybe they're called into the office with the CEO of their company, and they learn that they're about to be promoted or they're about to get a nice raise or bonus.

It could be they've now been single for a while; they've done a lot of work on transforming themselves, and they walk into a restaurant, social gathering, or someone else's business and next thing you know, they end up meeting the love of their life.

They didn't see it coming. It happens completely unexpectedly. And yet when it happens, they know something spiritually significant, something stunningly beautiful, just happened for them. That's the reward. It's that extra support. It's that extra grace that just shows up. It's coming from this trust account.

The beauty here is that whatever our trust account currently holds, it is always in relationship or partnership with the Divine. In other words, it's the Divine that basically gives the green light when the timing becomes right for whatever the reward is to be bestowed upon us.

Many of us have already had an experience like this, where something of this magnitude has shown up in our lives. It has physically manifested, and we can pinpoint it because we can see that it had these elements of the unexpected in the way in which it showed up.

And then, of course, what we choose to do with that now also becomes our choice. As in, do we choose to get excited about this? Do we choose to be grateful for this? Do we choose to celebrate this? Do we choose to fully embrace this?

Or do we choose to subconsciously sabotage this? Or maybe start to doubt ourselves? Or become stressed with this? Do we possibly even take it for granted or squander it because maybe we don't feel deserving of it? Do we choose to discard it or put it down? These too are choices. And we are completely at choice (consciously or unconsciously) with what we do next.

Should I choose to push this away, as in attempt to sabotage it, that too becomes another experience for me. Because now, as I'm choosing to do that, there's going to be a consequence. It's going to throw a monkey wrench into this blessing, this reward. Just as we've seen, for example, with companies, when they do their year-end conventions, and they recognize their top performers or people that did something significant in their company. These types of people get recognized in front of their peers. This can become a wonderful experience. And yet there are some that will have that experience, and for some reason, they will begin to sabotage it or push it away because they don't feel worthy of that level of recognition. They feel undeserving due to something that hasn't yet been healed or resolved inside of them.

So when this reward comes, how will we choose to be with it?

Let's go back to my earlier example of the parent who leaves a lot of money in a trust account for one of their children or all their children. Let's say something happens to the parent. The parent leaves this plane of existence, and shortly thereafter, the trust account is released to their children.

> Your spirit in partnership with the Divine is in full control of your cosmic trust account.

All of a sudden, their child, who is maybe twenty-four years of age, comes into a lot of money. Maybe they come into a lot of responsibility too—maybe they have to take over the company or all the real estate that's left behind. As is often the case, within months of receiving this inheritance, the heir has now begun the process of sabotaging themselves and/or what they've been given. Suddenly, they're drinking more alcohol, they're partying more, they're spending recklessly, all as a way to push this away.

Now, they might be more unconscious about what they're doing than conscious, but nonetheless, if that's what they're doing, that becomes a choice. They're pushing it away because maybe they don't feel comfortable in their own skin by suddenly having all of this. Or they're overwhelmed with the responsibility that comes with it.

So once again, they start to choose. And every choice must be followed by a positive or negative consequence.

So, as exciting as it sounds to have these types of things come upon us, it's also important to recognize there is tremendous value and real significance for us to be ready to receive it well so we can really embrace it, be responsible for it, celebrate it, and work with it in a way that brings us more joy, a little more peace, and in a way that brings us a little more empowerment.

KARMIC POTENTIAL

You were born with at least one purely positive karmic line. As previously mentioned, that karmic line is made up of a natural higher ability. It's made up of a gift or a talent that you have already earned, achieved, or been gifted from a previous time, based on your choices and actions. Again, you had some kind of remembrance of it in your first years. You weren't shown the whole of it, but you were shown a piece of it in your earlier years. Say you're styling someone's hair and you're doing it almost perfectly—but you're only four years old. Or you are inclined to pick up an instrument—a guitar, a trombone—and you just start playing it almost perfectly. Or you pick up a pad and start drawing—by the time you're done, others that are watching think you've just created a masterpiece. Or you start your own business as an entrepreneur at an early age—and your Kool-Aid stand morphs into a franchise among all your friends...you get the idea.

When you re-discover these talents, gifts, or abilities, you might want to refine them by taking what you've learned or earned to another level. Whether you do that or not is a personal choice. Some people have two, maybe three positive karmic lines, but everybody has at least one. In that karmic line, you either have a gift, a higher ability, and/or a talent. Each soul is going to be unique. Just like the soul chooses to bring forth what the negative karmic line is going to be, the soul also chooses what the positive karmic line coming forth is going to be.

The positive karmic line is a significant part of your karmic potential. This is beyond your higher potential. This has potential that's been destined. It's been written. It's already been scripted by your soul. This is the reward for a life of consistent and disciplined work over a sustained period of time. This is where your dream relationship or partnership could be. As you're clearing and coming to a point of mastery, it's going to start opening up to you again.

One of my positive karmic abilities that came from a karmic line is that I'm a mystic. I didn't know I was a mystic up until only a few years ago. When I lived in Sedona, one of the most world-renowned mystics on the planet and one of the top-level shamanic astrologers lived two doors down from me. When our paths happened to cross, the mystic told me he wanted me to run his entire mystic school as the head instructor. He was just blown away with me and said he had been waiting for me.

Now this caught me by surprise because I didn't even know this about myself yet. It just happened naturally. I didn't take him up on this at the time because even though he could see it in me, I couldn't see it in myself. And I definitely wasn't ready for it yet.

I wasn't searching for my higher abilities, but over time, one by one, they just started coming online. I would simply be doing something with somebody, and there one was. That's because I was resolving my karmic patterns. I had been learning my lessons, and my higher abilities began to surface out of the blue. It wasn't on my day timer. I didn't go to a meeting and say, "Okay, in this meeting, we're going to figure out what Dale's higher abilities are." I'm so done with that figuring-out business. Hopefully, you are too.

Your karmic abilities are already inside you. You've just got to chip away at your karmic lessons. Like the sculptor with the block of ice, your work is chipping away and forming the sculpture that is unique to you. Your work is rresolving your karmic patterns, learning and mastering your karmic lessons. Get that down properly, and your karmic potential—whatever it is—is just going to reveal itself to you naturally.

Whatever our trust account currently holds, it is always in relationship or partnership with the Divine.

You're going to be engaged with someone, probably in the name of service, and you won't even see it coming. Suddenly you'll realize, "What did I just do? Wow! Who the heck am I? This is amazing! What is this? Where did this come from?" Then it will happen again a couple more times, and you'll start to remember. You'll realize, "Oh my gosh—it's been inside me all along. I was born with this and now, forty-eight years later, I'm having a full remembrance of what I was born with that I completely forgot about." That's the beauty of the positive karmic line.

322

As this happens, the karmic potential is really the reward—meaning you have a karmic destiny. You might have a karmic destiny with a person. You might have a karmic destiny with a family. And by the way, the karmic destiny with your family might not be your birth family. You might have a karmic destiny with a dream mate, as in your true beloved—but you don't get her or him until this gets released. That person could even be somebody you know right now. You're struggling through whatever you're struggling with, and then, when you clear all that up, you realize they've been there all along. You couldn't see them before, but now you can.

Whatever it is, your karmic potential is hidden from you on purpose until such time that you prove you're not going to sabotage it. If you are dealing with a karmic wall, then you've got to dissolve it. If you are dealing with karmic lessons, then you've got to master them. If you are under the rule of karmic patterns, then you've got to dismantle them. Do that, and this potential is waiting to reveal itself to you.

You've got to let go of all that no longer serves you and then you grow into your full potential. You've got a bigger potential that lies ahead of you, just waiting to reveal itself.

If there's something going on in your life that you're resisting, and you know you've been resisting it for the last ten years, then that resistance is producing a karmic wall. And by the way, if you're doing that in this life, then you've probably done it in a lifetime before this as well. If that's the case, remember that what you've been given, you can also clear, or you wouldn't have been given it.

Let's remember that if we've created the karmic wall, what that also means is we can dismantle it and we are destined to do so. When it comes to our karmic patterns and karmic lessons, we've been given what we need in order to clear and master them. This is us moving towards achieving self-mastery.

EXERCISES

Write out your responses to the following questions in your notebook.

1. Have you had an experience that led you to believe in past lives? If so, describe it.

2. Have you had a dream that you felt was from a past life? If so, what was it?

3. Has there been a time in your life when you interfered with someone else's karma and ended up taking it on? If so, describe what happened.

4. Has there been a time in your current life that you had karma return to you? On a scale of 1-10, what was the intensity of it? 10 being a lot, 1 being a little. If there was a lesson to learn from it, what would you say it was?

5. How do you go about contributing to impersonal karma that is impacting the environment? As in, do you recycle or do you litter? Do you waste water, and if so, how might you change that?

   If there was something else you could be contributing to in light of helping the environment and Mother Earth, what would that be?

6. Have you had the experience where you clearly received a gift or a blessing from your cosmic bank account or your spiritual trust? If so, what was it? How did it show up in your life? And in what way did it help you?

7. Write on a notecard, "I relax. I surrender. And I let go." Adopt this mantra by posting it in a visible place. Repeat this out loud daily every time you are feeling challenged or resistant. And

when you do this, activate your imagination by seeing and feeling yourself relaxing into whatever it is you might be resisting. Then surrendering to whatever that is you are to be surrendering to. And when ready, take a deep and slow breath, and then on the exhale, repeat out loud, "I let go," while seeing yourself letting go of whatever it is you know in your bones you are to be letting go of.

You can take this exercise a step further by journaling your feelings each time you feel resistant and you repeat the mantra out loud.

CHAPTER 11

UNDERSTANDING THE SOUL

W̶e don't have a soul; we are a soul. We have a body, and in this body we are having a human experience. This chapter is going to take a deeper dive into your understanding of yourself as a soul.

THE KARMIC STATUS OF YOUR SOUL

The karmic status of your soul is a handful of its genuine needs that the soul came in with. Most souls only have up to three genuine needs. Now this is not the same as the needy energy of your ego. This is not like a need for affection that someone hooks into their partner and then, no matter how much affection they get it's never enough. This, rather, is a genuine need of the soul.

For example, you could have a need for freedom. The soul already knows you have a divine birthright of freedom, but it may also know that for the last five lifetimes, you've buried or been resisting your divine birthright—and have avoided it like the plague. So, now the soul has set a status for itself based on a genuine need for freedom. It's what's prompting you, in this case, to move through all these karmic lessons, karmic patterns, and possibly a karmic wall.

Your soul might have a genuine need to experience love. There are people on the planet that your soul is connected with, and your soul is waiting to plan meetings with these other souls. When you come into the presence of these other souls, you are going to be met with a tremendous amount of love because your soul carries the genuine need to experience it. Your soul wants to experience what it's like to fully give and receive love unconditionally.

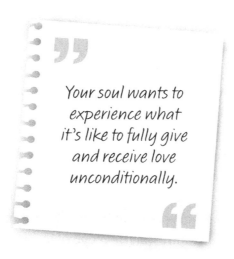

Your soul wants to experience what it's like to fully give and receive love unconditionally.

What happens if you have a karmic lesson around control that you're still in a state of resistance towards? Can you rise to the karmic status of your soul if the karmic lesson or karmic pattern is heavy? How can you do it? You've got to get to the heavy lesson, the karmic lesson, or the karmic pattern. Then, you've got to clear it out.

If your karmic pattern is a pattern of controlling, and your lesson is to learn how to trust and surrender—and you really master that lesson and dismantle that karmic pattern of control—then somewhere in that process, you'll begin to realize and actualize the genuine need of your soul.

If your soul's need is to experience love, and you're working your way out of your karmic lessons and patterns, then, next thing you know, people will start showing up that you just don't have that same level of conflict, confusion, or dysfunction with. You can now get on with the real business at hand and experience love—not hate, division, separation, hardness, cheating, betrayal, nor being taken advantage of.

The reward for rising up to the genuine needs of your soul is the karmic potential. The soul came in with these needs, lessons, and patterns, and the soul waits until we master whatever those lessons or patterns are—at least until we prove that we are well underway—which then begins the revealing of our karmic potential. Once the soul becomes convinced that both feet are in towards the mastery of those lessons, that's when the prompting comes from within, and you'll feel it through a sensation. Something will start to emerge. You'll feel it coming up. You are rising up to the status of your soul.

The genuine needs of your soul will permeate your life. In that process, those who have been manipulating, those who have been taking advantage, those who have been dividing, those who have been dysfunctional, those who have been difficult to be around, those who are filled with hatred and don't want to let go of it—they will all fall away from your life. What's even more interesting is that you will no longer feel the need to go find somebody else to replace them. That's another sign that you're rising up.

Now, if you're still playing out your karmic patterns, then your rising hasn't started yet. You're probably not even fully aware of what your soul's genuine needs are. But, if you really are on your way and you really are resolving this, then at some point, you're going to feel that rise.

If the genuine need of your soul is to experience pure love, you'll know when you are starting to rise into it, as your nighttime dreams will begin to reflect it and you'll start to feel a ray of hope that enters into your being that encourages you to continue on your journey. All of a sudden, you'll start getting messages that it's coming, she's coming, he's coming. You'll just know because the rising has now begun. It's a rising up into your Greater Destiny. You're rising in frequency and vibration. In that comes the reward. The types of people that are now in that new vibrational resonance that encompasses the genuine need of your soul will suddenly start to show up, if they're not around already. You'll recognize it and think, "Holy cow—there's no dysfunction between me and this other person. It's like that's been replaced with flow and ease—as in everything is just easier. I completely trust them as they do me. I know they love me just as they know I love them. There's no confusion here. It's clear. I just feel so supported. I feel strengthened when I'm around them or when I hear their voice."

When someone does embody their karmic status, things just flow for them.

That's because it's in alignment with that genuine need of the karmic status of your soul—or both of your souls, for that matter. This is where you get to experience a family type of relationship, a business type of relationship, and/or a love type of relationship at that level where there's just no dysfunction. That doesn't mean you'll never come across challenges, but the difference is that everything will smooth out and become easier because you've now embodied this higher frequency at the karmic status level of your own soul.

This is a very different way to live life. Right now, the percentage of people who are living at this level on the planet is minimal, but increasing. In fact, I invite you to look outside yourself right now. Look at your family members. Look at your friends. Look at your clients. How many people would you say, for real, are actually living this way currently? How many people do you know who are the walking embodiment of having achieved this status thus far—the karmic status of their soul?

When someone does embody their karmic status, things just flow for them. There's more smoothness, light, and a higher vibration, which they're now living their life in and from. They're also much easier to work with or be with. You completely trust them because they're worthy of your trust. They show up with great integrity. They show up with all these higher qualities, and inside themselves they're really happy because that's another one of their divine birthrights that is now fully active.

GENUINE SOUL NEEDS VS. NEEDY ENERGY

The first distinction between our needy energy and the needs of our soul is that they're two completely different frequencies. They vibrate at two very different levels. One is very dense, and the other one is very light. One moves very slow, and the other moves very fast. One of them pushes people away or pushes the very thing we really want away, and the other one actually calls it in. And it calls it in with the right people—the people who can really give us the love that we deserve to have, or that we as a soul want to experience.

Your soul is not needy for anything. Whereas your ego is needy for everything. For example, when you're operating from the neediness for love, one of two things will happen. First, you might be with somebody who could have an ability to love you, but you won't be able to receive it. You might not even be able to recognize it because your needy energy will block your vision from being able to see it and block your heart from being able to receive it.

Second, if you're needy for love in that way, you might end up with somebody who doesn't even have the capacity to love—period. Then, if you hook that need for their love into their psyche and into their subconscious, you're going to be in that impersonal karma range. Now you're going to be at effect of their karma, which means it's going to bring you down. It's going to weaken something inside of you. It's going to cause you to start separating from who it is you really are and distract from what you're really to be doing. And it could weaken your ability to manifest finances and even cause unnecessary struggle. That's the needy energy for love.

Now if you have a genuine need for love, as in the soul has set forth prior to this life that it has a need to experience love—and if you really are accessing and embodying the karmic status of your soul—then one of a couple things is going to happen. First, someone will show up who not only has the capacity to send love, but they also have an equal capacity to receive love. It will be love without the entanglements, without hatred, without manipulations. It will be love without the division and separation stuff. It will be a pure love. It will be somebody who just really gets you, who loves you unconditionally, no matter what you do. And they're also here to experience real love, not the dysfunction that goes along with love when someone desperately needs to be loved by a particular person.

The soul attracts this because the soul already has it. Your soul has an ability to merge with somebody else's soul any time it wishes. It can do it in your dream space, your meditation space, or your waking space at any time. But it's not going to do it if you're still doing the needy stuff because you'll end up sabotaging it. Your needy energy will come on, and then you'll push love away. Unless, of course, you're recognizing this needy energy and actually releasing it.

If, in fact, your soul has love as a genuine need and you rise to that karmic status, you'll know it because a family member (as in a birth family member or a soul family member), or even someone within an organization, or a friend will somehow show up, and there'll be an element of ease, grace, and love where you'll literally experience being loved and giving love. It's going to affect everything in the biggest and brightest of ways. More importantly, there'll be an element of ease and grace because this is literally destined by the soul.

EMBODYING THE SOUL

When the soul is planted into your body, or when you embody your soul, it's like it has its own tractor beam. To become your soul or rise to the karmic status of your soul, you're going to have to deal with your karmic patterns and lessons because your soul is not going to allow the rising to occur until you do. This is because the moment you start to experience the sensations that enter into your physical form with this level of pure love, your needy self or ego will get in there quickly and try to sabotage the entire thing. And, from the soul's perspective, that would be like the soul tormenting you. The soul doesn't operate that way.

If you've ever felt like you had your soul fully inside your body, even if it was only for ten minutes, you'll know what I'm talking about. Your soul does not fully come into your body until you're ready for its vibration, but you might get an aspect of it. You might get an inkling that comes into your body for twenty-five minutes in linear time. And I assure you, you might even think you're on drugs—but you're not. You will have some kind of Godhead experience, and your outer life will directly reflect it. And you'll think you're in heaven because your soul vibes at the frequency of heaven, which is very different than the frequency of dysfunction.

Your soul is waiting. It's saying, "Hey, come on over. You're to be on this path over here. Get going—start taking the steps. I'll help you. I'll support you. I'll be there. Parts of me, your soul, will come into your body and start supporting this whole movement." But until you choose it, it's just not going to happen. Your soul has a bigger plan here, so your soul is going to get involved. Once you're doing the right thing, it's going to let you know that it's clearly supporting you.

> When someone does embody their karmic status, things just flow for them.

RISING TO THE KARMIC STATUS OF YOUR SOUL

When you are able to rise to the karmic status of your soul, things just start happening naturally. You find yourself in the right place at the right time, doing the right things and connecting with the right people. Things just fall into place in the best and easiest of ways, the most synchronistic of ways, and the most serendipitous of ways.

But you've got to get on board, and you got to prove worthy to your soul. You've got to say to your soul, "I'm ready to go, even though I know I'm not completely you just yet here in this physical form. I've got some lessons here to learn, but I'm in the game. And I'm done with just doing these Lower-Destiny things because I need this or that. I want to start doing the things that are right for me to be doing. That's what I want to start committing to. So, what is the right thing for me to be doing now?"

In this case, the right thing for me to be doing is to recognize my needy energy. For example, sometimes when we think someone is making us wrong, that thought in itself can be incredibly activating or triggering because it brings up some of our old ways that are rooted in that needy energy, which is a pushing-away energy. If I stay in this pushing-away energy, that is what makes this continue to not work for me. When, and only when, I'm able to identify the needy energy that is influencing a lower energy pattern and I actually go to work on clearing it, this is when it starts working again in a way that is in alignment with my soul as I'm rising up to my Greater Destiny.

Out of this, if it turns out that your soul has a genuine need to experience love, you'll begin to experience it in various areas of your life. Are you aware that you can experience love in your finances? Your money is a living energy. Are you currently experiencing love with your money? If it's true that your soul carries a genuine need for the experience to be loved, then part of where that's going to express itself is in your relationship with money. You're going to feel like you're loved by money, and you're going to be more loving towards money. How about that? Your whole experience with your money just becomes more loving, which means it becomes more graceful. It becomes a little easier. Oh, and by the way, you'll get a lot more of it. That might be one of your definitions for freedom—as in your divine birthright to be financially free.

SHOULD THE SOUL CHOOSE TO END THIS LIFE EARLY

If the soul chooses to check out of this life early, it's because we've crossed the line and there is no more going back. We've traumatized ourselves to a point where it's just ridiculous for our soul to allow us to keep on going because all we're going to do is further the buildup of trauma and karma. We're going to further the buildup of the resistance, and that's going to be counterproductive and possibly even destructive down the way. The soul recognizes that. So, the soul comes in and makes the decision, saying, "That's it. We're pulling the cord—bottom line." But it's pulling the cord in the best of ways—in the healthiest of ways—because it recognizes this needs to happen. Staying in this life at this point would only increase the odds of more karma that would have to be cleared at some later point along the soul's journey.

> *Your soul has an ability to merge with somebody else's soul any time it wishes.*

When the soul chooses to exit this life early, this could be the person who keeps on making the same destructive choices over and over again. Or possibly the person that gets swallowed up in their own pain that they are clearly no longer interested in clearing or healing. Their soul has been prompting them, but they just resist and resist. What can happen before the soul makes that choice is the person can be stripped.

This is the soul's last attempt to say, "Okay—I have given everything that I could possibly think of to support them in what they're really to be doing, but they continue to resist it. So, now it's time to bring them to their knees as a last resort to hopefully get their attention."

Now, this is different from the stripping that I referred to earlier in this book, as that type of stripping is done from the perspective to get us to embrace the message that it's time to change. Whereas in this case the stripping is being used as a last attempt to get our attention before the cord is pulled and we exit this life.

Some people can't handle this type of stripping, as this is where they can lose hope versus build hope. They can begin to destroy themselves versus strengthen themselves. They possibly become too negative in their thinking. This is where they might turn to alcohol, drugs, or eating too much food in one sitting or consuming non-beneficial foods and too little of the foods that would be most right for them to eat. Or possibly they raid the sugar bowl even more, and then have a heart attack and die. This is usually because their way of dealing with the stripping is not productive. Whether done consciously or unconsciously, their way is to add more resistance or destruction to the stripping.

There are others who not only don't wake up but who literally can take their own lives. Now they might do this unconsciously, but they check out because they just can't handle it and they don't want to handle it—they're done.

However, for some people, the stripping works magically. They get the wakeup call, and they begin to change their lives for the better from that point on.

So, when the soul says that it's time for the stripping, and we choose not to wake up and not to navigate well through that stripping process, then we can consciously or unconsciously sabotage our life. In this case, the soul is allowing us to sabotage our life because it has called upon its last resort. We're being given one more chance to see if we might wake up and start paying attention. And to actually start doing the right thing that we are being prompted to do by that of our own soul or Higher Self.

The right thing might be to leave a relationship, change some part of our diet, stop investing our money unwisely, change careers, or to deepen our commitment with the career we currently have. The right thing might be to unhook from our husband or wife and stop trying to make them be our dad or mom–or it could be to stop trying to change them. The right thing might be to choose a counselor, healthcare provider, coach, or psychologist and start getting some help. Only you will know what the right thing is if you're ever in this situation.

THE PURPOSE OF THE PERSONALITY IS TO SERVE THE SOUL

Earlier in Chapter 5 we learned about the ego self (a part of the personality) and the soul self. Now we are going to take a look at how the purpose of the personality is to serve the soul. It's the guiding light. You've already learned about some of the other functions of the personality, but this is its deepest purpose.

When you consider people at large, how many people would you say live in such a way that they're making sure their personality serves their soul? With this understanding, you're now going to see this everywhere. You're going to see this with your kids, your ex, your current husband, current wife, your friends, or your associates. You're going to get a front row seat to see just how many people have this positioned properly and how many don't. It's going to be like you've been given a set of bionic eyes. At this juncture, I simply invite you to observe them. Then, go inside and ask yourself, "How is my personality serving my soul?"

Remember, the ego is an aspect of the personality. When the ego is being transcended, it's the best parts of the ego that integrate into that of the personality—the soul. If our ego were to take over our personality, then our personality could no longer be used as a way to serve our soul. So, the question here is: Will the ego take over the personality, or will the ego be transcended? We, of course, want to transcend the ego and not have it take over.

If you're going to transform your destiny, then you'll want to reach the point of transcending your ego, so the personality keeps only the best of the ego, and then the ego is truly able to serve the soul.

Your soul is not needy for anything. Whereas your ego is needy for everything.

Are you being tricked into believing that your personality exists for some other reason than to serve your soul? Is it showing up in your actions? Is it showing up in the words that come out of your mouth and how you express yourself? If you're devoted to your needy self, you'll find yourself thinking things like, "I've got to make sure I get approval from my kids at all costs, so, therefore, I've got to keep on sacrificing and denying myself or competing with my spouse for my kids' approval." If that's how you're using your personality, that means you're disconnected from your soul. You either haven't begun the process, or you've disrupted the process of moving towards teaching your ego/personality what its real role is. It's here for the soul—period.

When we're needy at the level of personality, we have addictions that want to be fed. What you might or might not know is that there is an opposite side to the ego, which is the inner child. Now both the ego and the inner child live inside the body. What does this mean? Your ego and your inner child will speak to you and will attempt to get you to do things that might not be in your highest and best interest to do. This is where the body can become utilized by the ego and the inner child, as in using the body's favorite addiction—whatever that might be. An addiction to the body is equivalent to a lower energy pattern from that of our inner child, or even a karmic pattern. Meaning depending on the strength of the pattern or the addictive behavior, it will more than likely determine how many times we will play out that addiction.

With the ego, it will more than likely go for its favorite strategy of the day, week, or month. As in a lower energy pattern of going non-present or spacing out on promises or commitments you made to others, whether that is a ten o'clock morning appointment with someone, or not following through on what you said you were going to do, or holding back on someone as a way to punish them—as in not calling them back right away or giving them the silent treatment for several days. Whatever the strategy or the pattern under the influence of the ego is, it's holding us back from rising up to our Greater Destiny.

This is where learning how to tame and teach both our ego and inner child is critical when it comes to moving forward towards manifesting the life we truly desire. For if we do not do this, we will get more of the same. In my course on Transcendence, we go much deeper into gaining an understanding of the ego, the raising up of the inner child, and how they can affect the body both positively or negatively. These are critical parts which hold some of the most important lessons we are to be mastering in order to transcend.

An example of taming or teaching our ego and inner child would be in speaking to them directly, like you would in teaching a new dog. When you become really good at teaching your dog to do what you want it to do, the dog will pleasantly surprise you. It will respond to the directive or whatever you are asking it to do. It is the same with your inner child and ego—when you get really good at taming and teaching your ego and inner child, they, at some point, will pleasantly surprise you with how well they now listen to you.

If your dog is not well tamed or trained, more than likely your dog will be running you rather than you running it—the same holds true with your ego and your inner child. If my ego or inner child is still running me, they will more than likely hold me back from rising up to my Greater Destiny. They will also direct what occurs in my body, meaning I'm probably going to have a challenging time being master of my own body versus my body being master of me. And therefore, I could find myself living at the level of Lower Destiny for the rest of my life, mainly because I have been letting my ego and/or my inner child run the show.

When under the influence of the ego or inner child, we can find ourselves wanting what we want and wanting it right away. And yet if we were to step in and engage in disciplining this part of ourselves, all of this could change for the better.

So, if our personality is being utilized by our ego or inner child in the way previously described, this will create some doo-doo for us to clean up in our life. For example, let's say we start a new relationship with someone as a way to fill some void that we're experiencing in our life.

More than likely, at the beginning of the relationship, we're going to think it's heaven. "It's so wonderful. This is the relationship of my dreams," we say. And now because we've been so desperate to fill this void of having no relationship, then ten months later, we're potentially going to begin feeling like we're in a hellish situation, asking, "How did we get here?", implying this is not the relationship of our dreams. That's because we haven't positioned our personality properly at a deeper, core level just yet. We have yet to line it up correctly nor have we recognized one of the key purposes of our ego and inner child within our personality—which again is to serve the soul.

> When the ego is being transcended, its best parts integrate into the soul.

We can't destroy our ego, nor can we destroy our inner child, but we can tame them, we can teach them, and by doing so we can then transcend our ego and ultimately raise up our inner child. Whether we achieve this in this life or a future one gets to be our choice. Now there's no quick fix here, and it's going to take some work. But it can be done. Why? Because this is part of our Greater Destiny to do so.

Training and teaching your inner child and ego while learning how to get better at disciplining these parts of yourself along with your body might take you a year, a couple of years, or even a lifetime. If you've allowed your body to control you through the needy self which is under the control of your ego and inner child, then this is more than likely going to take longer. You might have a physical body that's been ruling your roost by saying things like, "I want what I want, right now!" (As in the sugar fix, the adrenaline rush, the sex addiction, the immediate gratification, the need to be right, etc.), "I do not want to wait longer than 30 days. So there! I want the results immediately. I just don't want to wait, and I clearly don't want to do that level of work."

If that's how your inner child or ego influences your personality, in tandem with your body, then you've got some work ahead of you to tame and teach them, thereby learning how to pull in the reins when it's most appropriate to do so. But now you're getting the higher education. Which means you can change, heal, and transform all of this. You see, it is up to you to take this education and utilize it in a very direct way where you're consciously teaching your ego, your inner child, and your body. By learning and choosing to do this, you're now, at the very least, working towards that greater purpose of being here in service to your soul. Isn't that cool?

To learn more on how to raise up your inner child and transcend your ego to where they can meet their higher purpose in service to your magnanimous soul, I invite you to check out information on our Free Transcendence Master Class at the back of the book.

SERVICE TO SOMETHING OUTSIDE YOURSELF

Over the last fifty years or so, we've been coming out of the dark ages, the age of Pisces, into the age of Aquarius. We're in a real auspicious time period right now, but a lot of people don't see or feel it that way because they're getting activated with their own lower energies, such as their anger, fear, jealousy, or judgment, and they perhaps don't understand what's actually happening here. Or maybe they do understand this, but they're not yet managing their own activated energy properly or efficiently in the most productive way possible.

What's happening is we are experiencing a shift in consciousness. We are shifting from one way of being to another whole new way of being. Similar to what we're doing while we're transforming our destiny, we're rising up from our lower vibrational energies to the embodiment of our higher vibrational energies.

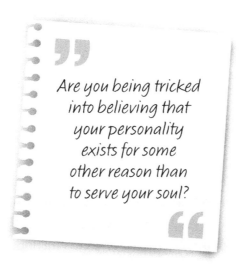

Are you being tricked into believing that your personality exists for some other reason than to serve your soul?

To do this, we are here to transform those lower energies. We're to heal our anger. We are to transform our fear and judgment. We're to transform those lower energy patterns, such as patterns like not having good boundaries, taking things personally, mentally building a case towards someone that you're in judgment of, being impatient, or the pattern of defensiveness. I can participate in this shift by looking at myself and then choosing to transform. Then those lower energies that reside in my Lower Destiny begin to rise up into those higher energies that reside in my Greater Destiny.

When someone is repositioning their personality to get back into alignment with its deeper purpose, which is to be in service to the soul, that person will suddenly find an organization they'll fall in love with, and they'll decide to serve that organization or the people who are in it.

This has been one of the saving graces for many people throughout the years. What's happening is they're stepping outside of their personality and devoting themselves to something that they believe has a bigger mission. People who join the priesthood or a convent are examples of those who want to serve something larger than themselves.

When you are in pure service to someone or to something outside yourself that is larger than you, something awesome ends up happening for you. There are some people who don't even need an education on this. As soon as they find that person or organization that they're in alignment with, the decision gets made. The devotion and dedication comes online, and their lives start to change rather quickly. What's happening unconsciously is the personality's being repositioned to its deeper purpose and the ego is beginning to be tamed.

This is one of the many ways to make your soul happy. This is also a way to help your soul thrive—and the cool thing is, anybody can do this. It doesn't matter who you are. We see people who are confined to a wheelchair, and they'll find an organization or a person whose values are in alignment with theirs. Next thing you know, they begin benefiting from these awesome changes that start to happen within them and around them. Situations like this can be very inspiring because these individuals have this obvious physical handicap, but the magic gets released inside of them, and they are able to do incredible things.

It's because when this happens, your soul literally comes to you and change suddenly starts to happen for you in the best of ways. Transformation starts to happen for you in the most beneficial of ways.

You get a few more blessings that start showing up on your doorstep. You get a little more of that third divine birthright—grace.

This is a really difficult concept for the self-centered person. Frankly this could be like a nightmare for them. They probably wouldn't go further than a couple of months, and then they would sabotage the situation. The deeper purpose of their personality gets completely buried because they're not able to serve from this pure place. What might the karma be for that? What would the consequence be for the person who chooses to remain in their self-centered ways? The consequence would be severing the connection to their Higher Self. That's the biggest and most painful consequential effect of this choice. They end up dividing their personality from their soul.

When you are in pure service to something outside yourself that is larger than you, something awesome ends up happening for you.

Globally, self-centeredness has become an epidemic all its own. Perhaps it's one of the reasons why the suicide rate is increasing at an alarming rate. Another dynamic that's also increasing at an alarming rate is entitlement. This causes people to push their souls out. In all fairness to them, they're probably completely unaware of this—but nonetheless that's what they're doing. And what are they experiencing as a result of this entitlement? More struggle, stress, anxiety, depression, anger, rage, and more resentment. Are you able to see this?

Again, self-centeredness on this planet has been spinning out of control, and as a result it's been creating division like a life-threatening disease or a big bad weed in your garden. Up until now, no one has seemed to be able to stop it. But the truth is, we are stopping it. This is all part of the cleansing because there's something much bigger, much brighter, and much better coming—and we are all part of it. For those of us who really are stepping up to the plate and taking responsibility for ourselves in relation to our souls, this is the game changer.

The last piece I'll say on this is that if you are in service to someone or something outside of yourself, remember to use your own discernment. Run it up and down your own inner flagpole to make sure this is a person or organization that's right for you to serve, and then get and stay devoted.

PURPOSES OF THE SOUL

The purpose of the soul is different than the greater purpose of karma, but these two purposes do intersect. The purpose of every person's soul is also going to be unique to the individual. Now let's explore some common purposes.

Actualization

Actualization means you're going to incarnate your Higher Self. You're going to embody your soul, or your true self—your most authentic self. This could be a deeper purpose of your soul in this lifetime. Meaning your soul contracted, before you took your first breath, that it's going to actualize itself here in the physical. In every century, there's always

346

been at least one master soul who has pulled this off and gone public. But we have reached an era where this is possible for many more to accomplish. We are being supported by the Divine to do this and the time has come where this is available to the many.

Our masters who have walked the face of this earth prior to this time who have achieved this are Yogananda, Buddha, Lao Tzu, Quan Yin, and more.

When you understand what's involved to do this and the importance of the education, elevation, and empowerment, you'll know that you need somebody outside yourself to help you to pull this off. This is a big deal. It's super big to the soul because it becomes the lifetime where the soul actualizes itself here in the physical. In other words, this is where you become your soul—your true self, as in the Divine Human. You become the person you were meant to be from the very beginning. It's going to be very unique to you. It is your higher truth.

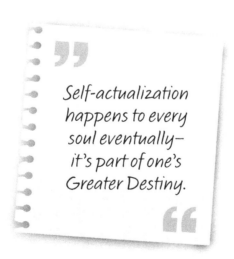

Self-actualization happens to every soul eventually— it's part of one's Greater Destiny.

Self-actualization happens to every soul eventually. That's part of one's Greater Destiny. Up until now, this has not been an easy thing to pull off, but it's all within someone's greater potential that resides at a higher level within them. So as they're transforming their destiny into that of their Greater Destiny, a significant part of that transformation is where they become their most authentic and abundant self. Your world naturally rises up to your Greater Destiny as you fully become who you were truly meant to be.

Enlightenment

Another purpose of the soul could be the purpose of enlightenment. For the longest time, this has been the purpose for certain souls who have come before us. They achieved an enlightened state of being to the point of where we could literally see their halos. But once again, not many people have done this because of the amount of self-transcendence work it takes to achieve it.

If this turns out to be a purpose that your soul has put into motion, then you're already halfway there because you've got your soul on your backside; you know something bigger is going on with you. Once you wake up to this purpose, it changes the game. And now since you have this awareness, the quality of your choices can level up rapidly.

The difference between actualization and enlightenment is, with enlightenment you might find yourself sitting in a cave, simply radiating out into humanity. Enlightenment is a higher consciousness in which you can access the higher realms. As an enlightened master, you're able to access other dimensions of a much higher magnitude while in physical form. And, should it be appropriate, you can bring it through and share it with some of your students.

Completion of Karma

A soul can also come into this life exclusively for the resolution of karma. In order to get to actualization or enlightenment, how important would it be for you to resolve all your lifetimes of karma, or at least the majority of those lifetimes? Do you know of a truly enlightened master who still has negative karma? Do you know of a fully actualized soul in physical form who still has negative karma? Have you ever heard of such a person? Of course not, because they don't exist.

When Yogananda, the founder of the Self-Realization Fellowship Center in Southern California, was in physical form, he would sometimes teach that for a soul to become fully enlightened in physical form, on average, it would take the initiate seven lifetimes. Now this is not intended to scare you. The intention here is honesty and to share with you the significance of what we're now talking about. In order for you to actualize, you're going to have to get off the wheel of karma. Maybe you've already been working on this for several lifetimes and aren't aware of it just yet. So if you believe this is up for you to do, then just set your mind to it and get to work on the steps you need to take to get off the wheel.

To Become a Conduit for the Divine

Enlightenment sets the stage to advance to the next level of purpose, which is to become a clear conduit for the Divine. Decades ago when I was studying Emerson, one of the things that he would often write about in his works was teaching people to become a conduit for the Divine, or for the Universe.

Gandhi also became a pure conduit for the Divine. He was able to move an entire nation of people. Think about the magnitude of that. But, when he was alive, it did not look good for him because the resistance was so overwhelmingly intense. Do you know what it's like to have five or ten people resisting you at the exact same time? Can you imagine what it would be like to have a whole nation resisting you? We're talking about a very different level here.

In order to operate on that level, you don't necessarily have to be fully actualized or fully enlightened, but you've got to be crystal clear as a conduit. It's the Divine flowing through you that's doing the work. It's the Divine flowing through you that moves a nation.

> Our deepest purpose at soul level naturally becomes revealed to us as our karma becomes healed and resolved.

It requires a lot of work to become a clear conduit. This would be somebody who is able to get themselves out of the way, even if it's only for a couple of hours, and be a complete, clear conduit for the Divine to flow through them. If they're doing the self-centered thing, it's going to be difficult. They've got to figure out a way to take their self-serving tendencies and put them on the back burner for a couple hours, which means they can't be needy. The only way the Divine can use them is when they're totally clear for a sustained period of time. Do they have to be crystal clear 100 percent of the time? No. They can be clear for a few hours, and that's when the Divine comes through them, should it choose to, and does whatever it needs to do.

THE COLLECTIVE SOUL ON THE PLANET

Just like we have a collective ego on this planet, we also have a collective soul on this planet and always have. We have billions of egos on the planet, and all of them combined would be the collective ego—like a command center for all egos. The same applies to the soul—all of the souls combined are the planet's collective soul. This collective soul can send out a broadcast energetically; it's like a message that goes out. Same with the collective ego.

Think of the show *Star Trek*, and specifically of the Borg. There are all these individual Borgs, but then there's the collective of them and the command center that ultimately controls all of them simultaneously.

Does this mean that all individual egos pick up the message from the collective ego? No. Does that mean that all individual souls pick up the message from that of the collective soul? No. Because in order to pick up these messages, there's gotta be some level of receptivity.

If the collective ego, or the command center, wants to ramp up the fear on this planet, for example, it might send out a collective broadcast which causes people to become more afraid. And if we as individuals are receptive enough with our ego to pick up that message, next thing we know, we might find ourselves feeling a little more stressed or experiencing a little more anxiety because we picked up on that fear that was broadcasted out.

The soul, on the other hand, might send out a message to the souls on this planet that it's time to wake up. We are seeing this currently more and more on the planet. We're experiencing a global awakening where many people are literally waking up to their own souls.

If you have a healthier, more vibrant, more conscious relationship to your ego, the odds now are when that broadcast goes off, you're going to feel the message coming in and you can do something constructive about it when it does. In other words, you don't have to take it on at all and let that broadcast that's rooted in fear become even stronger inside of you. Rather, you could begin to clear out some of your fear and even ward off that fear that was being broadcasted toward you. This is another reason why it's so important to develop a conscious relationship with your ego because if you don't, this type of a broadcast will affect you unknowingly.

> Just like we have a collective ego on this planet, we have also had a collective soul.

Then, of course, the same would hold true with your soul. When a broadcast is coming in from the collective soul and you have a healthier relationship to your soul, then likely when that broadcast comes through, you're probably going to feel some kind of an uplifting, as there's a higher message coming from the collective soul and the planet as a way to help empower us at an individual soul level or to help further awaken us.

Now is the time for us to show a greater appreciation for the collective soul by helping more individuals to start honoring their own souls in the best of ways. From the very beginning, the Universe was crafted so that the people would have the power, and then collectively they would move into a deeper, greater, and larger evolution.

Yes, we went off on a detour for a while, but the time has come back around, and now those who really understand how this has been set up are coming in to support this much larger movement. Over the coming years, we are going to see more advanced, ancient, and master souls that will arrive or step up to assist in the advancement and expansion of our soul's evolution on the planet.

When you begin resonating with the true purpose of your soul, you start to align your life.

The part your soul could play in this may be in taking advantage of this opportunity for you to advance as a soul. The wave is coming—and you will have the opportunity to ride that wave up to the next level. Are you going to be positioned properly so that you, as a soul, can fully step into the ascension of us as a race and benefit from this rising up to the next level of the soul's evolution? Is this something that is speaking to you right now? Does this resonate with you? Again, it comes back to these choices, and that's why it's so important to make the type of choices that will help us rise into our Greater Destiny.

BECOMING AWARE OF THE TRUE PURPOSE OF YOUR SOUL

When you begin resonating with the true purpose of your soul, you start to align your life. You make the arrangements and reorganize your life in a way that's completely in support of the unique purpose of your soul. This is one of the reasons I'm so dedicated to this work. It's because I'm very aware of what the deeper and greater purpose of my soul is. I've known about my purpose for some time. I'm not here to play games. I'm not here to screw this up. I'm here to accomplish something that's worthy at soul level. And because I'm aware of that, it's so much easier for me to make choices that are in alignment with that.

To share a little more of my journey in what it took to get here and to help you realize that if I can do this, so can you, let's go back to the days when I wasn't aware of this. I was the person who'd go to the bar to pick somebody up, and we'd have sex. I wasn't even thinking about what the consequences were. And when I was in a relationship, I was the type of person that would move from one relationship to the next relationship rather quickly. You see, I had that pattern in spades because I was really afraid of being alone.

I hadn't come far enough along on my own journey to know the consequential effect or the potential negative implications. I was just like many people on the planet; I was making choices that would create big distractions under the influence of my ego, but at the time I had no idea this is what I was doing. If I wanted to do something, I did it. And whether it was good or bad didn't matter to me. Many people on our planet, even to this very day, don't consider what the consequences of their choices might be. That was me back in my twenties.

But those casual encounters weren't the worst of it. The biggest issue was my food addiction. I got to the point where I almost died because

I was consuming way too many chemicals in processed fast food. I also got addicted to medication. I had no idea how it was plugging up my organs—how it messed up my liver. So, it shouldn't be a surprise that at the early age of 32, I was unconscious in the ICU. And I had already been hospitalized before for this.

I'd been constantly challenged with my respiratory system for most of my life up to this point in time. I was told that there was a good chance I wouldn't even make it beyond the next eighteen months, and there was nothing more they could do. They said my body was deteriorating from the inside out, so I'd best begin to get my affairs in order.

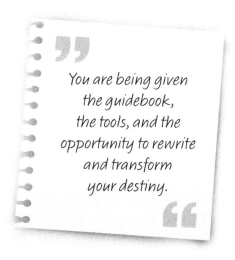

You are being given the guidebook, the tools, and the opportunity to rewrite and transform your destiny.

It was at this point that I came to a fork in the road, where either I was going to go down that path and at some point in the next eighteen months my body would fail, or I had to do something radical. The challenge for me at that time was I had no idea what the radical difference was ultimately going to be.

Obviously, back then, I had no idea as to the deepest purpose of my soul. I was definitely more unconscious than conscious and like many other people I had pretty much fallen asleep in consciousness. It took a little while, and then I started to access the truth. The truth had to do with the fact that I was really jammed up emotionally and hadn't even begun to become conscious of my karma at that point in time. In fact, part of my unresolved karma and its root being that of fear (which I had a lot of), had not begun to resolve yet. One of the fears sitting at the root within this unresolved karma was the fear of being alone. To be alone meant I'd have to deal with this constipation of emotional material inside of me, as in fear, sadness, grief, shame, anger, and so on. This was all there on purpose as part of my karma to heal and resolve in this life—I was about to begin to become conscious shortly after this period of time, but when this was going on it hadn't happened just yet.

I was all jammed up back then, and this eventually caused everything to jam up in my life. To cover up the areas that were jammed up emotionally for me, I became addicted to the chemicals that were found in processed foods, such as junk food or fast food. Between jumping from one relationship to another, to being addicted to these types of foods, those two things were serving as a way to keep me separate from all of this buried emotional material that I had jammed up inside of me.

The place where these jams showed up most intensely were in that of my physical body, which led to this fork in the road where it looked like, at the time, I was either going to die or have to do something radically different since my body was close to failing me. Now what's even more interesting here is that I would come to learn much later that this too was all part of actually resolving my unresolved karma.

You see, when I actually embraced making those radical changes, my choices just started to up-level. It wasn't so much a physical healing that I had a genuine need for; rather, it was an emotional healing. And once I was able to recognize this as a truth for me, then, as I fully began to embrace the journey that would lie ahead of me around healing myself emotionally, my physical issues began to clear up.

My choices continued up-leveling through my thirties, my forties, and my fifties. This had a lot to do with connecting to the deeper, greater purpose of my soul. It was during this time that I made a profound realization around resolving my karma, which was that I wasn't here to actually heal my karma; rather, I was here to fulfil my soul's deeper purpose—to fulfill my soul's contract in being here in this lifetime. You see, our deepest purpose at soul level naturally becomes revealed to us as our karma becomes healed and resolved. I know this because I've been at death's door more than once as I've related in several stories throughout this book.

The soul ultimately wants free reign when it comes to choice. Do you know what an exit strategy is when it comes to building a company? Just like creating an exit strategy for a company in advance, the soul creates a strategy for the completion of all lifetimes in advance of each lifetime.

Our soul wants the opportunity and freedom to choose whether to stay or go. The soul wants to say, "What do I now truly and purely want to do with this?" And whatever that answer is, it's celebrated. My soul signed on to stay in this lifetime, and I committed to doing the work to pull myself from a situation that modern doctors, at that time, labeled impossible. They had all but signed my death certificate. But I didn't accept that as my truth. I didn't give up. And my point here is that you don't have to give up either.

You are being given the guidebook, the tools, and the opportunity to rewrite and transform your destiny. It is at your fingertips should you choose it. So, the question is, what are you going to do next?

EXERCISES

Reflect upon the following questions and write your answers in your notebook:

1. Can you identify a genuine need that your soul has? If so, write down everything you can think of in describing this genuine need.

   If you were to integrate this genuine need into your day-to-day life, what's the first thing you would do?

2. Have you ever experienced "the stripping" or seen this type of event happen with someone else before? Write out a description of your experience, whether it was someone else's or your stripping that you were witnessing.

   And ultimately, what was the result and/or your response or theirs to this wake-up call?

   If there is something here for you to learn from this experience, what would it be?

3. Rate your personal truth of this statement: "I do selfless acts more often than self-centered acts." Score yourself on a scale of 1-10, 1 being very little and 10 being a lot.

   Why did you give yourself this number?

   If there was a selfless act you could commit to doing this week, what would it be? Write out your answer.

4. Think of a time when your inner child or ego really wanted something and they wanted it right now, and you gave into them. Describe what happened and how it turned out.

   And if there was something for you to learn here about your inner child or ego wanting something right away, what would it be? Whatever your answer, write it down.

5. Have you had a near-death or life-altering experience? If so, describe it.

If yes, what did you learn and/or discover from it?

Have you integrated what you learned or discovered into your day-to-day life ? If yes, what have you noticed in terms of how it has helped you move your life forward? If no, what's the very next thing you could do to help integrate what it is you've learned or discovered?

CHAPTER 12

SOUL THEMES

There's one more piece that you're going to want to know about when it comes to your soul—and specifically, to the resolving of your soul's karma in this life. This piece is on the soul theme and the life theme. I'm going to give you a few examples, and your job is to see what resonates with you. You can be assured, you have at least one soul theme. There are many, and you might even have more than one.

THE DIFFERENCE BETWEEN SOUL THEMES AND LIFE THEMES

A soul theme is different than a life theme. The difference is similar to karmic patterns versus lower energy patterns. A soul theme is something that you literally came into this life with. It's a carryover. Your soul is incredibly intelligent, and it carries some level of wisdom. As you ascend up the ladder, you can go from a little bit of wisdom, to a medium level of wisdom, all the way through to a more expansive sage-like wisdom. Your soul has gained this wisdom from previous life experiences where you mastered your lessons well in those lifetimes.

The soul theme is deeper than the life theme. Again, it's like a karmic pattern. A karmic pattern is much heavier and denser than a lower energy pattern. The soul theme has got weight to it, and it doesn't have to be a positive weight or a negative weight, though it could be positive in terms of its effect. The life theme is different from a soul theme because it was created in this life, whereas a soul theme is something that perhaps you as a soul have been attempting to pull off for a lifetime or two. That's what makes it more intense.

The soul theme is made up of your strongest karmic patterns and lessons.

Once you identify what it is, it's going to answer a lot of questions for you. The theme is already built into the soul. In other words, you can't change the theme. Nobody can—it's already there. However, you can be awakened to it, then learn how to bring it into your life and really work with it. It'll serve you well should you choose to do that. But you can't go in and simply change the theme. The theme is made up of your strongest karmic patterns. It's made up of your strongest karmic lessons. It's like a combination of these ingredients going into a blender, then you mix them up, and you get the theme.

The life theme is something that gets created in your childhood through that impersonal karma you learned about earlier. In other words, someone else's karma or something else outside of you can create a life theme. Children are sponges. The impressions that end up in your psyche due to your childhood experiences are enormous, and they don't go away until you go back in there and clear out the energy around those impressions.

It can get even more complicated if you end up creating a life theme and then choose to go to sleep and numb yourself out. If this happens, you can be assured that access to your soul theme will be temporarily blocked. That's how the soul carries the soul theme into the next life experience.

For the most part, the soul has been okay with this, partly because we've been going through the dark ages. But now that we're coming into a new age, the soul is going to start giving some swift kicks in the butt like we've never seen before. This process has already begun. That means whatever's not working in your life is going to get louder, and it's going to come back with bigger stings. It's going to come back like a Mack truck at 75 miles per hour. When you're struck with one of those, there's no way you can deny it or go off into your numbing strategy because you just don't want to deal with the pain of a blow like that again. You can exercise your free will, but in this new era that we've now entered, the soul is starting to kick butt. And, if that still doesn't get the person's attention, then more than likely the soul at some point is probably going to pull the plug.

Our death rate is climbing, and it's not just due to suicide. People's souls are pulling the plug because we're now in this new era, and these individuals want nothing to do with this transformation. They aren't in alignment with this type of transformation possibly because they are still self-centered, or they've been numbing themselves down with their favorite drug of choice, or they're downright stuck and possibly have been for some time along their life's journey. Any one of these things can leave us feeling exhausted and having thoughts of just wanting to

362

give up. And perhaps they've lost that ray of hope that, as I mentioned earlier in the book, is so important for us to have in our lives.

We're morphing into a higher, better place on this planet, and you're either going to level up to this, or you're not. If you're not honoring your soul theme or your life theme, then something else is going to happen. By the same token, if you are in alignment with this and really showing your dedication, you will be you will be graced in some way, somehow. It might be very subtle, but as you become more awake, you're going to catch it. You'll think, "Wow! I'm being graced again. This is so amazing. I love this. Just a couple of years ago, I was thinking of checking out. I couldn't stand it here. And now, all of a sudden, I'm actually starting to like it here–and even possibly love it!"

If you go through a lifetime and you learn diddly squat, your soul does not become any wiser. In fact, your soul might actually become trau-matized. One of the reasons the soul is here is to become wiser, and it knows that the only way it can become wiser is through experience—and more specifically, it needs to experience the lessons that you as a soul have come here to learn.

Again, it always comes back to the lessons we are to be learning here in Earth School. Are you identifying your lessons? Are you learning those lessons? And ultimately, are you mastering them? If you are, then good for you. You're on your way to something huge. IIf you're not, you want to be checking and re-examining this. You might consider going into some good self-inquiry here.

EXAMPLES OF SOUL THEMES

Soul themes are going to be unique to the soul. An older soul will have more than one soul theme. If you do have more than one, then one will be a primary and one will be a secondary. Once the primary soul theme becomes mastered, then if you do have one or more secondary themes, one of those will move into that primary position.

The following are a handful of are a handful of examples of some of the various soul themes.

Soul Theme of the Saboteur

Everybody has sabotaged some part of their life to some degree, but if somebody is coming in with a soul theme of the saboteur, their struggle is going to be high. It's going to be more than their next-door neighbor who doesn't have this as a theme. They're going to make poor choices that cause struggle because they're in the theme of sabotaging some part of their life.

If the theme is really strong—in other words, their soul has been attempting to resolve this for the last three lifetimes—then it's possibly going to morph into suicidal thoughts. Now if the person ignores this and doesn't get some help from somebody outside of themselves, then there's a possibility this is all going to get worse and they might even commit suicide. This is because a person can only handle so much struggle before they shut down. The ultimate shutdown would be to take their own life. Unless, of course, they were to recognize this theme, begin to embrace it, learn from it, and ultimately transform it. But let's assume for a moment that they don't transform this theme. Then this struggle would continue and increase in intensity.

Think of the people you know right now or you have known who have been greatly struggling in their life for quite some time. They've got the same health issue this year that they've had for the last five years, and they're no further along in healing it. Or, they've got a dysfunctional relationship going on, and they're no further along in resolving that dysfunctional relationship. Now, seven years have passed. They are not healthy. They're living in a toxic body. They're living in a toxic relationship. Or perhaps they're pursuing a career that they're not even happy with. They can't stand getting up, getting in their car, and fighting the traffic while driving to their office in the morning. They don't even like their boss. They've been working with their boss for five years and they can't stand them, but they stay with it anyway. They're struggling. There's nothing pleasant about it. They're in a constant fight.

The saboteur is the person who has been in resistance to their soul theme not just in this life, but they've resisted this theme for at least a couple of lifetimes. And now, in this present life, their resistance is off the charts. They exhaust themselves with the amount of resistance they live in on a day-to-day basis. They drain themselves.

An older soul will have more than one soul theme.

Some people end up with adrenal gland problems. The adrenal glands are the part of the body that produces physical energy. When you turn resistance into a lifestyle, you're going to be exhausted all the time because one of your adrenal glands is more than likely going to start to malfunction and may even begin to shut down. You could get nutritional supplementation, which would be a good idea to help replenish them—but the problem is, that's not really going to help them long term. In this case, it's all energetic.

With some there is no let off on the resistance, meaning that the resistance they are in is pretty much 24/7. Now they may be unconscious towards this, but one of the ways they can spot it is that they can't sleep at night, and when they do, they can't get into a deeper sleep because even in their sleep, they're still in a state of resistance. This person is usually in a constant fight—not just with others but with themselves or some part of themselves. They can even be putting up a fight against their own resistance. They can often fight others verbally, mentally, or emotionally. And when they do, it will be a power struggle—and that struggle can go on sometimes for months or even years, to the point where something they really value is destroyed.

The saboteur will start to succeed at something, and next thing you know, they're sabotaging their own success. They'll start a project but never complete it. They'll sabotage themselves and then get angry at life. Sometimes they'll get angry at God or the Divine. Sometimes they'll get angry at somebody else outside of themselves who's actually there to help them. If you were to let this theme run your life, it could consume you.

This is a theme that will wipe you out if you're not aware of it and haven't taken responsibility for it. The problem with that is you might end up going through an entire lifetime without moving the needle forward. That means your soul is now set up to have the exact same theme in the next life. This does not make the soul happy. In fact, this could actually weaken the soul. Some people with this theme have been dragging it out for multiple lifetimes, and now this theme is very intense. They might end up committing suicide, either consciously or unconsciously. They usually have an earlier death because it's so freaking tough. When someone is living their life at this level of resistance, whether they're aware of it or not, over time, their energy will be drained.

If you're in a relationship with somebody who's always resisting, then at some point, you'll say, "This is exhausting. I don't know if I can go on another week. Every time we do something, you're in resistance. Or, if we say we're going to do something, two weeks from now, you'll completely forget and be onto a new project. I'm so tired of your new ideas. I'm so tired of your new projects because you always abandon them. You never succeed, and then you get mad at the world for it. But you won't even look at yourself!" This person won't look at their own karmic pattern. They won't look at their own theme. They're here to heal their self-sabotaging ways, and if they don't do this, the struggle is going to increase. They're going to get into fights with other people, especially significant relationships in their life. The fights will go on because the struggle is constant. It's nonstop because it's all resistance. This theme can start taking complete control and literally consume them.

When we transcend sabotage and get to a point where we appreciate life, it starts to smooth out. We get to a point where life starts to have a little grace in it. And eventually, we get to a point where there's not even a part of us that wants to sabotage anything because we're actually happy to be here. But in order to do that, we've got some lessons to learn. We might have a lesson in gratitude. Maybe we're more miserable than we are grateful. And if there's any truth to that, then we probably have a lesson to learn around how to be grateful for things—including the struggles that have created an opportunity for us to clear out our karma and to learn something of value about ourselves.

Soul Theme of the Victor

The soul theme of the victor is more positive than that of the saboteur, but it does have a negative slant to it. If you have this as a theme, then you're going to be dealing with the lower rung of the victor archetype—and that is the victim. These themes can play out individually, and they can play out collectively. I'm going to give you an example of a collective one at play. There are individual soul themes and collective soul themes. When a collective soul theme is at play, there are two or more people involved.

I was called in a while back to work with a school—a group of teachers, the principal, and the administrators. I ended up working with them for about a year or so, but on my very first day, the theme of the victor became obvious to me. It wasn't as obvious to any of them because at the time they had all but lost awareness around the victor archetype, mainly due to the fact that they were pretty much under the influence or the spell of the victim archetype.

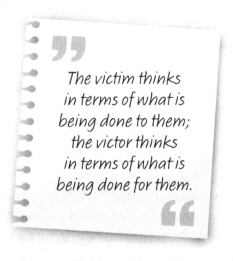

The victim thinks in terms of what is being done to them; the victor thinks in terms of what is being done for them.

Now this was a well-structured school that did great work with kids, but there was dysfunction in the way that the individuals worked together to be of service to the community and their students. From a collective energy point of view, division was running rampant at the time, at the level of the administration and the faculty.

Let me back up a bit and explain that the collective soul of two or more people is made up largely of the individual souls, so when we're looking at a company, we've got to consider the mission that it carries in the essence of itself, and we've got to take a look at its core values. The individuals of this collective soul are all contributing and participating in this movement. One might ask, "What is the essence of this company that brings these two or more people together to represent it?" Now that company also has a collective ego. And like the soul, the ego of the company is partly made up of the individual egos that represent the company from the top down and the bottom up. So, if the ego is really strong in that organization, then you're going to have some type of theme, like this victim archetype that I was speaking of. This would mean that the people within that group or at least some of them are victimizing one another. Whether they're blaming, criticizing, or being negative or hurtful to each other, some type of victimization will occur.

At this school, at first, a few of them fought me like a plague—a couple even stood up and yelled at me. It got pretty intense, but eventually we punched through, and those people came back and apologized later.

Why did they have so much complexity? Because they had an established soul theme, having been a school that had been around for quite a while. Whenever you have history and you're dealing with older dynamics at the level of their Lower Destiny, it can become very complex. A few decades later, something clearly had happened, because somehow they weren't picking up on the soul anymore. The soul was there, but you could say it had been pushed off to the side or pushed down and then replaced by those other dysfunctional ego-driven dynamics.

The victim archetype had become super strong in the organization, whereas the victor archetype had gone off in the background. So, it was like the ego was out front and center. What we needed to do was to reverse that and get the soul out in the front; get the victor archetype leading the way again with its influence on the people that were representing the school.

369

Some people got triggered, and some of their more unpleasant shadow stuff came out during this process. That's because now I had been with them for a few days and that shadowy part of them knew they weren't going to fool me about what was going on.

As a result, it started to settle down in a way that was moving towards working together more synergistically. There was more of a relaxed willingness to work together towards a common goal.

When someone is playing out the victim archetype, odds are they'll reverse roles and victimize somebody else.

I look for patterning when I'm working with organizations, taking them back into the past. I get them fully involved, and then I prove to them what I'm seeing. I have developed many techniques for doing this so that there's no room for doubt. I get them to the point where they can't deny what's actually going on. That's usually where the breakthrough happens.

I was able to prove to the faculty of the school in the previous example that over the last twenty-three years, the same scenario had played out three different times—and they were now on the fourth. I was able to show them the karma that got created for the school the first three times this happened. At this point, they were feeling sick to their stomachs. It resonated with them because they were starting to open up. We had the breakdown and were now moving into the breakthrough.

Next, we got to the place of identifying that the victim archetype was basically ruling the entire roost. It was the victim archetype that was sitting in the captain's chair of the collective unit of these wonderful human beings, and it was in the process of destroying them as a team and/or organization. A lot of people previously had already been hurt financially, emotionally, and spiritually. And now, this group was about to take the same path. But these brave souls decided to stand up to it. Some of them chose to leave, so there was a bit of a cleanup that needed to happen. People who really didn't belong there got cleared out because they were not in support of the victim archetype, or it was simply their time to leave by choice. And as they did, we were able to start moving the school towards the positive aspect of the archetype, the victor.

After we accomplished this, the parents were happy. The kids were also happy because now the pressure was off. They no longer felt like they were on the edge. Instead of letting the victim archetype consume the organization, they were now recognizing and taking full responsibility for it. They were doing what needed to be done in order to reorganize and clean it up, and then began to rise up to their greater theme, which was the victor archetype.

An individual, or an organization like in this example, can have this as a positive soul theme but completely mess it up by getting swallowed up in the victim archetype. This is the person who thinks, acts, and talks like a victim. They blame the world like they're the victim. They're always being done to. The victim thinks in terms of what is being done to them; the victor thinks in terms of what is being done for them. It's just nonstop. It becomes a question of time when the next victimizer is going to come in and victimize them yet again. They operate this way in order to continue this dysfunctional, lower-energy storyline where other people are always wronging them. Talk about being trapped in that of their Lower Destiny and being completely unaware of it!

Meanwhile, this person who is acting like the victim could have the soul theme to be a victor. But they may go through an entire lifetime and never move into alignment with their soul's positive theme and they may remain a victim. Does this make their soul happy? What happens now? After that life, the soul has to come back and put them, once again, face to face with this victim archetype.

> *The victim thinks in terms of what is being done to them; the victor thinks in terms of what is being done for them.*

Around 90 percent of the populace is in some way riddled with the victim archetype. It wouldn't take anybody a long time to figure this one out once they know what to look for.

An example of what you might be looking for could be blame. Once you spot the blame, how strong is it? Another example might be defensiveness, as in someone defending themselves based on whatever feedback you might have just given them. Not that defending someone or something is a bad idea. There are times in life where it's appropriate to defend someone who genuinely needs to be defended. But that's not what I'm referring to here. Rather, this has to do with a situation in which you attempt to bring up something in a conversation with someone you care about. Then they begin to defend their position to the point where they can't even hear you nor do they want to hear you. If this person has this as a lower energy pattern—as in a pattern of defensiveness—then somehow the relationship, friendship, or partnership they are in now gets sabotaged, as it is almost impossible for them to have a two-way conversation. You can spot this by simply noticing what happens in the conversation, meaning it takes a turn down a very different path than that of how it started.

It's very common for that victim mentality or that victim consciousness within us to either come out swinging, as in blaming somebody, or to take a position of defending as a way to make sure nobody gets in. The third indicator of what to look for in the victim consciousness would be reactivity. If I'm highly reactive, I am under the influence of the victim consciousness. Whatever I'm reacting to hasn't been healed yet. If it had been, I would be responding, not reacting. And I would be responding with a certain amount of conscious awareness, responsibility, and calmness. But in order to do this, I would need to get better at recognizing and acknowledging the part or parts of myself that have been hurting. Some time ago, I heard a teacher say, when teaching on the Kabbalah, "Hurt people...hurt people." In other words, if I'm hurting inside, there's a good chance I will then hurt someone else in my external world. You see, if I were to hurt someone else, its more than likely because I've been unconscious to the part of me that's been hurting.

Now the last indicator would be the language of the victim archetype. "You did this to me" or "Why did you do this to me?" These are victim statements.

To take whatever it is that we're experiencing from whoever or whatever and to be able to see it as something that's being done *for* us puts you in contact with victor consciousness or the victor mentality. This is also somewhere inside of you. It just might need to be called forward by you.

The more we're living under the victim consciousness, whether we're aware of this or not, the more likely it will be to live our life in and from that place of our Lower Destiny. Whereas when we're accessing and ultimately embodying that victor mindset, that victor consciousness, this in itself sets the stage beautifully for us to live our life in and from that place of our higher and Greater Destiny.

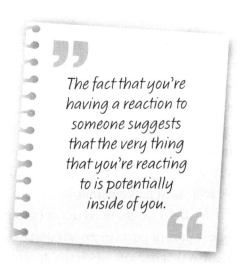

The fact that you're having a reaction to someone suggests that the very thing that you're reacting to is potentially inside of you.

Not everyone who engages with the world like this has the soul theme of the victor—we all fall victim to playing out the victim from time to time—but for the ones who do, the struggle to get out of victimhood is going to be more intense. They just have a difficult time letting go of the victim archetype. Often this is because they are identifying themselves with the victim, meaning they think this is who they are. They can even victimize you when you bring it to their attention. Which is another application of hurt people hurting people—through the victimizing of someone else.

When someone is playing out the victim archetype with that level of intensity, odds are they'll reverse roles and victimize somebody in their life. They're the victim who's being taken advantage of, and then, the next day, they shift to victimizing—as in now they're being overly reactive, pushy, or condescending. They're being way too critical or too judgmental. Maybe they get in someone's face or even do something to hurt someone. Or maybe they take something from someone. When someone is victimizing, the odds are they're creating karma. It's just a question of time when they're doing this that they're going to hurt somebody. You see, if we're still doing the victim thing, regardless of how pitiful our story is, then we've also victimized some people. Therefore, we've created some karma for ourselves that we might not even be aware of. Because if we really are aware of the karma that is created as a result of our choices and actions around victimizing someone else, we wouldn't be victimizing anybody at all anymore, including ourselves. If I'm victimizing someone, I am being self-centered. I'm trying to get something for myself at the expense of hurting someone else. Talk about the perfect recipe for creating negative karma.

The person who has this as a soul theme, or a life theme for that matter, is going to take the victim archetype and literally put it on steroids. In the process, they'll more than likely create a lot of extra karma for themselves. Even though this theme can have a negative slant and sometimes people can get swallowed up by it, at its higher octave it is a 100 percent positive theme.

Now let's remember, once again, that we really are to be rising up and completely aligning the way we're living our life with that of the victor archetype. To authentically empower the victor archetype from within us through the healing or transforming of the victim archetype is a game changer.

Soul Theme of Love

Another positive soul theme that can also have a negative slant to it is the theme of love. If you have the theme of love—and more specifically, you're here to master it because you've got lessons encoded in this theme—then you're probably going to experience its opposite, like fear, resentment, or even hatred. It's like the victor theme, where you'll experience the victim in order to really appreciate the theme of the victor. If it turns out that you have a soul theme for love, then somewhere in that theme, you've got to figure out where you are weak and where you are strong and then begin to balance them out.

Someone that has love as a soul theme is either not very good at giving love or at receiving love.

Are you giving love to the point where you're taken advantage of all the time? If you are, that means you've got a weakness around receiving love. People can come in and downright use you. They could steal from you—as in steal your ideas or take credit for them. They might rip your heart to pieces. They could even cheat on you. This is not because you aren't good at giving love.

It could be that you are really skilled at giving love, but you choose someone that can't give love back to you, or someone that can't receive it. Or maybe it's you that is not very good at receiving love, even though you might ask for it. But can you truly receive it? Is it possible that you have an issue around receiving love?

For someone that has love as a soul theme it's either they're not very good at giving love or they're not very good at allowing themselves to be loved. So therefore, they are not yet experiencing love from both directions. This is happening partly because they have yet to identify those karmic lessons that are unique to them.

If I'm still not learning my lessons just yet, then more than likely I'll only get the type of people who look like they love me and then once I fully commit, I realize I got a dud. Should I be deeply financially invested with this person—or better yet, I've got a child with them—then this relationship is more than likely going to become more complex.

Or maybe you own a bunch of real estate together, or you own a business together and you've got twenty employees on your payroll. This too can become complex if you have a deeper issue around giving or receiving love. As in you now might find yourself staying in this thing and possibly having your self-esteem go down to where perhaps you don't like your life or even yourself anymore. If you are aware of your feelings and you have a fairly good relationship with them, you'll more than likely begin feeling resentful at this stage. And in and from this place you might even begin to complain about how much love you always give. At some point, the story could become about how people always take advantage of you or are taking advantage of you.

If my giving is out of balance with my receiving, this will cause these types of experiences in my relationships to manifest. Because if I'm strong at giving love but somewhat stuck in receiving love, then I'm living my life out of balance. One of the emotional gauges that can let us know that we are out of balance is in that emotion of feeling resentful. In other words, if I start to feel resentful with whatever relationship

I'm in—either to someone or to something, the resentment that I'm now feeling is telling me that my giving and receiving towards them is out of balance. You see, giving and receiving are on the opposite sides of the exact same coin.

As an example, if someone is always giving, as in the act of giving, that act is covering up a deeper issue—the issue of receiving. On the other hand, if someone is always willing to receive, the deeper issue that gets covered up here is giving. So how could this play out? If I have an issue around giving that I'm just simply covering up with the act of taking (or always receiving), then the energy of this issue will attract its opposite to itself. Meaning now someone will show up that has the opposite issue. Deep down if I have an issue around giving, then the person I'm now in a relationship with will have an issue in receiving. So now one person is going to go over the top with giving and the other person will go over the top with receiving. This shows the imbalance going on not just within the relationship with this other person but also within me.

Another way to look at this would be that if one person has a receiving issue on one side of the coin, then the other person on the other side of that same coin has the giving issue. Regardless of the side of the coin you are on, each person will have two or three karmic lessons that are unique to each of them as an individual. In other words, if you are the one who has the receiving issue, you might have a lesson in trusting or in surrendering, or possibly even in learning how to give up the control. If you're on the giving side, you might have a lesson in learning about equality. Or perhaps it's a lesson in humility, fairness, or giving selflessly.

Whatever the lesson, it will be 100 percent unique to the underlying issue that the person is carrying within. And this is regardless of whatever side of the coin you are on.

Whether it's the act of giving or receiving in this theme, it's covering up the deeper issue—receiving love or giving love. If the issue is around receiving love, then the type of person we attract in will more than likely have no problem receiving—because that is what they use to cover up their deeper issue around true giving. So they now look for someone (even if they are completely unconscious towards doing this) that gives since they can't receive. This is where the other person that has an issue around not being able to give takes and takes until it possibly drains you. As in they have no issue with taking your money. They have no issue with taking your heart. They could care less because they're receiving, receiving, receiving, taking, taking, taking.

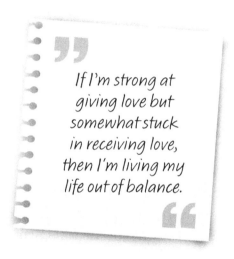

> If I'm strong at giving love but somewhat stuck in receiving love, then I'm living my life out of balance.

Remember this is the cover up—this is how they cover up their issue around giving; by taking or only receiving. And you, on the other hand, are just giving, giving, giving because that's your way of covering up your deeper issue in not being able to receive. You are to be experiencing love—but more specifically, when you have a theme for love, it's different than just the genuine need to experience love. Since this is a theme, it means there's a part of love that you're weak in. There's a part of love that you're jammed up in. It can eventually affect both giving and receiving. So, in this case, when you're jammed up, it affects the balancing of these two forces within you of giving and receiving. At this point in a relationship, the complexity becomes more immense. Everything would be heavy and thick like quicksand. Both parties would probably feel like they're drowning. Both parties potentially would get to the point where they can't stand the other person. And now, they're going to create some wedge of separation between them. Even though they stay together, the desperation can then become stronger, more intense, or possibly all-consuming, which can produce a greater level of confusion between the two of them.

If this is your theme, you've got to look at what side of love you're strong in and what side of love you're weak in. You've got to get brutally honest with yourself. And it would be a good idea to be completely honest with one other person. This could be your transformational life coach or mentor, your guide, or your dearest best friend. It's got to be somebody you trust—somebody who's not going to use this information against you. It's got to be somebody who's got your back. They understand, and they're not judging you.

They're going to support you through whatever you're about to go through because if it turns out your weakness is on the receiving end, then you've got your work cut out for you. There's no quick fix. If your quick fix is to jump into another relationship right away, then you're basically going into round number whatever. Not that you shouldn't date and still have a companionship experience, but just be aware of where you are along your journey.

The best thing you can do is stop thinking you're so far along when, in fact, you're now recognizing this is a theme for you. Recognize what side of the love equation you've got a serious weakness on. Or maybe you need one more round to wipe you out, and that'll be the last one that makes you say, "That's it. I'm done until I've cleared this inside myself. I'm done until I really get on the path to learning my lessons and I have the results to back it up. I'm not doing commitment with this type of a relationship or partnership anytime soon."

Like I said, this is not an easy road. It's one of the reasons people want to jump the gun into another relationship. They'll say to themselves, "Hey, I've already waited for three months." Yeah, but what have you done in those three months? Can you really say you've learned all your lessons in three months and now you're clear, centered, and your giving and receiving has now been properly balanced? Can you really say that you know this other person is your dream partner, business partner, or new best friend? If you really know that, then pull the trigger and go for it. If they're not, however, you're probably going to find out within a few months and regret being so hasty.

But in those few months, you might get invested in another area with them and get burned. This is what somebody does who is not really learning their lessons. They'll eventually get to the place where they say, "That's it—I'm just not meant to be loved." This is like a life sentence they've just given themselves. And, of course, it's nothing more than a distorted perception. It's a misplacement of their energies because they haven't learned their lessons yet. They'll start to believe love is not meant to be for them, and then decide they're going to shut down and turn off to the world, by saying, "No more—I'm done. I'm going to live by myself with my dog, my cat, my bird, or my fish. Or I'm going to build my business or my career all by myself."

Are you identifying your lessons and mastering them? Are you iden-tifying your karmic patterns and dismantling them? If you are, then at some point, you're going to end up with the right person regardless of the type of relationship—as in a friendship, a business partnership, or a love relationship. The right person is not going to take advan-tage of you.

You're going to be able to genuinely and fully receive the love they're showering you with as well. In other words, there's not going to be any part of you, consciously or unconsciously, that's going to resist them. You won't have to suddenly step into the driver's seat and take control to be their mommy, their daddy, their provider, or something they're so desperately needing in life—all as a way for you to lock down the relationship. Rather, you'll let the relationship show you exactly what it is.

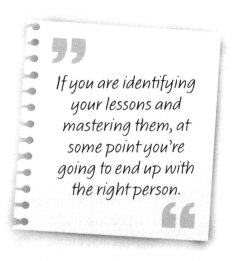

> *If you are identifying your lessons and mastering them, at some point you're going to end up with the right person.*

And, if it turns out to be the relationship, friendship, or partnership that really is most right for you, then you'll commit to it. But only then will you embrace it full on. If it's not the right relationship, then you'll get out of Dodge, and you won't take six months to do it either. It becomes a very simple decision when you're learning your lessons.

If you're not learning your lessons, however, the decision will become incredibly complex because you've got your unlearned lessons that you're possibly still in resistance of or you're not even aware of that are in the mix of this thing, and your ego is making it even more complex. This has all been set up for you to learn your lessons so that eventually, you can have those relationships that are truly right for you.

Remember, the greater goal here if you have this as a soul theme is to balance out your giving with your receiving. Giving is yang—masculine, and receiving is yin—feminine. Another part of the significance of having this as a theme at soul level is in recognizing that your masculine or feminine is out of balance as well.

One of the ways you can determine that you are healing this theme is you begin to notice a balance within you when it comes to you not just giving love but also in receiving love. If you were to have somebody in your world that has the giving and receiving of love balanced out within them, but you on the other hand are still lopsided—meaning you only give or receive and haven't balance them out yet—then it will be extremely challenging to be with someone who has.

So when our giving and receiving is out of balance, what this means on yet an even deeper level is the masculine and feminine within us are also out of balance. When this theme has been completely healed and transformed, we will know it because our inner masculine and feminine will have fallen in love with each other once again.

Soul Theme of Devoted Service

If you have a soul theme of devoted service, then there's a good chance you're going to have to deal with your self-centeredness and/or narcissistic ways. Narcissism is the lower rung of devoted service. Devoted service is where you literally step out of your ego.

When this happens, you start to remember who you are, and you find yourself in an organization, a family, or community where you start devoting yourself with no expectations. You just know it's the right thing to do. In this context, it's the right thing because the soul wants you to get a handle on this. You have some big karmic lessons when you're doing the self-centered thing, especially if you've been doing it for a long time.

It's up to you to uncover what those lessons are. Why are you so self-centered? Why are you narcissistic? Ask yourself these questions without beating yourself up or making yourself wrong. Go into it. If there's a lesson you're to be learning around self-centeredness—if there's a lesson you're to be learning around narcissism—what is the lesson?

Maybe you attribute narcissistic or self-centered behavior to others and think, "I can't stand narcissism. I can't stand the ego. I can't stand it when he or she is so self-centered. I hate that." If you find yourself thinking things like this, and especially if you have a negative emotional energy around this, then you more than likely have some deep lessons to learn here, meaning they're probably karmic.

Self-centeredness can literally block you from anything and everything that would be considered good to have in your life.

When you're reacting to somebody else's self-centeredness or narcissistic ways, you possibly can't see these dynamics inside yourself just yet. The fact that you're having a reaction to this person suggests that the very thing that you're reacting to is potentially inside of you. Not that the other person can't be narcissistic or really self-centered, because they most certainly can be, but the biggest challenge you're having is within yourself. Which is why you keep hanging around it or just can't let it go—as in you've got to keep on talking about this other person that has this awful problem.

In order to truly get to this and ultimately change it, you've got to stop focusing on everyone outside of yourself and you've got to go within and really begin looking at yourself. You've got to identify this correctly, connect with it, drop into it, and feel your way into your own self-centeredness. And, if it makes you sick, then get sick. You might feel like you're going to vomit because it's a sickening sensation when you realize, "Oh my gosh—I am so self-centered!"

But this is you now choosing to get onto yourself—and this is a wise choice. It's a very empowering choice. Now it might not feel good as you're going within and connecting the dots, so to speak, but it's what allows you to start accessing the lesson. Until you do this, you are completely numbed out to what the lesson is. And, if you're numbed out to what the lesson is, then are you learning the lesson? No way. If you're not learning the lesson, what does that mean? It gets louder and simply repeats—not because you're being cursed; rather, you're being blessed. If you need to go another round, then you'll go another round. If you want to complain about the pain, then go ahead and complain, but while you're complaining, instead of consciously working through it, then more than likely you're going to create more pain for yourself.

Self-centeredness, in all fairness, is ugly to look at. There's no question about it. It's just ugly. It's distorted and it can even be weird. It's all those things, especially if you have the theme of devoted service and you haven't stepped into it yet.

The high end of devoted service is in you consciously confronting your narcissistic ways so that you can access the lessons you are to be mastering. Remember the deepest purpose of the personality is to serve the soul, and you start that process by finding someone or something to serve in a devoted way. When you do that, you've got to get out of the way, which means dealing with your own self-centeredness.

Your self-centeredness can literally block you from greater finances, from true love, from a more vibrant and radiant body, or from having a good night's sleep. It can block you from anything and everything that would be considered good to have as an experience in your life. Self-centeredness is a disease. When someone is self-centered, it means they are no longer at ease with some part of themselves.

When you're no longer at ease with yourself, this is where the ego can seed and grow narcissistic ways like a bad weed in your garden. The upside to this theme, however, is if you get into devoted service, especially with the right organization or the right community, it's a powerful way for anybody to live. It's a beautiful way to live because at the very least, it gives you a breath of fresh air from all the self-indulgence. When you get this transformationally and understand that perhaps this is one of your soul's themes, it takes you to a whole other level in terms of your conscious evolution as a soul. Talk about ascending into your Greater Destiny!

Soul Theme of Manifesting

If you have the soul theme of manifesting, you're going to be born into this life having a difficult time manifesting the things that you genuinely want. It's going to feel like something is always holding you back.

Your soul wants you to master the art of manifesting with precision and clarity. For some, this is very challenging. We've got people in their forties right now who are struggling with something in their life that you might think would be relatively easy to manifest. But for the life of them, they cannot manifest it. Maybe they have a health issue, and they cannot manifest the solutions to resolve it. No matter what they do, no matter how many doctors they go to, how many times they've been hospitalized, or how much medication they put in their body, they just cannot manifest that positive result.

This is the person who makes ten resolutions every New Year's Eve, and by February 26, the resolutions have all gone out the window. This person has very little ability to be precise with what they're manifesting. Therefore, they don't manifest all that well on a conscious level. The result of not being able to manifest all that well is revealing this soul theme to the individual. Maybe they say what they want, but they keep on saying the same thing year after year. They have not moved the needle forward at all. This theme will make itself known to them because there will be something they've said they wanted more than once, and they're still saying it again and again to the point where they get frustrated.

If you get really good at this, meaning you manifest like a master, then you'll manifest with great precision.

Maybe they've even stopped saying they want something because they started feeling like perhaps it's just not meant to be. It might very well be divinely meant to be, but they're not recognizing, acknowledging, and ultimately taking ownership for their theme. Therefore, they're not working through their theme, which really means they're not getting to their lessons. They're not resolving their karmic patterns, at least just yet. And if that's the case, then this is going to be an ongoing theme, until, of course, they get what's really going on here.

There are some people who haven't been able to take their income beyond $3,000 a month. There are other people who have an issue manifesting love, a relationship, or even a friendship in their life. They struggle with this because it's a theme for them.

Most people have some kind of a theme that relates to manifesting. This is a common theme for pretty much all of humanity. This is why we take a much deeper dive into the conscious world of manifesting in the very next book of the Transformation Trilogy, *Manifest Like a Master*.

Now the majority of people on the planet, at the very least have this as a soul theme, and especially if they're a younger, less experienced soul. Perhaps they picked it up from Mom or Dad in this life. Mom and Dad ridiculed or dismissed manifesting with their own individual language, so they basically programmed their kids to be very weak at consciously manifesting. Then it became a lifestyle or a life theme for their child who's now twenty-seven years of age. They're having a difficult time paying their rent, month after month, to the point where they're forced into having to move back home. Then Mom and Dad might even start to complain after they've been around for a couple of months.

When you understand the lower vibrational frequency of the matrix that's been set up in this 3D world, and how the matrix is designed to shut us down and block certain things inside us, this is going to make a lot of sense to you. With this theme, you can be assured you've got some lessons to learn here. If you've got the theme of manifestation, you probably have at least a karmic theme of the saboteur. You've possibly got a pattern of not being able to commit to things, or the pattern of having only one foot in the game, or maybe the pattern of impatience.

The lower energy pattern of impatience is a common pattern of the individual who has manifesting as a soul theme.

If this pattern has been running my life, then no matter how positive I am, this will affect my ability to consciously manifest whatever it is I have a genuine heartfelt desire for. A pattern of impatience can produce a series of poor choices and bad decisions. And as you now know, consequences or blessings will always follow our choices or decisions. One of my favorite Chinese proverbs says, "One moment of patience may ward off great disaster. One moment of impatience may ruin a whole life."

Now a significant choice or decision we make in our life under the influence of this pattern could produce a consequential effect that might take us years to clear up. Talk about a distraction! "A distraction from what?" we might ask.

You'll know when you start clearing this theme because when you look at whatever part of your life you've been struggling with around manifesting what you genuinely want, it'll be like the clouds have cleared up, and next thing you know, you'll start manifesting the things you really want on a conscious level. If you get really good at this, meaning you manifest like a master, then you'll manifest with great precision.

By the way, manifesting is in everyone's Greater Destiny as a soul. Think about it for a moment. If you were the oversoul of all the souls on the planet, wouldn't it be a good idea to have them learn how to manifest with precision? What would that do? People would be genuinely happy because they'd be manifesting or creating the life of their dreams.

As I said, manifesting is something that's already inside of us. In fact, nobody can stop this process. The truth is we are always manifesting. The question is: Where are we manifesting from? As in, are we manifesting from our conscious self or are we manifesting from our subconscious self? Are we manifesting what we really want to have or what we don't want to have in our world?

What could we accomplish if we knew we could actually get better at consciously manifesting? Creating those experiences that we have a genuine heartfelt desire to create in our own day to day world? I created a master class on this subject some time ago. This Manifestation Master Class is available to you for free—just look for it in the last pages of this book. I invite you to check it out—I think you'll be really glad you did!

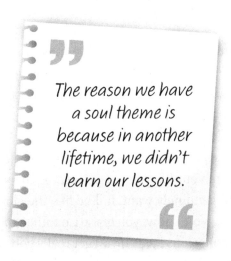

> *The reason we have a soul theme is because in another lifetime, we didn't learn our lessons.*

Again, as a reminder, these examples we just covered are themes you could have, or maybe they inspired you to connect with whatever your soul theme actually is. Keep in mind there are many more of these themes than those previously mentioned, such as: the theme of humility, the theme of respect, the theme of optimism (a.k.a. the theme of a positive attitude), the theme of balance, the theme of focus, the theme of trust, the theme of believing in yourself, the theme of the underdog, etc.

Soul themes are unlimited, but most importantly, the themes we have just covered here might be one of yours, or your theme will come to you as a result of learning about these other themes. Your theme is inside of you waiting to be revealed, for you to discover and ultimately remember. Once you do, this is where you can really work with your soul theme and ultimately heal and transform it. If and when you do, this is you now rising up to your Greater Destiny.

SOULS WITH MULTIPLE THEMES

You'd have to be a really old soul to have multiple themes. To take on one theme is a big piece on your plate. That in itself can pretty much consume you. But, if you are at the first level of an old soul, then you could have a couple of themes. The themes can overlap and interface, partly because you've had each one of these themes in at least one lifetime, probably two or three lifetimes. In each lifetime, you didn't complete a theme. You didn't honor it. You were still in denial of it, and now they're all starting to interconnect, which can create a whole other aspect of heaviness, density, or complexity to punch through.

If by chance you have multiple soul themes, then the bottom line is, your soul wants you to work on this because your soul set this up. The intention of your soul is never to overwhelm you, so if you do have three different themes, your soul is going to come in and emphasize one of them as a primary theme. That theme is interfacing with the other two as well, but the soul is going to put a little more focus onto one theme, as in the primary theme. And perhaps one of the other two become a secondary theme. As you get closer to resolving the primary theme, then the secondary theme becomes the primary theme. The soul takes one to three of our karmic patterns and/or karmic lessons and from them creates a masterpiece. Once it puts it all together, it gives us the theme. This theme will more than likely be one that you've already attempted to clear in one or two other lifetimes.

That's why for some, the theme can be very intense. That's the soul's way of saying, "You're not getting off this time, and if I need to kick you in the butt, I'm kicking you in the butt because there's a lot at stake here right now." That's when things get louder, or something comes in your life and stings you as a way to grab your attention. If you're not willing to wake up on this round, then you can be assured the next round is coming in louder. It's going to come in with a bigger sting, but that's not because you're being cursed. Rather you're being blessed.

LEARNING YOUR LESSONS FROM YOUR SOUL THEMES & GRACE

Whichever theme or themes we're in resonance with, we can be assured there's at least one lesson. That's why it's a theme. It's been set up on purpose by the brilliance of our soul. Our experiences or our circumstances with different people influence our life themes. There's a lesson in those too, but those lessons will be a little lighter. They don't carry the same weight as the soul theme, meaning our karmic lessons are encoded in the soul theme. Remember, the reason we have a soul theme is because in another lifetime, we didn't learn our lessons. So, it's like we're being given another chance. For some of us, this may be a third or fourth chance to truly master it once and for all. Until we come to that place of mastery, we'll experience small doses of grace when on the right path and moving in the right direction.

At some point, when you master your lessons, both the lighter lessons and the karmic lessons, you will have grace all around you. It'll be ahead of you, behind you, and beside you. It'll just show up, and you won't have to do anything for it. That's the best part. You won't have to do anything because you've already done everything. You've mastered what your soul put you on a mission to master. It's like you're honoring your soul and your true life path. This also opens up the doorway for you to learn more lessons, for this is the way for the soul to continue and even accelerate in its own evolution and expansion.

When we are genuinely excited about something, that's the Divine flowing through us.

Once you've discovered what your soul theme is, ask yourself the question, "If there was a lesson I am to be learning here as a result of this theme, what would that lesson be?" Can you start to get excited about this lesson? When we are genuinely excited about someone or something, that's the Divine flowing through us. It's the Divine igniting within us. We could say that's our soul flowing through us because our soul is of the Divine. Your soul is going to benefit when it's fueled by that genuine enthusiasm.

A soul theme is not heavy in the context that it is intended to weigh you down; it's heavy in the context that it's old and neglected. It's been around for a while. As you move into alignment with these soul themes, your life will change for the better in ways that you might not even be able to imagine right now. It'll be significant and lasting because your soul is completely on board with you.

Whether you've had this experience or not, the most important piece is identifying the lessons, honoring them, and working through them.

Stop fighting the learning of your lessons. Stop avoiding or resisting them. Remember, wherever you go, there they are. Stop pretending like they don't exist when they really do.

When we're really learning our lessons, that's where we'll have more grace in that part of our life. It's our divine birthright. It's just waiting to reveal itself to us. But it can only reveal itself to the degree that we are truly learning our lessons.

So now, be honest with yourself and get onboard with really learning your lessons. When you are truly learning your lessons or want to learn them, you might refer back to the section in Chapter 7 on The Five Essential Keys to Personal Transformation, or reach out to your coach or somebody who can actually help you. Whatever you do, make a decision right now that you're no longer going to allow yourself to remain stuck.

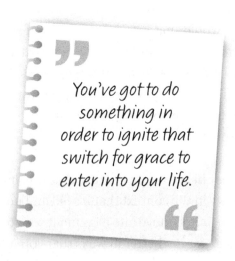

> You've got to do something in order to ignite that switch for grace to enter into your life.

If you're not getting a lot of grace in your life, you can be assured you're probably not learning your lessons well. Perhaps you've put your foot on the brake pedal. Maybe you're holding yourself back. Or you're holding yourself hostage (perhaps at an unconscious level) from actually learning your lessons in this life. You'll know this because you're not getting the grace. When you learn your first lesson completely, you'll know it because you'll be graced. You'll actually be experiencing one of your divine birthrights. It gives me God bumps to think about the possibility of you experiencing grace in your life in this way—because you deserve it. We all deserve it. But you've got to do something in order to open up that doorway. You've got to do something in order to ignite that switch for grace to enter into your life. It's waiting for you—all you have to do is choose it.

Grace can also serve as a gauge. It lets us know whether or not we're really getting it. If you're not experiencing it, maybe you're not really going in and actually embracing the lessons. One of the traps of the ego here can be that we are convincing ourselves on an intellectual level that we are learning our lessons when, in fact, we really aren't. Remember, it's going to be uncomfortable. Spiritual enlightenment is found where it's most uncomfortable. It's seldom found when you're in the privacy of your own space in your comfort zone. When you and I are learning our lessons, there are periods where it can get downright uncomfortable because it challenges us. But again, what challenges us is designed to change us.

EXERCISES

Reflect upon the following questions in your notebook:

1. How quickly do you spot blame in yourself or in others? If you were to give it a strength level, on a scale of 1 - 10, 1 to 10, 10 being really strong, and 1 being not so strong. What number would you give that blame energy?

   On a scale of 1-10, 10 being very well and 1 being not so well, how well do you receive feedback from others? What number would you give yourself?

   How much do you defend yourself when getting feedback from others? On a scale of 1- 10, 10 being really defensive and 1 being not so defensive. What number would you give yourself?

   How quickly do you spot defensiveness in yourself or in others? On a scale of 1 - 10, 10 being real quick 1 being not so quick. Write down your number.

   And why did you give yourself these scores for these questions?

   Finally, think of the Victim Archetype, describe the last time you noticed yourself using victim language? What did you do next?

2. Can you identify any life themes that came on during your childhood? If so, what are they?

3. Is your giving in balance with your receiving?

   If you were to slant more towards one than the other, which one are you more prone to do, the giving or the receiving?

   If you were challenged or weak in one of these two areas, the giver or the receiver, which one would it be? And what is it about your answer that challenges you?

4. How good are you when it comes to manifesting what it is you would like to have manifest in your life personally or professionally? On a scale of 1-10, 10 being really good, 1 being not so good. Why did you give yourself this number?

   Can you think of a time when something manifested in your world that you did not want? If so, describe what it was.

   When was the last time something manifested in your world that you did not want? Describe what that was.

   And if you were to become better at manifesting what it is you really want to have manifest, what's the very next thing you could do to get better at it?

5. Have you identified your very next lesson that you are to be learning? If so, what is the lesson? If not, set the intention to have your next lesson be revealed to you.

   Have you identified your very next lesson that you are to be learning? If so, what is the lesson?

6. Which soul theme from the examples mentioned in the chapter resonated with you most?

   If you were to choose a primary soul theme for yourself right now, what would it be? Why would i be this theme?

   And if you were to choose a secondary soul theme, what would it be? Why would this be your secondary theme?

CHAPTER 13

WHY FORGIVENESS IS NECESSARY FOR THE SOUL

Forgiveness is a big one for a lot of people. Just reading the title of this chapter may have activated you. However, to go deeper into our transformational experience, we're going to have to confront this idea of forgiveness. We're going to have to look at others in our lives who we feel have wronged us, but while keeping forgiveness in mind. We may also have to look at ourselves with forgiveness if we have made choices in our past that were met with strife, struggle, or pain that we've been holding ourselves in judgment for.. We're going to have to honestly confront where we're at with choosing to forgive and then get committed in that choice of mastering our lessons. That's because what forgiveness will do for us physically, emotionally, psychologically, and spiritually will greatly assist us in our rising up to our Greater Destiny. Forgiveness is one of our greater strategies for transforming ourselves and our lives. Forgiveness is also a significant contributor to embodying our divine birthrights.

FORGIVENESS AND THE VICTIM ARCHETYPE

We've become way too comfortable in identifying with this idea that we've been "done to." Again, this is the victim archetype, and if you have not healed yet, then clearly this lesson on learning how to forgive is going to be a challenge that's worthy of investing your time into. Perhaps you have not yet begun the process in learning this powerful lesson because you're possibly still committed (consciously or unconsciously) to keeping the victim in play, as if, somehow, that victim consciousness is doing something good for you. The truth is that all the inner victim is doing is helping to strengthen the needy self.

So, if that is what you want, then keep on doing the victim thing. Keep on feeding it, supporting it, nurturing it, and finding others in your life to help reinforce it. The recipe to continue to do just that would be to think, speak, and act like a victim. Then when you're upset, and your victim comes out, you will more than likely try to justify it in your head shortly thereafter. And when we try to justify the things we've said, what we're really saying from our own unconscious is, "Please don't call me out on this because I'm a victim—and I don't want to let go of my victim status. I need more pain to serve as my teacher. I'm not quite ready to let go of my victim just yet."

That is the bottom line to this whole story. People just don't want to let go of their inner victim. And it is because they love their victim—this is what that old saying "misery loves company" means. Our victimhood allows us and encourages us to keep on telling the same story that we're obviously not sick of yet. Others might be sick of it, but we're not. It's because we have a deep-seated need. Remember that needy self and how it might be hooked in—and in the deepest of ways, to this inner victim. One of the ways in how we spot it is we've got to tell that story one more time to somebody else, hoping to get something from them in return.

This is something that a majority of the populace struggles with. Way back when, I struggled with it too, so I get it. But I've also come to know that the more you keep yourself in the victim mindset, the more suffering you're going to bring upon yourself.

Forgiveness is a significant contributor to embodying our divine birthrights.

You have to go within and take a look at what is happening. If we go to the two sources of pain that you're experiencing, the first source is the original pain. And ultimately, none of us can avoid that. So, when it comes to resisting the original pain, the original trauma—whatever that might be—our resistance is futile. But then, there is the second type of pain, which is the unnecessary pain—and that is when you're hanging on to your victimhood. Hanging on to your victimhood means that you are refusing to learn this powerful, transformational lesson on how to forgive. But this is a part of your Greater Destiny—to learn how to deeply and completely forgive—to master the art of forgiveness.

If you could feel that in your bones, would you keep hanging on to your unnecessary pain and victimhood? Would you keep hanging on to all these old storylines, made up of hurt and pain or "what was done to me," "who did it to me" or "this person's a jerk" and all the rest of it? It just goes on and on. It's all a part of the victim archetype—this lower-level personal agenda, or storyline, in which someone just refuses to let go. Talk about getting stuck in one's Lower Destiny! You can spot these people from a mile away because they're suffering, and their suffering never seems to stop. If you were to go and have coffee with them today, then a month from now, they'll still be repeating the same old story.

Now, if you're really hanging onto your victimhood as a part of your identity, you might not want to hear or accept this just yet. When you're in love with your inner victim, you're just not going to let that inner victim die. In a lot of ways, being in love with your inner victim is like being in an abusive relationship. Many people will not let their abuser go. They just won't do it. Again, misery loves company!

If you go visit a domestic violence shelter, the directors will usually tell you that many of the men and women who are being abused will go back to their abusers. They will not let them die, so to speak. Then, when they have been abused again, they will have something new to talk about. And when they tell their story, they will whine and complain and groan about how hurt they are. Their suffering just simply continues, but they cannot transition out of the cycle because they do not want to let go of their inner victim.

When we identify with the inner victim—we then think we are a victim. But that's where we're off. We are not the victim, just like we are not our feelings. We are not our thoughts. Heck—we're not even our body that we're currently in. We are none of those things. Now, it is our body, and our thoughts, and our feelings communicating with us, but none of that is who we *are* any more than we are the victim archetype.

If the victim archetype is still living within us, and we are still feeding it, nurturing it and propping it up, that is on us; that is us choosing more pain, even if it's at an unconscious level. When a person is really attached to their victimhood, they will often fight you tooth and nail.

When you tell them that this pain is unnecessary, they'll accuse you of not hearing them—of not understanding them.

But I do understand them. What they can't see is that they are doing this to themselves, and then projecting their feelings and thoughts onto me because I'm bringing this to their attention. Then they often dig their heels deep into the earth and say, "I'm going to hang onto this victimhood no matter what you say because you clearly don't understand what's going on here." It's all part of the victim archetype; the victim never, ever feels heard. The victim thing runs rampant throughout the lower octave of our humanity's consciousness.

Our victimhood allows us and encourages us to keep on telling the same story that we're obviously not sick of yet.

All I can say is: get over it. If we're doing the victim thing and feeling like we're never being heard and that people never understand us, then we're being hoodwinked. The victim archetype is kept in play because we identify with it. We think that's who we are. And if we think that's who we are, we're going to pay homage to it. And we're probably not going to let the victim go. Because to let it go, we would have to let go of what we believe our identity is.

You can always tell when someone is doing the victim thing because you'll watch their suffering continue to increase no matter what; it never decreases. That external result speaks volumes to what is going on within us.

But when you're playing the victim, you don't want to hear that. You are still absolutely convinced that you are the victim; that this is the truth of who you are. This is not the truth of who you are. This is just something that you are simply believing is who you are. In truth the real you is greater than this victim that has been residing within you.

Remember, if the victim archetype within the soul theme of the victor is a theme for you, what that means is that you've been doing this for a least a couple of lifetimes prior to this one. And this more than likely has become a serious blind spot for you. Others can see it, but you cannot. That is why it's been so difficult for you to even be able to consciously connect with your inner victim—even when you're doing the victim thing, you just cannot see it. And when others who can see it try to tell you that what you're doing is self-destructive, it likely would be difficult to receive that message because you've already curated your story through the eyes of the victim. You'll be operating in your own basic Lower Destiny where the inner victim resides and you're not even close, at least just yet, to your Greater Destiny, where access becomes readily available to the inner victor.

If someone recognizes that you are truly unconscious to the victim that's inside you, at some point, they are going to make a choice as to how much time they want to spend with you and how many times they want to listen to you tell the same story around what's being done to you. That is because the story that is under the influence of the victim never goes anywhere. It exaggerates and elongates, but that's all. So, they get bumped out of your life, and you possibly go into isolation. And a few months or maybe even a year or two later, there you are, still attached and committed to this storyline that your inner victim simply repeats or adds to.

So, in this scenario we are just continuing to victimize ourselves. We're just repeating it to the next person who comes into our lives. This is how our victim story gets revived and revamped: it is constantly being regenerated until, of course, we step in and say no more—no more of this type of suffering. It's time to learn my lessons and rise up from this old storyline.

WORSHIPPING THE VICTIM

Living through your inner victim represents a total denial of the lesson that you really ought to be learning, which is how to forgive. Why do people do this to themselves? Well it's because they've begun to worship their inner victim. They distort it, turning their inner victim into their victor. Naturally, the victim feeds off this and just grows stronger and stronger. They're suffering, and it affects the people around them, causing them to suffer as well. And so on and so on. They're creating more karma, and the deeper challenge here is they can't even see the effect this is having with their own destiny—at least just yet.

It's all because they're in a state of refusal. Unconsciously, they are refusing to learn the lesson of forgiveness. Your soul has already decided that it's going to be evolving and transforming in this life, and in order for that transformation to happen on a deeper level, you must learn to forgive. If you've been resisting this lesson for thirty years, this is going to challenge you to the core essence of your being.

If you've been resisting for so long that your resistance has become a habit, and you've taken a position to hold this resistance in place, you might not even get through it—at least anytime soon. For this type of resistance is what I refer to in my previous book as the silent killer. This type of resistance, if held onto long enough, will destroy something in our lives that we greatly value. "What does this resistance look like?" you might ask. It looks like judgment, hatred, blame, revenge, etc. An example of this might be judgment, which is making energy wrong (accompanied by thoughts of "I'm not going to let this go"), or even hatred (with thoughts of, "I will hold onto this until the end of time if that's what it takes to make this person pay")—these are temporarily blocking us from being able to forgive. Not to mention the torment that we end up creating for ourselves while we are holding onto these negative thoughts and feelings in our stance of believing that to forgive is somehow wrong, weak, or that the other person is undeserving of it, regardless of whatever I perceive that they have done.

Forgiveness is one of our greater strategies for transforming ourselves and our lives.

Forgiving someone or something in our life that we feel has wronged us all begins with the choice to consciously choose to learn how to forgive. And then to remain conscious of this. The lesson of forgiveness is not fully learned overnight. Just like any of our lessons, there will be a process that we will go through in learning that lesson well. This is why the choice, once made, to learn how to forgive must be followed by a regular practice or ritual of renewing it at or on a conscious level.

When people are hell-bent on hanging onto their inner victim, what they fail to see is how self-centered they're being. It's like they're saying, "I don't care what my soul says. I'm going to hang onto this victim consciousness no matter what. I don't even care what anybody else has to say about it, even those that I say I care about. I'm still going to hang onto it."

It's this distortion—this misplacement of feelings—that causes suffering, and that suffering will continue as long as we choose to remain locked in that position of holding onto our victimhood.

The truth is, when we are truly in our centered self, we would not even perceive things this way but rather we would actively be learning to completely forgive whoever or whatever lay at the heart of that victim archetype.

THE LAW OF FORGIVENESS

There is a law known as the Law of Forgiveness. It says that we are mentally, emotionally, and spiritually healthy to the degree in which we can forgive and forget the grievances against us.

Now, I know that some of you are thinking, "Hey, I'm just beginning to consider the idea of starting to forgive. I don't know if I can also forget." That's alright—ultimately, you are going to get there, and even though the process often begins with and through the intellect, the reality is you're not going to get there through just the intellectualizing of what or who it is you are to be forgiving. Eventually, you'll get to the place where you're not just going to forgive; you're also going to forget the experience as well. You could say that when you arrive at that stage of your journey, you'll just let go of the whole enchilada.

Now when you arrive at the last doorway in this act of forgiving that opens up for you in your own personal or spiritual transformation, you'll know this place, as this is where you'll see the perfection in it all. And when this happens, there will be no reason within that of your Lower Destiny for you to remember it anymore. It won't be because you'll be forcing the memory out—you'll more than likely just be done with it. Because at this place you've become at total peace with it. It's like a leaf on a tree when autumn rolls around. When it's time to fall, it just simply falls away gracefully and naturally.

That is what it's like when you come to the final state of forgiveness. This last doorway opens, and there's no more hanging on. There is no more attachment. There is no more judgment. There is no more anguish. Since you have already done your forgiveness work, at this juncture, you arrive at a place where you no longer really want any of that in your consciousness anymore. Like the leaf, when it's time to go, it just…goes. It falls away. It just dissolves. It's really a phenomenal, beautiful thing.

Forgiveness is love in action. Now, we can say the opposite of that as well. When you are not in a state of forgiving, you are not acting out of love. That is when you are holding on. Resisting. Resenting. Judging. Grudging.

That is why forgiveness is one of the transformational keys to inner peace, freedom, balance, health, and happiness. But the victim does not want any of these things. It in itself doesn't want inner peace or freedom, and it certainly doesn't want happiness. Rather, the victim wants pain. Why? Because pain builds the story and allows the victim to continue to be fed by that story.

There will always be someone willing to listen to that victim story and feel sorry for you. But that doesn't help you, as it keeps you in a discordant energy, which keeps you away from a higher state of harmony. It keeps you away from living your life in that much richer place where you can manifest more of what you as a soul most genuinely desire.

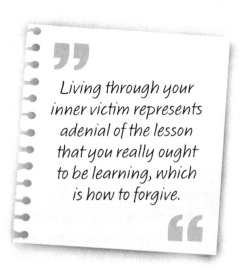

> *Living through your inner victim represents a denial of the lesson that you really ought to be learning, which is how to forgive.*

You may keep saying that you want harmony and happiness, but if you are operating out of the inner victim at the level of your Lower Destiny, your actions will often say something completely different—as in you won't do the types of things that actually produce that state of harmony or genuine happiness. The inner victim doesn't want these things because they aren't good for business, so to speak. Think about it—if you really did find inner peace, what would happen to your inner victim? Exactly! It would have transcended into the victor at the level of your Greater Destiny—meaning the victim would have to die off. Which is the last thing it wants. At this juncture another powerful transformational question you might ask yourself is: What do you want? Or to really personalize this you would ask: What do I want? Meaning, at any point, you can choose to shift the focus from what the inner victim wants to that of what you really want.

When you are in the presence of someone who has become the real deal and has achieved inner peace, where is their inner victim? Does it even exist? No—it's not there anymore. Push all the buttons you want on this person, but you will never see their inner victim because it has transcended to its higher octave, the victor.

FORGIVENESS IS A PROCESS

The idea that you are going to forgive today what has been haunting you for the last ten years, just like that, is pretty much ridiculous. Remember, forgiveness is a process.

Let's say that something happens in a company that affects two people who work there. They are both upset over the experience, but one is able to forgive it after a month or so, while the other might take years to find forgiveness. Why would that be? It's because forgiveness is unique to the individual. The person who needs years to forgive might still not have forgiven their parents or their siblings. They may not have forgiven their first lover who cheated on them. They possibly haven't forgiven any or all of those things, and now, many years later, they find themselves in that company, experiencing a similar event as the person who could forgive after a month or so.

The other person has been in the process of forgiving grievances from their past little by little, slowly but surely. So, when they have negative experiences in current time, they actually roll up their sleeves rather quickly and begin to work towards forgiving them. You see, they have been cleaning up their issues along the way. They've gone the distance and have been putting in the effort. Which means the act of choosing to forgive is no longer a foreign concept for them—it's no longer something they take a position in resisting. This is why they can forgive this new experience rather quickly—because they have literally been developing the transformational habit of forgiveness in their day-to-day life.

Wherever you are in your understanding around the Law of Forgiveness, you'll discover it is so empowering to deepen your commitment and recheck your commitment to consciously choosing to forgive on a regular basis. At the end of this chapter are several forgiveness exercises that will assist you in moving the needle forward in this area of your life experience.

SEEING THROUGH THE SOUL'S PERSPECTIVE

When you practice forgiveness and that last doorway to transformation finally opens up for you, what are you going to see? Perfection! Now I know that might sound strange. After all, how can there be perfection when somebody is destroying someone else's life? When you have thoughts like these, what you have to remember is that you are seeing the perfection in the imperfection through the soul's eyes.

Whenever I'm teaching about perfection, I often say, "The best perfection is imperfection expressing itself perfectly." In other words, everything is perfect. An example of this type of challenge could be when somebody is hurting someone else. How could that be perfect? But what we don't see, or we are not in touch with, is that these two souls that are playing out this dynamic right now may have played this out several times in this lifetime together already. Or it could be that they are playing out a similar dynamic from a previous lifetime. All we see is what's happening on the surface. But what we perhaps don't see are the lessons these two individuals are to be learning as a way to balance this out and more than likely heal and resolve some of their karma. In other words, we could say there's a real good chance that these two came together as a part of their destiny, as each needs the other to help them get a handle on perhaps what their lessons are that they really are to be learning.

Now I'm not saying that we should just stand by and not do anything, because there are times when we are prompted from within and we feel we need to step in—if that happens, then that's what we need to do. The deeper point here is to be open to the idea that there might be more at play than what meets the eye. There are other dynamics that are living somewhere in the underbelly of this experience, and whatever it is that's going on from within, this might very well simply need to be played out. And somewhere within all of this is that element of perfection. Can you see it yet?

> Pain builds the story and allows the victim to continue to be fed by that story.

I have a whole body of teachings just around perfection because it's such a misunderstood topic on this planet. Too often people are so quick to jump the gun because they think they know exactly what's going on, but they're only using their physical eyes. They'll be quick to react to whatever it is that they're seeing and then completely miss the perfection behind what it is that's actually going on.

And as always, if we miss something, then all that means is that it's more than likely going to repeat itself yet again. And it will continue to do so until, of course, we rise to the level of recognition where we can clearly see whatever it is that needs to be acknowledged and ultimately embraced on all levels. As in physically, emotionally, mentally, psycho-logically, and spiritually.

So when you can see at the soul's level, you can see that even when you experience wrongdoing, there is something else going on. The soul is not the victim; it is the personality that the victim comes through. Believe it or not, the soul really knows what it is doing.

Ideally, we want the soul to fully come through the personality and take complete possession of the personality. But pulling that off is usually a pretty major undertaking. So, it's the victim that flows through the personality, and you'll see it because the person will act like a victim. They will think like a victim. They will speak like a victim. And they can even walk like a victim.

That's why it's easy to spot this once you know what to look for. It's easy for us to spot somebody who's got the victim consciousness coming through their personality—through their physical body or their physical actions. Say your son is hell-bent on doing something and you know in your bones that what he's doing is potentially going to hurt him or somebody that he really cares about.

We sometimes have a difficult time when some person is hell-bent on doing whatever it is they're going to do and will not let us influence them. Even if it would be in their best interest to do so. This could bring up our control issues, and if it does, one of the ways we will know is that we get immediate pushback. This contributes to the elongation of the experience we're having as a soul with that other soul. But again, what you possibly are not yet aware of is that there is a chance that your soul and theirs have played out this exact pattern before—only now the roles have been reversed.

Here in the Western world, we for the most part don't understand reincarnation and how it really works. Many of us have been programmed to believe that there is only this one life, on this one planet, in this vast universe. We have been programmed to shut down to the greater truth so that we cannot see what's going on at soul level. But intuitively, it just starts to make sense. Take the scenario of a murderer and a murder victim. You see these two souls that are having this conflict with each other, where one is the perpetrator and the other one is the so-called victim, but what you cannot see is the possibility that those two souls were together before, in a previous lifetime, with the roles reversed.

We don't see events and conflicts like this from the greater perspective. We see them all from the smaller perspective, which is like viewing life from 3,000 feet when you could be seeing things from a perspective of 44,000 feet. If you're at 44,000 feet, your vision is going to be greatly expanded. You're going to see other aspects of what is going on. But if you're only seeing life from a 3,000-foot view, you're probably thinking what you see is what you get. You cannot even imagine seeing life from 9,000 feet because as far as you are concerned, you're already at the top of the mountain. But that's just your ego tricking you.

We are constantly evolving. And when we evolve, it allows us to see more and more of the world within us and around us. When it comes to forgiving, this changes everything. The last doorway that opens up to you, when you come to the crest of your full-on forgiveness of a person, is going to feel like a grid has emerged around you. You're going to see all these dots of light on that grid—and then, suddenly, all the lights are going to connect, and the whole thing will appear to you as one great masterpiece. You'll be in awe of it and wonder why you never saw it before. Well, that's because before you were at 3,000 feet, and now you're at 11,000 feet.

You have raised your frequency because you rid yourself of all the anger, judgment, resentment, and grudging that was blocking your vision. You will feel like you've had the epiphany of all epiphanies where you can see much more of the perfection that is at play here.

When we see the perfection in all of its detail, within the experience that we have been struggling to understand, we become free of that trauma or pain from our past which we were enslaved to. Talk about freedom! This is another way in which we reclaim that birthright. You see, once I am in the complete recognition of the perfection at the core of the experience, all can now become well in my world—as the recognition of the perfection restores balance and harmony.

If we aren't willing to forgive, then we won't be able to see this. We'll think that we have the largest vision of anyone on Earth, when really we are only seeing a fraction of what we could be seeing. We will have been tricked—both by our own ego and by the collective ego here on Planet Earth. We'll even forget that there is a much larger pattern at play here. We'll only be in touch with the lower patterns, but we won't know that they are the lower patterns.

BEING IN A STATE OF FORGIVENESS

Forgiveness is a very powerful practice. But living in a state of forgiveness is even more powerful. Being in a state of forgiveness means that we have already forgiven whoever it is that is *going* to hurt us before it even happens. When you live in this state of forgiveness, then quite frankly, no one can really hurt you. They might do something nasty. They might sting you or cheat you. It might hurt in the moment, but it's not going to affect you for the rest of your life. Why? Because you're now living in a state of forgiveness.

When you're living in a state of forgiveness, you will not hold a grudge against anyone or anything, as you are no longer holding onto the hurt or possibly even the resentment that you carried for however long. Rather you work through it fairly quickly, learn whatever there is to learn, and you let it go. This is what allows you to continue moving forward in your life. In other words, you're not going to let someone who hurts you affect you or hold you back from the life journey that you are on.

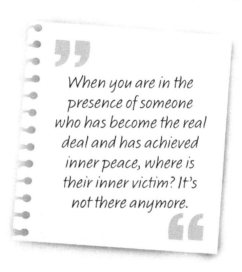

> When you are in the presence of someone who has become the real deal and has achieved inner peace, where is their inner victim? It's not there anymore.

Your soul wants you to live in a state of forgiveness because of the implications for your soul. You see, when you are not able to forgive, it means that you have gotten snagged. Once we get hung up on something, at this juncture there's really no evolution for the soul. As in, it's almost impossible for the soul to grow and evolve. So now the question here would be: how long will you stay there? Or, how long do you want to remain snagged? As in the next year? The next decade? Or possibly for the remainder of your life?

If you're living in a state of forgiveness and someone cheats on you, it's going to hurt. But you know what? You're going to get through it rather quickly. You're not going to get snagged. You're not going to spend the next seventeen years being hung up on the same snafu.

And yet this happens every day to people in countries all around the world. Why do so many people get caught in these snafus? It's because they are not living in a state of forgiveness. The moment that someone stings them, odds are they will allow themselves to stay snagged on that hurt. Why would they do that? When we're not able to forgive, it's because we don't understand on a deeper level those dynamics that are happening within the underbelly of the experience.

I love what Buddha once said, "To understand everything is to forgive everything." So every time you feel yourself getting snagged on a hurt, simply ask yourself: "If I hold on to this hurt, will there be a cost? And if so, what might the cost be? How might this choice to hold onto this hurt for too long affect the way I'm living my life?" And probably the most transformational questions to ask are, "What's my current level of understanding of this experience? What do I believe has really happened here? And is it possible that my understanding of this experience around what I believe has occurred is somewhat limited?"

It's the deepening of our understanding of something that has happened to us that helps us in forgiving everything that we feel has been done to us. Which also means if I'm still not able to forgive whoever or whatever, it's because of my current level of understanding.

So as we understand something on a deeper level, we see more of the perfection at the core of the experience. For at the core of whatever we've been experiencing, its only when we are recognizing and understanding in a more expansive and deeper way, that this allows us to live our life in and from this state of forgiveness more frequently.

Jesus said, "Father, forgive them, for they know not what they do." Why would Jesus say such a thing? Because he was already living in a state of forgiveness. For him, it was a non-issue. He knew that those who were out there stinging others had no conscious awareness of it—that

416

they had no clue what they were doing. So he was asking God to please forgive them in advance. He didn't want them to get snagged and to have that snag affect the next five lifetimes of their souls' journeys. Jesus was dialed in; he was accessing a higher, greater truth when he declared this. And now here we are, two thousand years later in linear time, and we have a huge opportunity to learn how to do this as well.

> Being in a state of forgiveness means that we have already forgiven whoever it is that is going to hurt us before it even happens.

This is a common lesson for almost every soul on Earth. I say "almost" every soul because I have met a few people who were clearly living in this state of forgiveness from the beginning; they must have learned how in a previous life. Those types of people, when they show up, are here to plant into our collective consciousness. They're setting the example, which is just as powerful, if not even more powerful, than teaching it. As Jesus said in the Sermon on the Mount, the most powerful teaching is to be the example of what it is you are teaching others to move towards.

I knew a lady who, long ago, was a beautiful model with a stunning body. And she had the pictures to back it up. When she was nineteen or twenty years old, she was in a plane crash. Of the hundred or so people who had been on the flight, she was one of only a handful that survived this horrific crash. There had been negligence within the airline; and it was believed that this shouldn't have happened. But it did, and she found herself all bandaged up in the ICU. All you could see were her beautiful eyes, and a couple of her fingertips—she had pictures of that as well.

And right from the day it first happened, she met the entire thing with forgiveness. No one ever heard a single complaint come out of her mouth. She never griped or groaned. She never did the victim thing— even though other people would tell her she had the right to feel like the victim in that situation.

Later in life, when she was in her late thirties or early forties, she discovered singing. Her voice was so wonderful that she made it all the way onto the television show *America's Got Talent*. When she walked out on stage, you could see that her whole body was terribly scarred. But it took me all of ten seconds to become absolutely captivated with her beauty. I was so moved, and as she began to tell her story, you could tell that the audience was inspired by her as well. Everybody got God bumps, seeing the beauty of this woman and her magnanimous soul.

She was so inspiring because you knew that most anybody else who had experienced what she did would have died—not because of the plane crash itself, but because they would have been so negative and resentful in its aftermath. They would have died just from the sheer bitterness and toxicity of giving into their inner victim.

Not only did she not carry any of that toxicity with her, but she was blessed with this incredible voice that she discovered. Everything about her was stunningly beautiful—and a large part of that beauty came from knowing that she had not had a moment of complaint. Not one single moment.

The other remarkable thing about her was that when she walked onstage, she did not try to cover up any of the scars from her injuries. I can still picture her as clearly as if she were standing right in front of me. You could see her scars and see the missing fingers on one hand. But she didn't try to cover any of that up. She barely wore any makeup, much less than the other contestants who had appeared onstage. You could clearly see that her entire body had been engulfed in flames. And yet, if you were to close your eyes while she was speaking, you would never know it. You would just think that you were in the presence of someone truly beautiful—and she was. And so is anyone who is living in a state of pure forgiveness. This is one of the master keys to becoming a Divine Human.

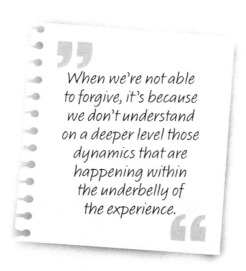

> When we're not able to forgive, it's because we don't understand on a deeper level those dynamics that are happening within the underbelly of the experience.

Remember again, the lesson in forgiveness. It is one of the keys that leads to inner peace, harmony, and your freedom. It is one of the keys that leads to health and happiness. So, if you are not experiencing these five things to the extent that you would like to, then there is a good chance that you have not yet learned how to forgive or how to live in a state of forgiveness.

Clearly, this is a lesson that many on our planet need to learn. It sure would make it a nicer place for all of us if the majority instead of the minority of people learned this lesson well and became the embodiment of this profound lesson on forgiveness. Talk about humanity rising up to our Greater Destiny!

FORGIVENESS QUESTIONS

The next few sections contain specific questions on forgiveness. These are presented in a different format than the rest of the exercises in this book and are done so on purpose. Keep in mind that they may challenge you. But if you choose to answer them, you will find a wonderful lesson and personal discovery within each of them. Get your journal out and record your answers to reflect on later.

Ask yourself where you are at with forgiving, on a scale of 1 to 10, 10 meaning you're really good at forgiving and you get there rather quickly, 1 meaning you don't even get out of the gate for months, or maybe even years after the event has happened. Where are you in your ability, in your willingness, in your readiness, to forgive a grievance? Write this down in your journal along with any other thoughts that come up for you.

Think of a person or some part of yourself that it would be in your highest and best interest to become forgiving of. If you haven't forgiven them, why?

Giving it as much detail as you can, describe the very last time you chose not to forgive. And how has that turned out for you?

Now describe the last time you chose to forgive. How did that work out for you?

Forgiveness Exercise #1: Am I Willing to Forgive Others?

The first question that we are going to reflect on is this: Am I willing to forgive others?

The key word here is "others." It's a yes or no question. Can you currently see the benefit in forgiving others? This might still be a process for you, and it might challenge you to the core of your being. But it starts with you choosing to forgive others from this point on, regardless of what has been done to you. Why? First and foremost, for your own salvation and the sake of your own soul. Because when all is said and done, you are not with them, you are with your soul—and ultimately, you as a soul must choose to be true to you.

When you are holding someone in judgment and choosing not to forgive them, all you are doing is further hurting yourself. Forgiveness is love in action—and in this case, forgiveness is self-love in action. Every time you forgive someone who has hurt you in the past, it is an act of self-love. It is a divine choice in giving love to yourself. When you are able to give love to yourself, this is what opens the doorway within you to give unconditional love to others.

Action Step: Letter of Forgiveness for Others

Make a list of up to three people that it would be in your highest and best interest to forgive.

Note: This letter of forgiveness we are writing to someone else is really for you. In other words, when you're done with this letter, you could mail it to them—or not. The whole purpose of this exercise is for you to have an experience so that you can get a deeper understanding of what this really is for you and to assist in moving the needle forward in forgiving this person.

This letter writing exercise is not dependent upon you actually mailing the letter or giving the letter to the person you are writing the letter of forgiveness to. This exercise is more for you than for the one you are writing it to. Of the thousands of people I have facilitated in this letter writing exercise, only a small percentage of them actually mailed the letter.

For each of the people on your list, write out the following:

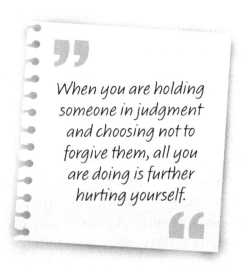

When you are holding someone in judgment and choosing not to forgive them, all you are doing is further hurting yourself.

Step 1: Start off by writing, "I forgive [FILL IN THE BLANK] for..." and then complete the rest of that sentence.

Step 2: For each person on your list, think about what lesson or lessons you may have learned from your hurtful or painful experience with them. Then, write about those.

Step 3: Now write the Letter of Forgiveness to each person on your list. Turn to a blank piece of paper so you'll have a fresh page to work with, and title it as if you were addressing a letter ("Dear Joe," "Dear Joanne," etc.). Then...just start writing. Let your thoughts go wherever they need to go onto that paper. Be real about whatever it is that's coming up for you to put to that piece paper or multiple sheets of paper. In other words, when writing whatever comes up for you in thought or feeling, just write it down unfiltered and unedited. No matter how critical or negative your thoughts are, no matter how angry or even sad your feelings are—that's all part of this exercise. Remember that the focus here is on forgiveness. You might need to express why you're forgiving them or share why it is such a challenge for you to forgive.

If you are still finding it difficult to forgive them fully, that's alright—just do whatever you are capable of doing, with the intention of moving the needle forward in your overall process of forgiving them.

As you are writing your letter of forgiveness, do be aware of the unique lesson or lessons that you are potentially to be learning as a result of this experience that you've had with this person. Even though a part of this letter will be about them, it's important to recognize that the real transformational power of forgiveness comes as we take whatever happened in the experience and bring it inward. This is where we access deeper insights into those lessons we are to be learning. Remember, as our understanding of this situation deepens, so does our process in completely forgiving them. Now you might want to consider the part that you played in the experience or acknowledge any responsibility you may have had in your interactions with that person. As you're working to forgive them for whatever they may have done, you might also want to forgive yourself for any errors you may have made in your interactions with them.

Whatever direction you choose to go in with your letter, take charge of your own forgiveness! Remember, you're not asking for their forgiveness—you're choosing to forgive them, to whatever degree you are able to do so, so that you can continue working to heal and to resolve these issues inside yourself for your own inner peace, harmony, and freedom.

Forgiveness Exercise #2: Am I Willing to Forgive Myself?

This is a great exercise to do just before going to bed, as it may activate a dream for you. The more important question to ask here is: "Am I willing to forgive myself?"

For this exercise, write down up to three things or experiences that you are willing to forgive yourself for, using the following template:

"I forgive myself for [FILL IN THE BLANK...]"

After you have identified those things or experiences you are willing to forgive yourself for, for each one, ask yourself: if there was a lesson I was to be learning from this experience in forgiving myself, what would that lesson be?

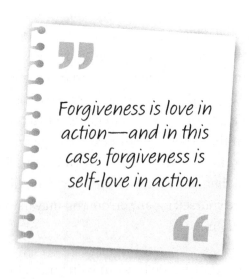

Forgiveness is love in action—and in this case, forgiveness is self-love in action.

Action Step: Letter of Forgiveness to Yourself

Just like you wrote a letter of forgiveness to other people who have affected your life, now write a letter of forgiveness to yourself.

Begin your letter, "Dear Self," and then write for as long as you need to until you feel a sense of completion.

This is not something you want to rush into. You are going to need to take some time to really let yourself have an experience as you go into writing your letter. If some emotions come up in the process, just go with them. If you need to write about any feelings or sensations that come up for you, then write about them.

Part of the forgiveness process is connecting with the feelings that come up in your body. Those feelings need to be felt by you. It is important that you really connect with them and become one with them, even if it is just for sixty seconds, because those feelings often release another insight or two that will be of value to you.

Forgiveness Exercise #3:
Am I willing to forgive some part of myself?

Complete this letter in a similar way to the letters you did in the previous two exercises, with the focus this time being on a specific part of yourself: as in the inner child, the ego, the shadow, or some other part of you.

Action step: Letter of Forgiveness to Some Part of You

Now write a letter of forgiveness by beginning with "Dear [FILL IN THE BLANK]."

Just like when you are writing a letter to yourself or to someone else, more than likely there will be feelings and/or physical sensations that will come up in your body as you address this part of you that you have chosen. Those feelings and/or sensations need to be felt by you. Remember it is important that you really connect with them and become one with them, even if it is just for sixty seconds, because as previously mentioned, those feelings and/or sensations often release another insight or two that will be significant to you.

Bonus Exercise:

Affirmative Declaration: Create an affirmative declaration that you can repeat over and over again throughout your waking day for the purpose of forgiving whatever or whoever you need to forgive. For example, "_____ (name the person, yourself, your ego or your inner child, etc.), And continue with: I forgive you for _____."

Once you've completed your affirmative declaration, repeat, preferably out loud, seven times in the morning and seven times when you go to bed for seven consecutive days. Journal how you feel after doing this exercise after those seven days as compared to when you first began.

CHAPTER 14

HIGHER DESTINY, LOWER DESTINY

I've referred to Higher Destiny and Lower Destiny at various times throughout this book. Now we are going to explore the different areas of the Higher Destiny and the Lower Destiny from a different point of view.

LOWER REALITY VS. HIGHER REALITY

Within our field of consciousness, both individually and collectively, a higher-reality and a lower-reality plane exist simultaneously. Most people end up in the lower reality—and for the most part, they remain there for the duration of their life experiences, most often due to a lack of awareness. The higher reality is, ultimately, our soul's destiny; that is where we are meant to be rising up to.

Now this could be difficult to do, particularly for new souls, unless of course someone has a mentor in their life that they trust and who listens to them. A trusted mentor will greatly increase the odds that they can level up and rise into whatever their higher reality is.

Believe it or not, master souls, ancient souls, advanced souls, and older souls are rising too! All souls are always intended to rise higher from their inception. As we know, there is really no end to this because we live in an infinite universe. How could there be an end? Is there an end to God?

This concept really freaks some people out. Others get excited about it because this means that the last frontier is the soul, and that is what we are now beginning to explore. So, how do we explore this frontier? What are we to be doing as souls? Well, first, we must get a handle on these concepts of a higher reality and a lower reality.

A higher reality operates at the highest, greatest truth. Now, remember that this always upscales; regardless of where you are at as a soul, there is always a higher reality to rise up to. This means that the truth becomes more refined and vibrates at a much higher frequency.

The lower reality is where we find truth's lowest rung or lowest octave. That is where most people are—they just aren't aware of it. That is where you find the unpleasant truths—the ugly ones, the heavy ones, the dense ones. An example of this might be where we've told someone a lie, such as "I'm not cheating on you," when, in fact, I am cheating on that person, or, "I'm protecting our bank account," and meanwhile I'm syphoning off the account without telling my partner, or, "This is your child," when in fact this child is by someone else. Or we might work at convincing others that we're really well when we know that we're hiding an addiction or an illness, or maybe we married or partnered into money and say we love the person we married, or love working with that business partner. But at the lower level of truth we are there because of the money this other person provides for us, etc. These are the types of truths that, over time, could destroy something that we really value and/or could kill us.

When I say this, I do mean that literally. If you have enough unpleasant truths buried in your lower field of consciousness—whatever that means for you and your soul—that could be enough to take you off the face of this earth. If you have three or four unpleasant truths buried in your consciousness, they could potentially cause you to turn to drugs or alcohol or whatever your numbing strategy is. Younger or less mature souls do not have the same strength as older souls, so they are more susceptible. The older soul that is also down in their lower reality can handle more unpleasant truths; however, in doing so, it is still playing with fire.

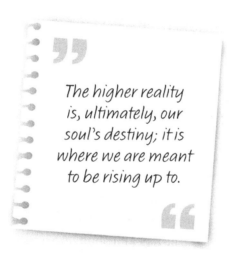

> The higher reality is, ultimately, our soul's destiny; it is where we are meant to be rising up to.

A soul can only hold so many unpleasant truths at the lower level of its consciousness at any one given time. If you get enough unpleasant truths inside of you, that means you've got a lot of weight, energetically speaking. These are all lower energy frequencies. Imagine being a powerful swimmer, getting ready to dive into a pool with a depth of eighteen feet—and then, right before you get ready to dive in, somebody ties a fifty-pound weight around each of your ankles. How powerful would you have to be in order to traverse that pool? How long could you stay above water before you found yourself in real danger? Of course, this is just a metaphor, but it allows us to consider a very important question: how long can you maintain the number and the weight of the unpleasant truths that are buried inside your consciousness before something takes you down?

The whole purpose of the lower reality is to see if you can be taken down. Why, you might ask? The why has to do with us becoming healthier, stronger, and wiser. You see when I rise up from having been taken down, this is a significant part of the process. For when I rise up, this is what now makes me healthier, stronger, and wiser. Because every time this happens, I rise up even higher, little by little, slowly but surely towards the highest octave. Now the greater purpose of the higher reality is to prop you up—even higher. Ultimately, the goal here is for you to rise into your higher reality and then to sustain it.

Think of your career, for example. At any point, you could drop into the lower reality with your career and your position in your company. While you're down there, it has the potential to really cause some harm. For example, you could become too aggressive in your company, and next thing you know, you find yourself behaving aggressively towards someone. Not necessarily physically, but maybe you are becoming aggressive with your words or aggressively sending negative darts to them mentally. Maybe this has morphed into a pushing energy where you're pushing too hard on someone or something. And while this is going on, you're probably not even aware. Now if you were to push for too long of a period of time, there could be a negative consequence coming your way. Maybe this affects your health, or a relationship with a colleague. Maybe it affects your relationship with your boss. Maybe you turn off a client. Whatever it is, if you're not aware that you're pushing, if you're not aware that you're aggressing on someone or something, and you stay in this lower reality for a period of time, at some point, this will produce a negative consequence.

By the same token, if you rise into your higher reality, who knows how far you could potentially go? How successful, how effective, how masterful could you become? An example of this could be a leader within a company that has been leading a small group of individuals. And now that they have risen into this higher reality of their career, they find themselves being promoted to a higher level of leadership and responsibility within the company. It becomes really obvious that this person has become more effective in their role as a leader and they've become better at what they do, which now produces a positive consequence, such as possibly an increase in pay, or maybe it's some form of recognition. Whatever it is, as we sustain this higher reality in our career, it just simply becomes a question of time; this will be followed by a positive consequence. It's the Law of Cause and Effect in action.

If one of this person's responsibilities is to hire new people into their department or into their company, they just start hiring better people. They get better at recruiting, or they get better at hiring the right person the first time. This is another place where you can spot that they're living in a higher reality, which means they're producing healthier, richer, more positive consequences for themselves.

And in the business world this is a positive consequence because it's such a beautiful result when you hire the right person right away. Maybe this person becomes better at problem solving as a leader. This is all part of that higher reality. And when you become better at problem solving, just like when you become better at hiring the right person, at some point, this will produce another positive consequence because from the company's point of view, you're now increasing the value that you're bringing to your company.

The two worlds of the higher reality and the lower reality are available to us at any time, but we have to be aware of them in order to remain in the higher one. We must be aware of what is either going to bring us up into the higher reality or pull us down into the lower reality. And when we are in the lower reality, the risk is in possibly getting stuck there.

431

In whatever higher reality that you as a soul are rising to, it is always love based and unconditional. When you are in a higher reality, and you are with your kids, your wife, your husband, your best friend, your lover, your family, or your business partner, you are always met with love because you are in a love-based world.

> We must be aware of what is either going to bring us up into the higher reality or pull us down into the lower reality.

The lower reality, however, is always fear based. What that means is that when you are in this lower world, the odds are you will find yourself in a state of reaction—as in you are either reacting to somebody or something or getting ready to. Maybe somebody cuts you off in traffic, and then you lose it in your car. Or you are having a tough conversation with somebody, and then you lose it on the phone because your conversation is not going the way you think it should be going. That is you operating through fear, not love.

In the higher reality, that world is based on love and unity. It's saying, "I'm loving you for the purpose of unifying us. I'm loving my child for the purpose of unifying with my child—or, if they are old enough, I'm loving them as a way to help them unify within themselves." It's saying, "I'm coming from love, always with the intention of unity."

LOWER ENERGY WILL RISE IN THE PRESENCE OF HIGHER ENERGY

I have two people that I have been working with for the last few years. As awesome as each of them are, let me tell you, at the beginning, there was nothing awesome about this union at all! When those two got together for the first time, they were really having a challenging experience. I chose to get involved more than once, and a lot has happened between the three of us over the last few years since then. There has been a lot of growth. But back then, I was coming from a place of love and unity, and the two of them were coming from a place of fear and separation.

They were completely repelled by one another, which showed itself in the amount of resistance they had towards each another. They would both make statements like: "He's abusive" or "She's an absolute b****" or "I don't know if I want to or even can work with this person." There was a tremendous wall there where the flareups would happen. They would avoid each other's calls, even if they knew they needed to talk about something for the company. That was all part of their resistance.

So I'd come on the team meeting, I'd ask them if they had spoken to each other, and they would both say no. And I'd say, "Well, how about we speak to each other now?" And I wouldn't get a response from either one of them, like they were frozen. I said, "Okay, so this is where we are. So it looks like we're going to stay here for at least another few hours." Neither thought that was funny at all, because they were in such resistance. And in that position, they're going to hold and hold and hold.

Then I ended up addressing both of them. One of them called to talk to me about it, and that's what opened up the conversation. And then, I reached out to the other team member and asked, "How long are we going to do this? Are we at a place right now where we can punch through this and start to have a conversation?"

433

Well that softened things up a tad, and then we had the punch through where they talked on their own. They already kind of broke loose with all of this, but I helped massage it along so that they eventually got to a really great place. And we've been in that great place ever since.

If they would have gotten their way, they would have separated, but love is the highest frequency. Unity is the highest frequency. And when you are in the presence of somebody who embodies love and unity, then the waters just start to smooth out.

With some concentrated effort and mediation on my part, we crossed over into a place where there is more synergy and it's more consistent, as everyone is interacting with each other in this energy of harmony on a more regular basis. There's a lot more reaching out to each other. The resistance that once was has been melting away and continues to do so. This has made it much easier and more enjoyable for us all to work together. There's a greater inclination to just reach out to the other team member, in both an immediate way and also in a more frequent, consistent, and honoring way. We get more done. And we get more done with fewer mistakes.

Now we're like one big happy family. They love each other—they're like brother and sister now. They now talk on the phone—sometimes at night, and even on the weekends. Neither of them knows this, but privately from time to time, they'll each tell me how much they appreciate the other one. That is exactly the way it's supposed to be. Yet in the beginning, the two of them were so stuck in their own lower realities that if left to their own devices, they wouldn't have even gotten to step one. One of them would have destroyed the other. But that didn't happen because I was there for them, in that higher reality; I was coming from a place of love with the goal of unity, and I did not waver.

There's a Universal Law known as the Law of Frequency that says all lower frequencies, when in the presence of a higher frequency, must rise to that higher frequency. Whenever they are in the presence of that higher energy, those lower energies naturally begin to rise to that higher octave. The higher energy serves like a magnet if you will—it just lifts the lower energy up to itself. And as long as that lower energy remains in that higher octave, it cannot return to the lower octave because there is no longer anything there for it to return to in that moment. An example of this would be with fear. Fear is a heavier, denser, and slower moving frequency which can manifest its like or show up in our day-to-day reality through worry, stress, anxiety, insecurity, etc.

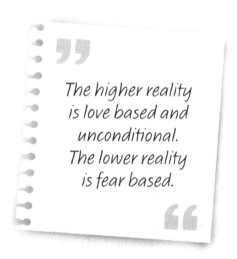

> The higher reality is love based and unconditional. The lower reality is fear based.

Whereas calmness, peace, harmony, and love are a higher and faster-moving frequency. So if someone is afraid but is now in the presence of someone else who is in a state of calmness and peace, in a relatively short period of time, that person who's afraid begins to calm down. They begin to feel safer and more secure once in that higher frequency of calmness, peace, harmony, and love. Another way to explore this would be to recognize that the frequency of your divine self, your greater soul, is considerably higher than your basic human self, your ego.

So if we are living life more egoically, then we are in that lower frequency and temporarily separated from the higher frequency of our true self—our divine soul self. Now if we're not able to sustain the higher frequency of our most authentic self, then more than likely our best strategy, for at least experiencing this higher octave of our soul, is to purposely find someone (as in a teacher, mentor, or guide) that has become the embodiment of this higher frequency—known as their most authentic self.

Think of someone you might know that whenever you are around him or her you just start to feel better. Or maybe you feel safer, or maybe you notice that your attitude towards life just becomes brighter. This is happening because you are now more than likely in the presence of somebody who has embodied that higher frequency. He or she is like a gift to humanity. You could be down in the dumps and as soon as this person shows up, regardless of whatever you might be going through—as in feeling negative, discouraged, anxious, insecure or just walking around with a bad attitude—as you come into the presence of this person, you slowly but surely begin to rise up. You notice that you've become lighter. You notice that your attitude has become brighter. And it's not because they, this person, this embodiment of this higher frequency, are forcing you to do anything. Rather it's because all lower energy seeks to rise higher when in the presence of a sustained higher frequency.

SERVING SOMETHING HIGHER

The higher reality is all about serving something greater. At the highest levels, it is all about serving the Divine. If you are not yet your Higher Self, then it is about serving your Higher Self. If you are not yet the embodiment of your soul, then it is about serving your soul. Even more specifically, you are serving the agenda of your soul, or the Divine Agenda.

Now in the lower reality, it is all about serving the self alone. There, you're serving the agenda of the ego. This is where the darker entities, the darker energies, and the darker influences all live. This is where entity attachments can happen.

Your angels and guides don't live in this lower reality. The reason why we sometimes doubt we have angels and guides is because we cannot connect with them when we're living in the lower reality; even though they can, for the most part, come down to that lower frequency, they generally won't. When you're in the higher reality, that is where you often get an inkling of your angels, or your guides. You might also feel a physical nudge sometimes. It will feel really cool when that happens because in that moment, you will have risen into your higher reality. You might not stay there—you might even drop back down rather quickly—but for that moment, at least, you will have connected briefly with one of your angels or guides because you will have elevated up to that higher reality.

Now, where do you suppose the powers-that-be, or the establishment—whatever you'd like to call them—wants everybody to be? In the lower reality, of course. And why would they want everybody to be in the lower reality? It's because people for the most part can't wake up, which mean they're easy to control. It's just the establishment's way of herding the cattle. That's why they oppose people like us—people who are waking up. We could say w're not good for business. Who's business? Their business!

But now many of us are inspiring others to wake up, by that of our own example. Then, where most appropriate, we're helping enroll them into their own process of waking up as well. We're also directing others to learn how to authentically empower themselves. As this continues to happen, over time, we're going to end up with even more people living their lives in and from a higher reality.

437

So coming back to the establishment or the powers-that-be, for the most part, they want everyone to stay at a lower reality, whereas the masters want everybody to rise up into a higher reality. You and I get to decide which reality we ultimately want to live in—and the first step is becoming aware that there are two realities to choose from.

> Many of us are inspiring others to wake up, by that of our own example.

The second step is to start dialing in to what reality you currently are in. Right now, while you're reading this, you're more than likely in a higher reality—and that's good! I want you to have the experience of what it's like to be at that higher frequency so you'll start getting the anchors going in your cells. The more you're here in the experiencing of what it's like to be in this elevated frequency, the more it just starts to become a question of time that you'll be living here much more of the time and eventually all of the time. You'll see that as you begin to appreciate what it's like to be at a higher reality, before you know it, you start to blend that more elevated state into how you're living your day-to-day life. This is where it starts to become second nature to you. And you'll want your family, associates, and your loved ones to get in on it as well, so you'll start to reorganize your personal and/or professional environment to where they're becoming more like your higher reality. This is where the real juice is—and I'm not talking about O.J.! And this is also where the greater truth exists.

Have you ever heard the quote, "Thy will, not my will, be done"? It's a very powerful command. It's important to understand and recognize that the higher reality is where "thy will" exists. However, in order to empower that, you must equally recognize where the small will, or "my will," exists. Only you and you alone can choose which reality to inhabit; nobody can make that choice for you. And if you try to choose it for someone else, you are the one who is going to end up with the extra karma. Because this gets to be a choice that everyone on an individual level gets to make. In other words, this is a 100 percent personal choice—and for you to live at a higher reality, it is a choice that you will have to make over and over again until you're able to sustain "thy will be done." Remember, it's "my will be done" that will suck you back into your own lower reality every single time.

LOWER DESTINY VS. HIGHER DESTINY

There are some questions that can be helpful to ask when working to figure out what pulls you down into the lower reality and what boosts you up into the higher reality.

In terms of your Lower Destiny, what do you struggle with the most in this current life? Do you struggle with addictive behaviors, negative thinking, self-doubt, insecurity, trying too hard or moving too fast, etc.?

As always, there is an opposite side to everything, and the opposite side to struggle is going to be found in the energy of purpose. Your deepest purpose is the opposite of your most challenging struggle. Whatever you have been struggling with, there is a deeper purpose within that struggle. You're not just struggling for the sake of struggling; you're struggling to come into the realization of the deeper purpose. When you are in a true discovery process, you're going through a struggle, and as you're coming out the other side of that experience, your deeper purpose around that struggle naturally reveals itself. It always does. Ideally, when you make that connection, you will see it—it'll light up like a Christmas tree within you.

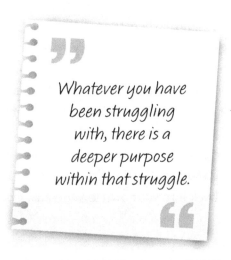

> Whatever you have been struggling with, there is a deeper purpose within that struggle.

We can look at our struggles like those of a caterpillar. When the caterpillar struggles, it's really just the butterfly struggling to get out of the caterpillar's cocoon. It's coming into realization; it's actualizing a higher part of itself. That's why our mindset is so important when it comes to addressing our struggles. The person who is making their struggles wrong, or approaching them from a negative mindset, is just locking themselves into the lower reality. They're creating their own hell.

Sometimes, it can be easy to identify your lower energy patterns, but you might find yourself struggling to identify your higher energy patterns. If so, then this is actually showing you the influence you've been under. If you are entirely under the influence of your lower energy patterns, and even hell-bent on playing out those patters no matter what, then clearly you have been sucked down to a lower reality. It's kind of like being swallowed up—and that is the intent of the lower octave or rung of the matrix: to see if you can be swallowed up, get completely lost, and then possibly even die.

OUR DARKEST PLACE VS. OUR SUPER STRENGTH

Another thing that will definitely bring you into your lower reality is your darkest place—and if you don't identify this properly, it can keep you there for days or even weeks on end. It's important to acknowledge what your dark place is. Trying to pretend like it does not exist is pointless because we all have one until we no longer have one anymore.

Once you have learned to acknowledge your dark place, the next step is to recognize the early signs when you are going there. The question is, do you *have* to go there? Do you *have* to go to that deep, deep, deep, *dark* place for days or weeks or even years on end?

It is important for you to remember that there is an energy on this planet that *wants* you to live at the lower reality. I've given it a couple of different names—the establishment, the powers-that-be, and the matrix, to name a few. Whatever you want to call it, if it had its way, we would all be living at that lower reality. Think about your mom and dad for a second. Where did they live? How much of their life did they live at that lower reality? Did they even get to experience the higher reality—and if so, for how long?

This is why you really must learn to identify your dark place and recognize when you are on your way there. No matter how deep you go into your dark place, ultimately, if you were to remain in that position of staying there, there would be no one else that could help pull you out. Unless, of course, you were willing to let someone help you. Remember that old adage, "When the student is ready, the teacher appears." The

441

emphasis here is on the student. We know they are ready because they are now willing to ask for help.

What I've noticed with some, prior to making this choice to ask for help, is they seem to require more pain. And in this scenario the pain serves as their teacher. You see, when we are hanging on to our dark place, whether we are aware of this or not, we are choosing to stay stuck. We are using our free will—or perhaps I should say, we are *misusing* or even *abusing* our freedom of choice.

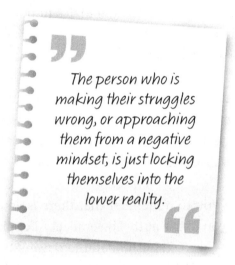

The person who is making their struggles wrong, or approaching them from a negative mindset, is just locking themselves into the lower reality.

Why would people choose to stay stuck like that? Well, there can be a lot of reasons. Maybe they're comfortable holding onto their dark place. Maybe they're addicted to suffering, self-abuse, or torment. And why not? These things can be like a drug sometimes. In fact, we can become addicted to our own pain and suffering. We can become addicted to our own drama. Heck, we can even get addicted to the temptations of the dark.

I say these can be like a drug because just like when someone is addicted to a drug, they continue to go back. At any time, of course, they could decide to choose something different, beginning with asking someone to help them. That in itself is a choice. They perhaps know they could choose to leave that dark place at any time, but often they don't. Rather, they might choose to stay in their dark place and possibly even beat themselves up for doing so. While in this dark place there is a good likelihood that they'll make some lousy choices during their time there.

Eventually, however, there's a possible chance that they will decide to choose differently, once they cross that threshold of where they've had enough of that type of pain. And then they'll choose to climb out, but that just begs the question: why did they drag it out for so long? They had the choice all along. They could have made that choice at any time. So why wait so long to do it? We're never boxed in. There's no law that says that we *have* to go into our dark place for weeks on end. We *always* the option to choose differently.

Now, when people choose to go into their dark place, it is usually because they haven't been learning their lessons. So, the question you have to ask yourself is: "If there is a lesson for me to be learning right now, what would that lesson be?" The answer will come, and it will show you where you went off track. Maybe you went off track a week ago—something threw you off course, you completely forgot what your lesson was, and you started going into this dark place. OK, so now what are you going to focus on? Are you going to focus on getting back into the process of learning your lesson and rising up out of that place, or are you going to dig deeper and deeper into that dark place? Which choice is more empowering—and more importantly, which one do you want to focus on?

When you are in that dark place, one of the things that could be really beneficial to do is to find one of your super strengths. Once you know what your super strengths are, this will help you shorten that gap between the time you start falling into that dark place and when you choose to pull yourself out of it.

443

Imagine if somebody came to you and said, "Hey, listen, you don't have to hang out in there any longer than 48 hours." Now if you have been hoodwinked into living at a lower reality, you will still find a way to stretch that out to possibly three weeks. You might even think that you belong in that lower reality because that is what the collective ego on the planet wants you to think. That is all false though—where you are divinely destined to be is in your highest reality.

As an example let's say that one of your super strengths is intensity. It's important to recognize that anyone's super strength can be misused. Even someone with an intensity like Bruce Lee had could have it used against them. At any point, the ego can move in and use that intensity to put them down and literally send them to their lower reality yet again. And if the external influence moves in to merge with it, such as an entity attachment or some aspect of the dark, because it wants to keep us down for whatever its reasons, then this becomes a double whammy.

But by that same token, when we are completely resolved and totally focused on using that super strength of intensity, this is where that strength becomes channeled and directed towards whatever it is we want to accomplish. When that happens, we can move mountains. Meaning whatever it is we are experiencing that was originally designed to take us down, as in finding ourselves in a darker place, we'll be climbing out so quickly it will make our head spin. And the next time we drop down into that lower reality, that super strength we now know we can access when we need it most will be there.

Once we have found our super strength, we are going to use it. Everybody has at least one—we just have to identify and acknowledge what it is. Another example of a super strength might be a highly developed intuition. Everyone has an intuition, but not everyone has a highly developed one. Somebody that has a highly developed intuition, knows this about themselves. They also follow through on the inner prompts from their highly developed intuitive voice without hesitation. This person will clearly make better choices for themselves. As a result, they are now better equipped to navigate through whatever they experience in their day-to-day life.

When we are completely resolved and totally focused on using our super strength of intensity, we can move mountains.

Some other examples of a super strength might be in being the coach of all coaches, if that's a person's chosen profession. Or in being an incredible parent. Maybe a highly attuned intuition ties into this; this parent's intuition helps them to always be in the know around what's going on in their child's life. They're now able to use that intuition in an effective way when it comes to caring for others. Or it could be an employer with his or her employees. It could be the problem solver, the clairvoyant, the clairaudient, the empath, the strategist, the entrepreneur, the leader, the healer, the psychic, the mentor, the mathematician, the mystic, the teacher, the mother, the father, the performer, the manifestor, the generator, the enroller, the super smart or intelligent... and the list just goes on and on.

It is similarly important that we each take a look at our weaknesses because we can get hoodwinked when we don't understand them. And as always, whatever your biggest weakness is, you can be assured that you are going to have its opposite. In this case, the soul is going to have a unique talent or ability. This could be anything from being a great listener to an awesome cheerleader, an incredible promoter, an amazing communicator, or a fantastic organizer. It could be a talent for music or writing or editing or even administrating. The point here is everybody has something that is very unique to them at soul level. The question now becomes: What is your something that is unique to you?

HIGHER AND LOWER DESIRES

There is a specific way in which we can be kept in a lower reality, and it has to do with something that we all have: desire. Desire shows up on two levels: a higher desire and a lower desire. When people get into a dysfunctional situation, often it is because they have been under the influence of a lower desire. So, my question to you now is: What are some of your lower desires? Or more specifically, if you were to name off up to three of your lower desires, what are they?

For a lot of people, their lower desires are going to have something to do with the more taboo subjects. They might center around sex or pornography. They might center around eating and drinking. It might have something to do with a desire to control people or to have power over somebody. The desire to hurt people is a lower desire. The desire to see someone punished is also a lower desire because it stems from a lower teaching: the old "eye for an eye." That desire to "see somebody get theirs" is definitely a lower desire.

Whenever you find yourself in the presence of somebody who is really purifying themselves, *this* is what they are purifying. They are purifying their lower desires because they recognize that if they are going to go to a higher reality, they need to be able to sustain that higher reality. In order to get there, all of those lower desires need to be transmuted—the whole kit and caboodle. The lower desires all fall within the realm of one's ego. Whereas the highest desires all have something to do with the deeper purpose of your soul. They will be in alignment with your soul and will help move you up towards the highest reality. So, once again, my question here would be: What are some of your highest desires? Or more specifically, if you were to name up to three of your highest desires, what are they?

> The question is not, "What should I be passionate about?" rather, "What am I most passionate about in the here and now?"

Once again, your lower desires will eventually pull you down and possibly keep you down in the lower reality for some time. As we know, the lower reality is fear based, and the higher reality is love based. That means that when you are accessing your Higher Destiny, you are going to translate that love into something that you are passionate about. You might be passionate about the love of your life, or raising your family, or about rising to a more expanded and higher level in your career. The question is not, "What should I be passionate about?" rather, "What *am* I most passionate about in the here and now?"

Finally, this last area is where the rubber really meets the road, and it has to do with your hurts and your pains. There are things in your life that have already hurt you or caused you pain. In your Higher Destiny, there is a direct correlation between the things that have hurt you and the lessons that you are to be learning.

Now, here's the higher truth when it comes to those two poles. Those hurts will pull you down into the lower reality—they have before, and they will continue to do so. But the lessons that you actually take the time to learn well will literally elevate you to the higher reality—they have before, and they will continue to do so as well. And this too is completely your choice. If you choose to focus on the hurts, even the hurts that have not happened yet, you will continue to suffer. Now should you choose to put your focus on the lessons—and more specifically, on learning your lessons as they make themselves known to you—then you will continue to heal, rise, and grow.

Those of us who are truly dedicated to healing and growth have been handed a golden nugget in the form of this book, *Transform Your Destiny*. For those who have found this book but have not yet found the dedication to your own transformation, you have also been given a golden nugget—in this case, it is in finding the answer to the question, "Why do I keep suffering? And what would it be like to put an end once and for all to the suffering that I have been enduring, whatever that suffering might be?"

As always, it all comes down to the direction you have chosen to point your energy towards. It is your choice, and it will always continue to be your choice. That external force, as in the powers-that-be, the darker influences, or even someone that's currently in your life that does not want you to know this—they want you to continue to live in that lower reality. But the higher force—the spiritual force, the divine force—wants you to learn this. It wants you to practice and ultimately embody this. It wants you to be conscious of this...it wants you to continuously become more conscious of this so that you can not only elevate yourself to the higher reality but eventually sustain that reality where you're now living your life from this higher place.

When that happens, not only will you be blessed as a result, but you will become a blessing to others as well. You will become the example for others to be inspired by. You will have demonstrated to them that the higher reality is truly possible.

EXERCISE

INSTRUCTIONS: The unfinished statements on the left column of the chart below are all designed to show what pulls you down into the lower reality. The ones on the right column are all designed to show what helps boost you up into the higher reality. Think about each question, and then write down one to three answers that come up for each one.

LOWER DESTINY	HIGHER DESTINY
What I struggle with most is...	My deepest purpose is...
My deeper ego needs are...	My true soul needs are...
My strongest lower energy patterns are...	My strongest higher energy patterns are...
My darkest place is...	My super strength is...
My greatest weakness is...	My greatest abilities or talents are...
My lowest desires are...	My highest desires are...
What I'm most afraid of right now is...	What I'm most passionate about right now is...
What actually hurts me is...	What I am to be learning is...

CHAPTER 15

DETERMINING HOW TO CHOOSE

One of the core themes of this book has been choices. By now it is pretty clear that our choices create our destiny. They shape our reality and have the power to lead us to a life of happiness or of misery.

Even the smallest of choices can turn the rudder of our ship that one degree that takes us in a different direction. If we can keep this awareness in mind when choosing, we can better keep ourselves on our Higher-Destiny path.

The Dalai Lama said: "I find hope in the darkest of days and focus in the brightest. I do not judge the Universe."

If we get stuck in the darkest of days or we're not processing that denser, darker energy correctly, this is where we can lose hope or be tempted to lose hope. And if we do lose hope, it becomes almost impossible to experience a positive focus in the brightest of our days.

HIGHER AND LOWER VIBRATIONAL CHOICES

We always have the option between a higher vibrational choice and a lower vibrational choice. A higher vibrational choice is always going to have a natural progression: it is going to bring you up to a higher reality. A lower vibrational choice is always going to bring you down—that is the natural consequential effect of making a lower vibrational choice. Over time, you will get really good at identifying a higher vibrational choice versus a lower vibrational choice because of their effects: one will naturally bring you up, while the other will just as naturally bring you down.

That means that when you and I make a lower vibrational choice, we are going to be on our way down to that dark place I mentioned earlier. Probably one of the most consistent things that will drive you into that dark place is when you make a lower vibrational choice. Maybe you drank too much alcohol or had too much caffeine or too many sweets. Maybe you had sex with somebody—your mate included—when the timing was off. You were coming from a lower desire rather than a higher desire and were desperately trying to fill a need from your needy self. That is a lower vibrational choice.

You will notice that every time you make a lower vibrational choice, or a few of them in a row, you will feel yourself starting to go down. It's like a downward spiral, or a negative vortex. If you make a few lower vibrational choices in a row, you'll feel like you're getting sucked down into that darker place. You will feel like you're powerless and like you can't do anything to stop it. But I promise you, once you have gotten back to a place of objectivity, if you trace it back a couple of days, you will find that you made two or three lower vibrational choices leading to that downward spiral.

Once you have already made those lower vibrational choices and have recognized that you are on your way down, the question then becomes, "What kind of choices are you making from that point forward? Are you making higher vibrational choices now, or are you going to continue making even more lower vibrational choices?"

Even the smallest of choices can turn the rudder of our ship that one degree that takes us in a different direction.

By that same token, if you suddenly find yourself feeling elevated and connected to your soul, try to trace that feeling back a few days as well. I can almost guarantee that you will find you have made two or three higher vibrational choices—you just weren't aware of them. Maybe you made a choice and gently told your partner, "I would rather not have sex tonight," because you could feel something was a little off. One of you was being extra needy, and you could feel it, so you found a nice, graceful way to tell them. That was a higher vibrational choice, and now the day after that, you can feel yourself elevating.

When we make a higher vibrational choice, we must be brought up. If we make a couple of higher vibrational choices in a row, then I can guarantee it: we'll be moving back up again into a higher elevated reality. It works like magic on both sides of the coin.

When you are in this higher vibrational place, you are choosing to do things like step into your true self. For example, you might choose to embrace someone or something that has been uncomfortable for you but which you know is the right thing to do. Maybe it is an activity that you have been resisting for who knows how long, and now you make that higher vibrational choice to embrace whatever it is that you have been resisting. Or you might choose to do something to restore your transformation, peace, or harmony. The next thing you know, you're being elevated. You're going to start to feel yourself being pulled up to the higher reality because you made the higher vibrational choice.

There is a real difference in the quality of these two choices. The majority of the planet has been making their choices from the lower frequency. And in all fairness to that majority, they haven't been all that aware this is what they've been doing. This is why they constantly live in the lower reality of fear, separation and even aggression—always trying to make things move faster. Talk about a lower energy pattern of impatience!

When you make lower vibrational choices, you start sending out negative energy. You start having conversations that are based on things like hatred, judgment, control, manipulation, or maybe even criticism—just to name a few. Of course, the moment that you go there, you start going down.

This is why it is not a good practice to stay too connected with the news channels. The majority of them are primarily focused on negative information. Isn't that interesting? What kind of agenda do you think they're operating with, a Divine Agenda or a personal agenda? Now this isn't to say that you should never choose to watch the news, but if you do, it should be limited, and you should be very aware and conscious that you are letting a flow of negative energy come in through that screen or that television set right into your nervous system.

Now again, I am not saying that you should never do that. But if you choose to turn this into a lifestyle where you're too focused on the news channels and have been taking in a lot of negativity, and then you go have a cup of coffee with your friend in which the conversation turns into a beat-up session over everyone you think has done something to you that you're in disapproval of—then you've been had. Meaning you have let that negativity get in there and influence a negative stream coming out of you. You are not in a higher reality when you do that because you are making choices based in fear, separation or judgment— and now you are contributing to that fear, separation, or judgment in others too.

> When we are down at this level, we are contributing to more fear, separation and judgment.

As mentioned before, you have a choice in whether or not you want to contribute to the world dividing itself even further than it already has. Or in helping to unite it by first and foremost healing whatever patterning you have inside of you that has been dividing or separating you from your true self. It's the healing of this lower energy patterning that brings us into a state of union with our most authentic self. As more of us on the planet achieve this place within ourselves, we will then have the collective patterning of us as a people morph into a higher state of a unified consciousness within our humanity.

Now, when it comes to world events and the news, you might think you're justified in having negative, critical, highly judgmental conversations about people that you have never physically met before. But do you realize what you are doing in terms of making a lower vibrational choice rather than a higher one? I mean, are we really going to get this person or that person out of office? Come on. Why would we want to continue using our creative energies to talk smack about this person once we realize the effect that it is having on us and our life personally and/or professionally? When we are down at this level, we are contributing to more fear, separation and judgment. We are contributing to the division that has been spinning out of control.

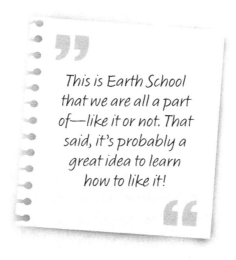

This is Earth School that we are all a part of—like it or not. That said, it's probably a great idea to learn how to like it!

Do you want to guess what else happens when we are doing that? We are getting a little bit of karma. Think about yourself and your shadow side. Is that how you heal your shadow side—by dropping into a lower vibration and becoming divisive, resentful, positional, or even judgmental? Of course not. That is being counterproductive.

For years, one of my friends would not even turn on her television set. She had no interest in the news; she thought it was all just bogus. But then, one of her friends got her all freaked out about what she thought was going on politically at the time—how one side was completely right, and one side was totally wrong—and somehow, she convinced my friend of this.

Now my friend is a very sharp and intelligent woman, but she became obsessed. It was just ridiculous—and no one, including me, could pull her out of it. She was like many people who get hooked in and contribute to the negativity and judgment on the planet. Can you see what type of a vibrational choice this was? Exactly! It was a lower vibrational choice. She was living in fear and separation of whatever she thought these people were going to do to the world and she had not made the connection that she was actually contributing to making it worse by giving it so much attention. She was already experiencing the consequences of that in her life, but she could not make that connection because she got swallowed up in it.

It is like there is this objective to make sure that everybody watches the news—as if the news is gospel and knows exactly what it is talking about. I said to my friend, "Listen: if you can come back and be objective for a moment, here is what I want to do. I want to sit you down and blindfold you. First, I'm going to play one channel, and then I'm going to play the other channel, and I want you to tell me exactly what you feel when you hear them." But, of course, she wouldn't do it. She was completely convinced that one of them had the truth, and the other was nothing but lies—just one lie after another. Meanwhile, there was somebody just down the street who believed the complete opposite. Which leaves the neutral bystander asking, "Well, who's right here?" Which brings us back to: "One of them is right, and the other must be wrong." Exactly! This is one of the more common ways in how we contribute to this dynamic of divide and conquer—where we can become more separate from each other in these two different camps implying that I'm right and the other camp is wrong. And if enough of us on an individual level are not aware of this, then this is where we as a race can get swallowed up by these lower vibrational choices. Which then affects our collective consciousness and how we interact with one another.

Remember, a lower vibrational choice is going to bring you down, while a higher vibrational choice is going to bring you up. In other words, this also serves as a gauge on the dashboard of your life. If I feel myself elevating, it's because I've made a higher vibrational choice prior to the elevation. If, on the other hand, I feel myself going down, it's because I've made a lower vibrational choice prior to that descent. If it's a true desire of mine to get better at making higher vibrational choices, then it would behoove me to decide who I want to be.

Grace is around the corner, and grace loves when you recognize it by acknowledging it and feeling appreciative of it.

Think about this: which movement do I want to contribute to? As in do I want to contribute to the creation of more fear and judgment on the planet or do I want to contribute to the creation of more love and unity? And which movement do I want to contribute to—the movement that is living in a 5D higher reality or the one that is living in a 3D lower reality?

If we are coming from fear, judgment, and separation, then we are contributing to more fear, judgment, and separation on this planet—and thereby attempting to keep humanity in a 3D world. But if we are truly coming from a place of harmony, love, and unity—which means we learn to love and unite *everybody* on this planet, then we are contributing to the manifestation of a 5D world. When our Greater Destiny becomes more important to us than our Lower Destiny, we will more than likely feel this harmonic resonance within every one of our seventy trillion cells, to the point where we can no longer deny it.

When you are making a higher vibrational choice, you are choosing to be yourself. This is you now choosing to live your life authentically. You are choosing to take back your power to reclaim yourself. And to, of course, renew this choice on a regular basis. What a beautiful way to live your life!

Now when you are choosing to make a lower vibrational choice, you are choosing to remain separate from you true self. You are choosing to live inauthentically. It is the opposite side of the same coin. This is why many on the planet have felt so powerless—it's because for some time, they have been unconsciously choosing to remain separate and divided from their true selves. This is where we can do the blaming, the judging, the shaming, the blocking, the avoiding, the resisting or the criticizing. Anyone choosing to do any of these things is not in that higher reality of the 5D world. Rather, they are in the old 3D world or that lower reality. And for the most part they want to pull everyone in their life into this lower reality with them. And, once again, they are probably not even aware of it. But that has been the conditioned program on our planet for thousands of years. It is only when you and I become acutely aware of it that we can learn to start empowering ourselves by upgrading the quality of our choices that we make in our lives.

I am not just talking about the bigger choices, but the day-to-day choices as well. For example, when I choose to go to bed early at night, I get a much deeper, better sleep. I just feel different when I wake up in the morning versus when I choose to go to bed late at night. This is why many people have their TVs in a room other than their bedroom. Now I'm not saying that you shouldn't ever watch TV. I watch TV—but I do it in another room. And when I'm done, that thing goes off. Then, I have my quiet time, or my reading time, and I go to bed. I choose to go to bed early because I value my day and I value my energy. Meanwhile, some people do have a TV in their bedroom—and by the way, if you have a TV in your bedroom, you might consider booting that thing out! Think about unplugging that sucker and putting it in another room. Why? It is not a good idea for you to go to bed with the TV on. It's just not. It can cause less of a deep sleep and a number of other things that you can do some research on if you are so inclined.

As I've alluded to in previous chapters regarding our dream space, here's another golden nugget on dreams for you: if you want to affect the lowering of the quality of the dream content in your nighttime sleep, then leave the TV on. If you want to heighten the quality of your dream content, leave the TV off or remove it entirely from your bedroom.

The point is that removing the TV from the bedroom will help you stay disciplined to go to bed on time, and it removes the temptation to watch TV right before bed and to risk falling asleep with it on. Many people have chosen to move the TV into another room, and so can you, should you choose to. Again, this is merely an example of a higher vibrational choice.

When it comes to a higher vibrational choice versus a lower vibrational choice: one is going to drive us to a lower reality, while the other is going to pick us up and raise us to a higher reality. This is what sets the stage for us to rise up from our Lower Destiny–from where our lower self is operating through that personal agenda. This is what allows us to rise up, slowly but surely, into our Greater Destiny. That is also where we get connected with our Higher Self and can start to become more of that divine human—this is where we unify our humanity with our divinity because we are now operating within and from the Divine Agenda.

This is where the real juice lies. When you are in a terrific relationship or business partnership, or you are working with a team, and together you are operating from a Divine Agenda, everything is just better. It's richer. Everybody on the team feels more connected to something that's bigger, something that's healthier, something that's empowering. Just compare that to the "I'm going to do everything myself" mindset.

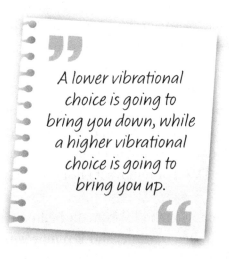

A lower vibrational choice is going to bring you down, while a higher vibrational choice is going to bring you up.

There is one final thought I want to leave you with about lower vibrational choices. There are two things that I have witnessed people doing over and over again. The first is to take a small piece of information and then choose to exaggerate it. The second is to manipulate the truth. Let's remember here that whenever we do these things, there is more than likely going to be an undesirable consequence.

A lot of times, I will see someone take information and manipulate it in order to get what they want. They might take something that someone said about another person and go up to that other person and say, "Hey, did you know he said this, or she said that, about you?" and then that person will get their feathers ruffled. But the information was either taken out of context or twisted in some way so the manipulative person could get what they wanted. Maybe they quoted the literal words that the person had said, but that person had said them with a different intention, or some important piece of context was being purposely left out of the retelling.

Exaggeration and manipulation are very common tricks of the ego and/ or the shadow self. Another way of saying this is that these are tricks that come from within the lower reality world to get you to make lower vibrational choices. Oh, and by the way, you might recall earlier in a previous chapter where we learned the lower reality is where the ego and the shadow reside. Coincidence? I think not!

The lower reality world is where we can be tempted to exaggerate or build upon some story so that by the time we're done, that story could be miles away from the truth. We might even believe that story is the actual truth, and we may get others to buy in and believe it as well. If that were to happen, now we have created some karma that will pull us back down to that lower vibrational place. This was the temptation. And if we fell prey to it, who knows how long we might stay there? This is also where fear and separation are rooted. Which means if we have not healed this at its roots yet, then there's still a chance that we are separated from the truth because we are still afraid to own up to something that is really ours to own up to.

This is something that has been going on with our humanity for a long, long time. Our job is to recognize where we are when we start descending into that lower place, and then choose to make the right choice—whatever that may be. When in this lower place, we are more than likely contributing to a lower vibrational choice. "How might we be contributing to a lower vibrational choice?" you ask. Well, we can do this whenever we are being divisive, too defensive, or too positional—or when we're blaming, projecting, criticizing, blocking, or judging.

It's these types of actions that will bring us down to that lower reality, all as a result of having made the choice, whether we're conscious or unconscious, to engage in these types of actions. In order to work with this type of energy consciously, we can choose to stay aware of any of these types of actions that we are about to engage in and ask, "Is this the person that I want to be or the person that I genuinely want to become? Is this what I really am to be vesting my energy into? And if so, am I prepared to embrace the consequence that will come as a result of this lower vibrational choice?"

If the answer is no, then choose to make a different choice. Choose to pull yourself out of that dynamic. If you catch yourself exaggerating some story, as soon as you recognize it, pull yourself back. You don't have to go the distance. You don't have to risk having somebody else make a choice based on your exaggerated story that ends up having undesirable consequences, and then having those consequences come back on you.

BE MINDFUL OF DISTRACTIONS

One of the ways we can work on being mindful of distractions is by asking ourselves what our greatest distraction is. So, what is your greatest distraction?

For some of you, it might be your kids. Maybe you have three kids, and one of them is just—well, let's say they're a handful. Or maybe you have an addiction, and that is your greatest distraction. Maybe you have a toxic person in your life that is just down all the time—and they're determined at an unconscious level to drag you down with them.

Whenever you do become activated by whatever your distraction is, the question now becomes: What will you do next? What choice will you make? When your anger, jealousy, frustration, depression, or fear is activated, will you take that out on somebody, or even on yourself? Or will you choose to clear it out? We're all going to get activated by our own distractions sometimes. Let's be real here: over the course of a week, we're probably going to get activated at least a couple of times. I know it. You know it. We all know it. It is what it is.

> Always remember that regardless of what you're experiencing, your guides, angels and your Higher Self are as close to you as your next breath is.

So the next question at this juncture would be: What will you choose to do the next time you become activated? Will you choose to move towards a place where you will work on clearing out that activated energy, or will you possibly act out on it instead? Maybe you will move towards your favorite strategy influenced by the ego, and then exaggerate or even manipulate that energy as a way to serve the needs or personal agenda of your own ego. Or perhaps you'll suppress it and go to one of your favorite numbing-out strategies such as sugar, alcohol, junk food or fast food, sex, compulsive shopping, etc.

You see, it is the choices we make which ultimately determine the destiny we'll take. In other words, raising the vibrational quality of the choices you are currently making would not only be a wiser thing to do but is something that your magnanimous soul wants you to specifically learn and master. As I have often shared in my seminars throughout the years, knowing what to choose and how to choose may be the most significant thing we'll ever learn how to do. This, in my experience, is an awesome decision, as this choice will serve you and your soul's journey impeccably well.

When our life becomes a classroom in which we're learning our lessons, this is where we're changing, healing, maturing, and transcending. This is where the rising up to our Greater Destiny is in staying in our conscious awareness and having it become a lifestyle.. This is now us rising up numerous times, leading up to the sustainability of our Greater Destiny. We're continuously becoming better, healthier, happier, and wiser. We're becoming who we were meant to be from the beginning. And as we become who we were meant to be, or inspired to be, our own personal universe rises up to our Greatest Destiny. This is also where our soul, spirit guides, and angels all get onboard—bigtime!

The decision to turn our life into a classroom is more than likely a choice that has already been made by that of our soul prior to entry into this life. So now when we're having an experience in our day-to-day world, and especially when the experience is somewhat painful or even uncomfortable, this is where we get to see what it is we're to be learning from that experience.

By the way, we've all had bad experiences. What we might not be aware of is that some part of us created this uncomfortable experience for us to learn something of soul significance from. Now if on the other side of this painful experience we say we didn't learn anything—rather we say "it was just a terrible experience, look at what was done to me, look at how mistreated I was"—what happens then? Well, it's pretty simple...we will get a do-over. Just like in high school, if we don't get passing grades, we will simply go back to the beginning of that class and repeat it again. Remember, this is Earth School that we are all part of—whether we like it or not. That said, it's probably a great idea to learn how to like it!

Now a good question to ask at this point would be: "If there was something that I was to be learning from this experience right now, what is it?" This is the master key to eventually getting off the wheel of karma once and for all. You might recall in one of our recent chapters that we're not here to heal our karma. Rather, we're here to fulfill our soul's purpose—our soul's contract. To do this, however, we must heal and resolve our karma.

Our best strategy for healing and resolving our karma is in purposefully embracing those painful, uncomfortable experiences. The degree that we embrace that experience is the exact degree in which the lesson or lessons that we are truly to be learning will become visible to us. If I was to make the experience wrong, attempt to push it away, or blame it on someone or something else, and there really is a lesson encoded in the experience, then I'm also making the lesson wrong and pushing it away. All this does is cause the experience to be repeated yet again.

Now there's another important viewpoint for us to consider about these types of experiences, and especially when they are karmic lessons, meaning there really is a profound lesson or two to learn from this experience. When our negative karma comes to visit upon us, it's doing so as a result of a negative energy that we put out into the Universe somewhere in a previous timeline—as in, we did something that hurt someone else or even hurt ourselves. When that happened, it knocked something out of balance.

Many times, when we at soul level have chosen to resolve this type of karma, we do so by experiencing what it would be like to be on the receiving side of this energy that we put out somewhere in our past. This is a greater strategy of the soul that assures we will get it this time. "What will we get?" you might ask. The lesson, or lessons, that we really are to be learning well. For as we do, this is what causes the rebalancing and resolving of that old karma.

> It's the highest path of the sacred warrior where we take the journey within and confront whatever it is or all that it is.

We must learn how to exercise our free will, also referred to as our freedom of choice, both powerfully and masterfully. At the pinnacle of all our lessons that we've come into this life as a soul to master, is one of the toughest lessons to learn...the lesson on how to choose wisely. Again, this is why I say knowing what to choose and how to choose may be the most significant thing we will ever learn how to do.

WHEN A SOUL COMPLETES ITS JOURNEY

As mentioned previously, one of the purposes of the soul could be for lifetime completion. What does that mean? If you, as a soul, complete your string of lifetimes, what does that mean for your soul? Well, it means it is off the wheel of karma, and now you as a soul have a choice whether you want to stay or leave.

As far as the Universe is concerned, it doesn't matter whether the soul chooses to stay or leave—either way, it is equally celebrated. What often happens at this point is that some souls choose to go back to their place of origin; meaning they return to wherever they originated from. They've accomplished their soul's deeper purpose. They've completed their service and they've succeeded in getting off the wheel of karma, as they have now mastered all of their lessons.

Another choice that is often made by a soul at this stage of their journey is they take on another mission or another way of serving. You see, there are other ways in which you as a soul can serve the Divine—this is suggesting, of course, that Planet Earth is not the only place in our Universe to serve.

Some of these souls have already left—and left with great celebration because they completed their journey. At that level, it's a bit like a martial art: the higher up you go, the fewer seventh-degree black belts there are because of everything that is involved to rise up to that level.

The way it's been, there has always been at least one master soul on the planet at any given time. There has also been a handful of ancient, advanced souls on the planet as well at one given time. Up until most recently that's the way it has been. Those higher vibrational souls were always here to serve. But in this new era we have now entered into, everything has changed dramatically. In the essence of this new era is

467

a larger movement where we are now seeing and will continue to see more advanced, ancient, and master souls here on the planet at the exact same time.

As more of these ancient souls materialize in this new era, you might not even know it. Usually they go unannounced; they don't like to call that kind of attention to themselves or make a big deal about it. They might be out there in the world serving and assisting people personally. Or, as I have previously said many times over the years, they might go live in the mountains and serve the many from there.

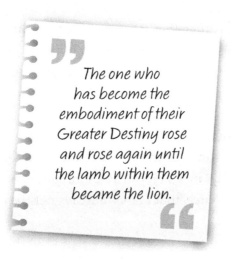

> The one who
> has become the
> embodiment of their
> Greater Destiny rose
> and rose again until
> the lamb within them
> became the lion.

So, the good news for us is that there are going to be more of these advanced, ancient, master-level souls on the planet during this time than ever before. These souls are here to both usher in and support this larger movement, and ultimately this will benefit *every* soul in the brightest, best and greatest of ways. All souls are going to benefit from this raising of consciousness. When a tide rises, it lifts up every boat, be it large or small... Souls are the exact same way.

This is an exciting time, and it brings with it a tremendous opportunity for you to understand where you are at with your own evolution as a soul. Now if you don't know or aren't quite sure, start asking—call in your Higher Self and ask for a clarifying nighttime dream.

LIVING IN GRACE

What happens when you do the right thing—or better yet, do a series of right things? You get grace. Grace is around the corner, and grace loves when you recognize it by acknowledging it and feeling appreciative of it. When you do that, you're also in recognition that you did the right thing. In that moment, grace is always right around the corner. It could be very subtle, so the key here is, when you're aware that you're doing the right thing and grace shows up, recognize it. And then, take a moment and simply shower it with gratitude. Let that gratitude be felt in every one of your seventy trillion cells that make up your physical body. Let yourself have that moment. Be fascinated by it. Be impressed by it. Be inspired by it. Be in awe of it. Be grateful for it. And let that gratitude lift you. As this will all set the stage for it to happen again and again.

MAKING A DIFFERENCE

Lastly, here is a reminder of the difference you as a soul came here to make. Now your difference doesn't have to be some grandiose ideal of having to be the one to change the world. For the majority of us, our greatest difference is found in how we live our day-to-day life.

- Every time you make a wiser, healthier choice you're making a difference.

- Every time you choose to learn one of your lessons well, you're making a difference.

- Every time you choose to forgive yourself and/or someone else, you're making a difference.

- Every time you choose to pull in the reigns of your ego, your inner child, or your shadow, you're making a difference.

- Every time you choose to help your inner child heal and grow, you're making a difference.

- Every time you choose to help someone or selflessly contribute to a greater cause, you're making a difference.

> *Every time you choose to forgive yourself and/or someone else, you're making a difference.*

- Every time you choose to embody more of your true self, as in the Divine Human you are intended to be at soul level, you're making a difference.

- Every time you choose to live your life more authentically, you're making a difference.

- Every time you choose to accept responsibility and fully embrace the consequence of a previous choice you made, you're making a difference.

- Every time you choose to courageously rise up to adversity, you're making a difference.

- Every time you choose to completely accept what is, you're making a difference.

- Every time you choose to change, heal, and transform yourself and/or your life, you're making a difference.

- Every time you choose to solve, resolve, and dissolve a chunk of your old karma, you're making a difference.

- Every time you choose love over hate or judgment, you're making a difference.

- Every time you choose to become a greater example for someone else, you're making a difference.

- Every time you choose an act of kindness, you're making a difference.

- Every time you choose to give someone a smile (including the Universe), you're making a difference.

CLOSING THOUGHTS

Along our journey there's a chance we might lose our faith or hope temporarily. There's a chance that we might even start to think, "What's the use?" or "I want to give up. Is this ever going to end?" Those types of thoughts can creep in. However, if you take the time to reflect on where it is you would like to be a year from today in relation to your Greater Destiny, and then keep this in your view on a day-to-day basis, this will keep you in that acute state of awareness of what it is you are moving towards. As always, moving toward something of a higher and greater nature will not only challenge us but it will also help to anchor us to that higher place we are moving towards.

I learned a long time ago that this path of transforming ourselves can not only be incredibly challenging from time to time, but it can also be a part of our journey where there will be times when we feel completely alone. Part of my journey was to learn how to accept this. Do remember though, that feeling of alone is just a feeling. When we're feeling alone, it very seldom means that we really are alone.

Remember, within your partnership to the Divine it's already been written at soul level for you to do this.

A quote that dropped on my path some time ago that quickly became another of my favorites is by an anonymous author: "You are never alone or helpless. The force that guides the star guides you too." Always remember that regardless of what you're experiencing, your guides, angels, and your Higher Self are as close to you as your next breath is.

Another way of understanding our feelings is that all feelings are temporary, meaning that they too shall eventually pass. Again, if we operate our life from this place that we will be challenged, meaning we know that there will be obstacles and hurdles—many of which are going to be uncomfortable and more than likely unpleasant—with this knowledge and awareness we will traverse them less turbulently. The temptation here, however, will be to bypass them. So it is best for us to embrace them as they make themselves known to us instead of attempting the bypass. For if we do bypass them, all that means is we're just simply going to have to come right back to the very place that we did the bypass and literally pick up where we left off.

When moving forward, it's critically important to be reminded of this truth that within every hurdle, every obstacle, there's always an opportunity to transform something about ourselves where we potentially either learn one of our lessons or advance the process in learning our lessons. Now there is another part of this truth that every time we transform something about ourselves on a deeper level, we awaken an aspect of that greater part of us. The next transformational objective is to now become one with this higher awakened aspect by embodying it.

We as a race are now in this process of awakening. With each deeper transformational experience that we have, this is what naturally has us become even more awake to who it is we are divinely meant to be, both individually and collectively—as this is what is now happening on the planet and will continue to happen. The Greater Awakening that some of us have been privy to and have been waiting some time for has now come upon us. Which begets the question: In this Greater Awakening that is happening within our humanity on a global scale, what is our part, and how do we step into it?

To once again quote the profound wisdom of Lao Tzu, "If you want to awaken all of humanity, then awaken all of yourself. If you want to eliminate the suffering in the world, then eliminate all that is dark and negative in yourself. Truly the greatest gift you have to give is that of your own self-transformation."

Just know that those who have gone before you have also confronted many obstacles, many hurdles—most of which were within themselves. It's the highest path of the sacred warrior where we take the journey within and confront whatever it is or all that it is, little by little, slowly but surely. We all have a Greater Destiny. In order to become the embodiment of that Greater Destiny, we must rise up to it—implying it does not come down to us. Another way in which we naturally rise is to get out of our ego self and give to someone else—simply for the sake of pure, unconditional giving. This causes a rising up to our Greater Destiny where our basic human status—our Lower Self can be slightly raised to our divine human status—our Higher Self. When someone has become the embodiment of their Greater Destiny, this is someone who has risen numerous times, usually over a long period of time.

There's a very powerful message in the 2010 *Robin Hood* movie starring Russell Crowe, where at some point early in the movie the character Russell is playing, Robin Longstride, shows up with his men on an ambush that is done with Sir Robert Loxley and his men. The message gets set up with this scene where Robin Longstride is standing next to Robert Loxley, who is now laying on the ground in his last moments of life. Just before he dies, he asks Longstride to return the special sword that he had taken from his father, Sir Walter Loxley. Longstride gives him his word that he will return the sword to its rightful owner. A little later in the movie, Robin and his men are sitting around the campfire whereupon he begins to peel away on the coiling that is wrapped next to the handle of the sword. As he does, he notices an inscription embedded onto the sword which reads, "Rise and rise again." That was on one side of the sword, and as he turns the sword over, the inscription continues to read, "until lambs become lions."

Robin eventually comes to the sword's rightful owner, Sir Walter. He then shares the news of his son Robert's passing and hands him the sword. Throughout the movie, every time Robin reads the message, he asks himself: "What does this mean?" There then comes a sequence in which he's flooded with memories from his past and future. They reveal visions of him in a courtyard. There is another scene later in the movie where he finds himself in the courtyard from his visions. He walks towards a stone that he instinctively knows to overturn. As he turns it over, there is the inscription again—it is in this scene where the answer to his question comes, as to what this means. Right at that moment, one of his men that is standing next to him also notices the message "Rise and rise again until lambs become lions" and he asks Robin, "What does it mean?" Whereby Robin immediately utters the words, "Never give up."

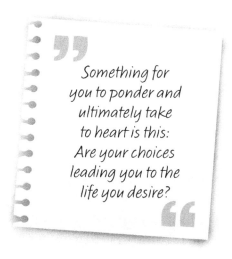

Something for you to ponder and ultimately take to heart is this: Are your choices leading you to the life you desire?

You see, the one who has become the embodiment of their Greater Destiny rose and rose again until the lamb within them became the lion. They never gave up. Rather they navigated their journey and eventually got through the many confrontations, the many times of rising up again and again until they achieved the sustaining of their Greater Destiny.

To become one with our Greater Destiny means that we do so incrementally. This rising up will happen over and over again. Until, of course, this larger process that we're in of becoming one with that Greater Destiny completes itself—as in we become the total embodiment of it.

Remember, within your partnership to the Divine, it's already been written at soul level for you to do this—for you to eventually complete this part of your journey. Simply trust that when the timing is right, for the next part of your process where you're rising up yet again, the "when" for this to happen next will be revealed to you because the "when" is also a part of the unfolding and ultimately embodying of your Greater Destiny.

Something for you to ponder and ultimately take to heart is this: Are your choices leading you to the life you desire? The quality of the choices you make going forward will determine that. You'll want to examine this periodically, now that you are finishing reading this book for the first time. Should you return to read it again, you will gain further insights each and every time you read it that you weren't able to absorb the time before.

The depth of the quality of those choices, of course, has to do with really getting in touch with the life you genuinely desire and then staying in touch with it. You already identified where you would like to be in relation to your Greater Destiny a year from today. And over the coming year, I suggest that you take the time to reexamine the choices you're making on a day-to-day or at least on a week-to-week basis, where you simply ask yourself: "Are the choices I have been making leading me to the life I truly desire? Are the choices I'm making TODAY leading me to the life I truly desire? Are they leading me to becoming the person that I want to become? Am I becoming that vision of my Greater Destiny, one year from today? And if not, what can I do differently?"

Again let's remember, in large part, choice, not chance, determines your destiny. In other words, how you Transform Your Destiny all comes back to YOU and YOUR DIVINE MAGNIFICENT SOUL.

A MESSAGE FROM DALE

At this point, you now have a great understanding of what it takes to get on and stay on your Higher Destiny path. I don't know how long it is going to take you to not only rise up to your Greater Destiny but to embody it as well. It all depends on your choice to do so and the resolve of your commitment you are going to apply in using this knowledge. What I do know is that you now have the tools you need for your training to be well underway. Always remember that at any time you can choose to take your journey of transforming your destiny to the next level. These are big things to take on, and they will have huge implications for your powerful, magnanimous soul.

So, with that, I want to thank you for being here at this time on our precious planet and also for taking the time you did to read this book in its entirety. I commend you on your act of courage for being willing to step into the hot seat during the course of our time together and to really go for it in the way that you did.

On whatever level you experienced them, all the insights, breakthroughs, and the "A-ha!" moments you have had will literally help you better connect with your soul. Perhaps it will be right for you at some point to move closer in your process of embodying your soul and even towards actualizing your Greater Self, or Higher Self, in this lifetime.

You are completely at choice as to the trajectory of your path of destiny. And now, as you go forward with this newfound knowledge, my wish for you is that you will remember these teachings as you make choices along the way to wherever your journey is leading you. Whether they are choices leading to your Lower Destiny or your Higher Destiny, only you can decide. And no matter what, from my heart to yours: "Never ever give up."

Until next time, my Aloha and Namaste...

~ Dale

Acknowledgements

I am so grateful to those who have generously supported my teachings, my writings, and my partnership with the Divine. I would specifically like to shine the spotlight on the group of amazing people who all, in their own special way, helped make this book possible.

First, I want to acknowledge Janell Simonson for her contribution in the very beginning stages of creating Transform Your Destiny. It was quite a few years ago when TYD first came into my awareness. I was doing what I've been doing for decades; I designed a three-day seminar on destiny, which, over time, morphed into a five-day class. Then, about two and a half years ago, we began the process of taking our transcript of what I had been teaching in these classes and turning it into a manuscript. My warmest gratitude to you, Janell, for being the first one to get us started in this process, as this was the first benchmark in having somewhat of a document to work from.

It was at this point Matthew Ross helped us complete this first version of the manuscript. In addition to completing this version of the manuscript, he was also instrumental in reworking a few of the chapters to give us a clearer document to move forward with. Thank you, Matthew. Your great writing skills and professionalism are a gift to this project.

Thirdly, I want to give special acknowledgement to Mycki Manning. Her contribution to book number two in our Transformation Trilogy was nothing short of huge. Once we had version number one of the manuscript, the first thing she was tasked with was to reorganize the chapters. This was no easy task. But she got it done along with what was her first round of edits.

Then we got it off to the publisher to have their editing team give feedback. This is where the more involved work began for us. It was at this point when I became engrossed in the re-writing and editing process alongside Mycki. Over the next few months, we dedicated, on average, four hours every day to this last phase of this much larger process of completing the manuscript. During this time, she not only had other projects to get done in our company, as well, but she also had several deeper transformational experiences (all of which took time to go through) as a direct result of being fully immersed into these teachings.

During the months of us working together with this level of focus and intensity, she never complained and she didn't give up. She simply stayed with me through to completion, which was not easy to do. I'm grateful and very happy she did, as we work really well together and she does good, quality work. I couldn't have asked for a better person to work with and have help me with the many rounds of editing and the rewriting than her. From my soul to yours...thank you, Mycki :)

Finally, I want to give a heartfelt thanks to Jesse Krieger, publisher of Lifestyle Entrepreneurs Press and his undying dedication to me as one of his authors. From our first meeting in 2016, Jesse's unconditional support and love of me and my work has only grown with each passing year. He knows and understands the many parts of publishing a book like no other. My deepest appreciation to you, Jesse, and everyone on your team for all that you do. I want to extend a personal thank you to Stan on the design team, to the lead editor, Zora Knauf, to Tracey Ashby for your support, and Irena on the layout team. You all contributed greatly to the creation of Transform Your Destiny. Please know that each of you made a difference in the production of this book. Thank you.

The Advice You Need Most When You Don't Know What to Do Next...

Get The Answers to Your Most Pressing Questions About Every Area of Life, Relationships, and Spirituality in This Top 10 People's Choice Podcast!

The People's Choice Podcast, *Ask Dale Anything*, contains the answers to the deepest spiritual questions you often think but don't know who to ask. On top of that, it gives you the guidance you need for doing what's best when it matters most in your life, relationships, and career.

In this weekly show, you'll gain insight into the mysteries of the spiritual world as well as practical advice for being more equipped to navigate the challenges of daily life.

Join us each week for a refreshing new episode that will lift your spirits and recalibrate your perspective towards a brighter future for yourself.

Go to www.AskDaleAnything.com to subscribe today and peruse our vast collection of episodes.

Is It Time for Change?

Discover the Virtually Unknown Secrets to Easily and Gracefully Create an Exciting NEW Life for Yourself and Let Go of Everything That Has EVER Held You Back!

Get Your Copy Today and Start Creating
The Life of Your Dreams NOW!

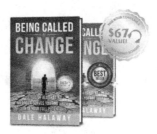

In my work over the last 40+ years with thousands of people, I've found 95% of them believe change is hard or scary The fact is, we've never been taught how to make change easy (yes, it can be easy) We're conditioned from an early age to unconsciously fi ght and resist change This is what restricts our happiness and prosperity

This fi rst book in the Transformation Trilogy, *Being Called to Change*, is being hailed as a guidebook for welcoming new and exciting things and for letting go of everything that has constrained your potential It dispels the false myth that change is hard or scary and off ers a step-by-step approach that makes change simple, graceful, and easy

Being Called to Change became a best-seller on its second day on the market and has sold out several times on Amazon since

As a bonus it contains a free audio program on 10 Powerful Secrets That Can Change Your Life for the Better in 30 Days or Less

To discover for yourself why this roadmap to spiritual prosperity is a must-have companion for transformation seekers all over the world, visit www BeingCalledToChange com

Are the Constant Pressures and Expectations of Your Fans, Your Community, or the Public Weighing on You?

Discover How Private Personalized Intensives for Celebrities, Influencers, and High-Profile Leaders Help Them Reclaim Their Freedom and Happiness from the Challenges of the Public Spotlight

Explosive growth, success, and devotion to serve the many comes with great pressure that can lead to stress, overwhelm, depression, some form of sabotage, or even health issues. Being in the public spotlight is not easy. No one taught you how to deal with the degree of pressure, scrutiny, and loneliness that comes with success, wealth, and fame. What most people don't understand is that you're no different than anyone else... You have to deal with the same thoughts and feelings that we all do – except with the added expectation of always having to look great, act perfectly, and deliver unrealistically.

Private Intensives are personalized solutions for leaders, celebrities, influencers, and policymakers who impact the many. The intensive happens in an environment that is conducive for becoming clear on the vision you are to be truly holding for yourself or your organization.

In my experience working discretely with high-profile individuals, I've uncovered specific strategies that empower them to effectively navigate and rise above the unique challenges they encounter from success, fame, and fortune. The tools you will learn in private, one-on-one intensives will teach you how to relieve the pressure, stress, and anxiety that can come with being in the public eye or under constant scrutiny. As a result, you'll experience a new level of personal freedom, joy, and happiness even while living a high-profile life. And you'll be more empowered than ever before to create a lasting positive impact and legacy for your followers, fan base, organization, and community.

If this sounds like something that could benefit you and you'd like to find out how I could assist you in achieving your goals and rising above the challenges you face, please reach out to my assistant at mycki@dalehalaway.com.

Discover the Secrets of Powerful Manifestors That Will Get You the Love, Opportunities, Friends, Money, and Good Health That Will Truly FULFILL You

FINALLY KICK LACK AND LIMITATION TO THE CURB
ONCE AND FOR ALL!

Are you ready to usher in a new life rich in love, good health, money, and anything else your wonderful heart desires? You are? Good.

As a thank you for reading this book, I want to give you exclusive FREE access to my Manifestation Masterclass, which will kick your conscious manifestation abilities into high gear.

This class takes a completely different approach to manifestation than anything else you may have seen so far...which is why it's so refreshingly practical and effective!

Learn some of the ways the most powerful manifestors on Earth create the life of their dreams at www.ManifestWithDale.com.

FREE Dream Masterclass Shows You...

How to Uncover the HIDDEN Messages Your Dreams Are Desperately Trying to Tell You!

Did you know there's a resource within your psyche that can help you heal your life faster, give you insight into your future, and tip you off when you're about to make a "wrong" turn in life?

That's exactly what your dreams can do for you... if you learn how to utilize them properly.

In this FREE masterclass, I'll show you how to access and decode the hidden messages your dreams are trying to tell you, so you can use that information to better navigate your life.

This class will empower you to uncover deeper insights into yourself that most people would need the help of a psychic or a psychologist to access.

To watch the masterclass for FREE, visit www.CrackTheDreamCode.com.

WOULD YOU LIKE TO GAIN CONTROL OVER YOUR EGO AND RAISE YOUR PRECIOUS INNER CHILD INTO THE SECURE ADULT IT'S ATTEMPTING TO BECOME?

Watch This Free Master Class Today and Learn
How to Rise Up to Your Own Inner Greatness!

In this FREE masterclass, you'll discover lost spiritual teachings that will empower you to transcend your life beyond the shackles of fear, negativity, and struggle that have become so common in today's world.

This class provides clear direction for transcending your Ego and raising up your Inner Child, which will open the doorway to a whole new destiny within you filled with joy, peace, harmony, and inner security!

Watch the class for FREE at www.TranscendingYourLife.com.

This Transformational Healing Modality Is Proven to Help You Release All That Is No Longer Serving You and Is Yours FREE!

My registered healing modality has helped countless people in transform-ing through the discovery of significant things about themselves. Through a series of probing questions, whatever is waiting to be revealed and released is uncovered to be processed with this proven technique.

As I referred to at several points throughout this book, these techniques can be used at any time you hit a spot where you are feeling challenged or your energy is feeling stuck and needs to move.

As a bonus tool to accompany the *Transform Your Destiny* book, we are giving you the TransCovery Process® Meditation ABSOLUTELY FREE.

To get your Free TransCovery Process® Meditation, visit www.transcoverymeditation.com.

Made in the USA
Las Vegas, NV
07 February 2024

85452115R00275